Critical Studies Series

General Editor: Anne Smith

NEW APPROACHES TO COLERIDGE: Biographical and Critical Essays

NEW APPROACHES TO COLERIDGE:
Biographical and Critical Essays

edited by
Donald Sultana

VISION
and
BARNES & NOBLE

Vision Press Limited
11-14 Stanhope Mews West
London SW7 5RD

and

Barnes & Noble Books
81 Adams Drive
Totowa, NJ 07512

ISBN (UK) 0 85478 294 X
ISBN (US) 0 389 20060 3

© 1981 by Vision Press
First published in the U.S.A. 1981

Printed and bound in Great Britain by
Redwood Burn Ltd,
Trowbridge & Esher
Typeset by Chromoset Limited,
Shepperton, Middlesex
MCMLXXXI

Contents

Introduction

by DONALD SULTANA

This collection of essays is a blend of biography and criticism
surveying Coleridge in relation to a wide range of his contemporaries in England, Scotland and Germany, and to his followers
in America in the nineteenth century. The essays present him in
various settings—at Highgate, Clevedon, Nether Stowey and
Malta—and in various roles: as poet, critic, philosopher, theologian, translator, lecturer, conversationalist and public servant.
The biographical essays form mainly the first half of the collection, although several of them are interspersed with sustained
critical comment, as in Geoffrey Carnall's fine essay on Coleridge
and Hazlitt. The longest of them is Alethea Hayter's essay on
Coleridge and Charles Maturin, which is placed first to justify at
once the title given to the collection, for no systematic account of
the turbulent episode involving Coleridge over Drury Lane's
rejection of his *Zapolya* appears to have so far been written by
Coleridgeans. The gap has now been fully filled by the person
best qualified to do so, for Alethea Hayter has not only written
extensively and perceptively on Coleridge in such books as *Opium
and the Romantic Imagination* and *A Voyage in Vain* but has also
edited Maturin's *Melmoth the Wanderer*. Moreover, her knowledge
of the Regency theatre arising out of her general interest in
drama and of her membership of the boards of governors of the
Old Vic and Sadler's Wells Theatres enables her to discuss
Coleridge and Maturin in a historical context, including the
different parts played by Byron, Scott and Hazlitt in this
'imbroglio', as she calls the episode.

Hazlitt more than Coleridge is the subject of Geoffrey
Carnall's essay, which is principally concerned with explaining
Hazlitt's complex attitude towards Coleridge, following the leads
on this subject from Professor Herschel Baker and, latterly, John
Kinnaird. Whatever one may think of Hazlitt as Coleridge's *bête
noire*—and the partisanship they continue to arouse among scholars of different political persuasions was again recently high-
lighted in a sharp review of Coleridge's *Essays on his own Times* in
the *Wordsworth Circle*—it is Geoffrey Carnall's strength as a

7

literary historian that he not only knows Coleridge and his period well but *understands* Hazlitt and his art even better. Accordingly his essay is full of insights as a blend of psychological analysis and literary interpretation. Technically, therefore, it performs a service, as an apologia for Hazlitt, in the tradition of the skills deployed so impressively by Coleridge himself as 'subtle-souled psychologist'.

Something of the same service—and as concisely—is performed for Scott in the essay on him and Coleridge by Eric Anderson, the editor of Scott's *Journal*. He has skilfully sifted a mass of references to Scott in Coleridge's letters and notebooks that collectively are far from unambivalent, and has supplemented them by Coleridge's marginalia on the Waverley Novels. By their means combined with his special knowledge of Scott he has drawn a more balanced and sympathetic portrait of him in relation to Coleridge than is implied in some of the comment on him by Coleridge's editors. Griggs, for instance, in his editorial notes on Scott in the *Collected Letters,* is certainly not free of occasional slight bias. The comment—not by Griggs—that Scott dissuaded Maturin from replying to Coleridge's criticism of Maturin's *Bertram* because Scott 'may well have felt a bit awkward' about *Bertram*'s success since he had himself promoted it for Drury Lane, although 'well aware of its shoddiness', discredits not Scott but its author—as a reading of Alethea Hayter's essay shows. Besides, Scott warmly congratulated Maturin on 'your splendid success' and felt gratified that *Bertram* had proved him 'a prophet'.

In place of such comment, therefore, it is good to have Eric Anderson's fair general comparison of Coleridge and Scott as two 'extraordinary' but very different men as well as his reassessment, in proper perspective, of Scott's alleged plagiarism from *Christabel* for *The Lay of the Last Minstrel* with particular reference to Coleridge's own pronouncements on the subject. It is also good to have Eric Anderson's very favourable view of Coleridge as a critic of Scott, whose American friend, James Fenimore Cooper, has provided Eric Anderson with a brilliantly dramatic opening for his essay in the form of a sketch of Coleridge as 'monologist' at one of William Sotheby's dinner-parties.

Scott's biographer, John Gibson Lockhart, is the subject of Marion Lochhead's essay, the ending of which matches Eric Anderson's opening with a description of Coleridge in a hilarious drinking-party near Highgate, attended by, among others, Lockhart and that clever, if somewhat venal, wit and entertainer, Theodore Hook. The description, in Lockhart's best vein of mild irony, is the sort of set-piece in which he excelled. Marion Lochhead, as Lockhart's biographer, is able to follow up her analysis of his correspondence with Coleridge over *Peter's Letters to his Kinsfolk* in *Blackwood's* with a contrasting outline of their careers before the development of their friendship in London during Lockhart's editorship of the *Quarterly Review*. As Coleridge appears himself to have perceived, *Peter's Letters to his Kinsfolk* marked a turning-point for both Wordsworth and Coleridge in the history of critical appreciation. The tide began to flow in their favour, particularly for Wordsworth. The musical quality of Coleridge's verse was the talent that Lockhart praised most in his attempt to convert readers of *Blackwood's* to a better response to the much-maligned 'Lake Poets'. This point is underlined at once by one of the opening quotations in Marion Lochhead's essay, which also relates Coleridge's own principles of criticism—as outlined in his correspondence with Lockhart—to *Biographia Literaria* with particular reference to his complaints against the critics of the *Edinburgh Review*. 'My unfriends' he called them in a characteristic coinage prompted by his admiration for the word-forming powers of the Greek and German languages.

The campaign of the *Edinburgh Review* against the 'Lake Poets'—roundly condemned by Lockhart in *Peter's Letters to his Kinsfolk*—had materially contributed to the hardening of Coleridge's initially mild anti-Scots prejudice, which had been obvious enough, for instance, in 'The Two Round Spaces on the Tombstone': a verse satire on James Mackintosh, another *bête noire* of Coleridge's together with David Hume. There is a hint of this prejudice, in fact, in the passage cited in Eric Anderson's essay expressing Coleridge's feelings on hearing of Scott's bankruptcy. Fortunately it did not come in the way at all of his friendship with Lockhart, to whom— in overflowing gratitude for *Peter's Letters to his Kinsfolk*—he went so far as to reveal his estranged feelings against Wordsworth under the name of 'Atticus' in an obvious echo of Pope against Addison. His complaint that Wordsworth 'withheld' praise for others, including Coleridge, is itself echoed in John Beer's essay on Wordsworth and Coleridge towards the end of this collection with reference to Wordsworth's 'unwillingness' to acknowledge publicly his debt to Coleridge. On the other hand, Wordsworth's *private* feeling for Coleridge is overwhelming—and extraordinarily articulate—on a mere reading of the tributes to him in *The Prelude* cited or referred to in the same essay.

Marion Lochhead, for her part, in pursuing the extremely embarrassing situation that followed the publication of Coleridge's 'Atticus' letter in *Blackwood's,* makes the point that Coleridge himself completely exonerated Lockhart of breach of confidence in passing it to John Wilson, the editor. The point needs to be made, as it tends to be obscured, if not overlooked, in Griggs's unqualified condemnation of Lockhart in the *Collected Letters.* Marion Lochhead's essay also implies that Lockhart's Tory politics reinforced his regard for Coleridge, who, in turn, warmed to Lockhart's wife, Sophia, Scott's elder daughter. He called her a 'love-compelling woman' in a characteristically 'chivalric' response to a lady that links him inseparably in one respect at least with Scott. His equally characteristic letter to her from Ramsgate, almost on the eve of his death at Highgate, lecturing her on Greek metres, constitutes his final testimony to a life-long passion that was partly responsible for drawing him so closely to John Hookham Frere as translator of Aristophanes. Margo von Romberg, herself a classical scholar, underlines this point in her essay on Coleridge and Frere, which can certainly claim to break new ground in its attempt to glean Coleridge's theory of translation with particular reference to Frere's 'Aristophanics'. Her essay presents his theory in relation to Dryden's dominant views and against a background of a cordial and profitable exchange of ideas analogous to the 'confluence' of minds that John Beer explores, in a different context, in his essay on Coleridge and Wordsworth during and for a few years after the period of *Lyrical Ballads.* If Coleridge regarded Wordsworth then as a 'giant', he came to esteem Frere as his ideal English gentleman.

Although Frere's *Works,* as Margo von Romberg explains, took long to appear after his death, when they did so, they included a useful Memoir by Bartle Frere, on which she has drawn not only to track the sluggish progress of Frere's 'Aristophanics' in England and Malta but to identify the hitherto unnoticed fragment of 'a religious and Philosophic poem' that Frere recited to an enthusiastic Coleridge at Highgate. Moreover, she has used a review in Frere's *Works* to trace the parallels between his and Coleridge's ideas on the theory of translation. Coleridge's own translation of Schiller's *Wallenstein* was praised not only by Frere but by Scott and Lockhart, as Eric Anderson and Marion Lochhead explain respectively. Although Frere's endeavours to obtain a sinecure for Coleridge from Lord Liverpool's administration were frustrated by events beyond his control in his absence from England after he had prepared all the ground for Coleridge, his patronage benefited not only Coleridge but his son Derwent at Cambridge. Frere's domicile in Malta owing to his wife's ill-health provided another link with Coleridge as well as an explanation for his taking Coleridge from Highgate to meet the Marquis of Hastings, the late Governor of Malta. Frere also introduced Coleridge to George Canning, his oldest Etonian friend and an influential minister for the sinecure. Canning as well as Frere had satirized Coleridge in the *Anti-Jacobin* for his radical politics, while Coleridge in turn had voiced the general public's feeling in censuring Canning for his duel with Castlereagh. In keeping with Coleridge's conversion to Tory politics, he eulogized Canning to Frere as 'the eminent statesman', and afterwards related anecdotes of Canning's wit heard at Frere's dinner-table. All this information—and much else—is now available in the *Collected Letters*, supplemented by the *Notebooks* and the *Table-Talk*. Only a portion of it was available to Gabrielle Festing as far back as 1899 for his chapter on Frere and Coleridge in *John Hookham Frere and his Friends*. A reading of Margo von Romberg's essay, therefore, should serve the additional purpose of suggesting that, although Griggs has contributed a brief general comment on Coleridge and Frere in the editorial introduction to volume five of the *Collected Letters*, there is now full scope for an up-to-date monograph or at least a substantial article to supersede Festing's chapter.

The beginning of Coleridge's friendship with Frere coincided with the arrival in England of Ludwig Tieck from Germany to collect material for his book on Shakespeare. The relationship that developed between him and Coleridge is recalled in Kathleen Wheeler's essay, which supersedes Griggs's shorter article on the same subject. Her larger design comprehends Coleridge's central tenets on Shakespeare as a topic of common interest to him and Tieck in the context of the distinguished contribution to Shakespeare studies by the Germans, notably A. W. Schlegel. Coleridge had made, over several years, his well-known borrowings from

Schlegel, but Kathleen Wheeler's essay is more concerned to show differences between Schlegel on the one hand and Tieck and Coleridge on the other. She exploits her knowledge of German Romantic literature for Coleridge's discussions and correspondence with Tieck besides drawing freely on Henry Crabb Robinson's diary and the *Collected Letters* for the framework of her narrative. Tieck, as reported by Coleridge himself in the letter she quotes about his translation of *Wallenstein,* appears to have been among the first to take part in the debate—recently revived in the *Times Literary Supplement*—as to whether the translation equalled or excelled the original. Behind Coleridge's discussions with Tieck loomed the figure of Goethe, whose *Faust* was still without a translator in England. Coleridge's projected translation of it for John Murray had fallen through. Goethe's *Sorrows of Werther* was better known, so that Byron had lately echoed it in canto three of *Childe Harold's Pilgrimage* on exiling himself from England. In consequence he severed his connection with Coleridge over *Zapolya* for Drury Lane, as Alethea Hayter explains in her essay on Coleridge and Maturin. Nevertheless, in virtue of Byron's celebrity on the continent, he too fell within the range of authors listed by Kathleen Wheeler in Tieck's discussions with Coleridge. Her essay is particularly timely in the wake of Rosemary Ashton's *The German Idea: Four English Writers and the Reception of German Thought: 1800-1860,* in which Coleridge is a seminal figure in Anglo-German cultural relations.

His influence across the Atlantic is discussed in the essay on the American Transcendentalists by Alexander Kern, who, drawing upon an impressive range of scholarship, updates such earlier surveys as Alice Snyder's 'American Comments on Coleridge a Century Ago' and Marjorie Hope Nicolson's 'James Marsh and the Vermont Transcendentalists'. Instead of focussing on Coleridge's literary influence—as Griggs mainly does in the section on 'American Associations' in *Coleridge Fille*—Alexander Kern expounds Coleridge's philosophical, theological and aesthetic ideas with particular reference to the impact of *Aids to Reflection* and *Biographia Literaria* upon Emerson, Thoreau and Poe. Moreover, he explains how Coleridge's ideas were adapted and modified to suit the American environment, traditions and aspirations. Coleridge, more than Carlyle or the German philosophers, is represented as having precipitated American Transcendentalism. The essay, as a blend of philosophy and literature, is designedly placed in the middle of the collection, for it serves to mark off the more biographical from the critical articles, all but one of which form a compact group and in several ways complement each other, particularly the essays by Ann Matheson and John Gutteridge.

Although Ann Matheson echoes George Whalley in explaining how Coleridge was led to William Cowper's 'simplicity' of diction by Charles Lamb, she goes very much further than Humphry House's Clark Lectures on Coleridge in her comparison of Cowper's and Coleridge's attitudes to Nature in *The Task* and the Conversation Poems respectively. Moreover, in tracing the ideas that Coleridge and Cowper had in common regarding the Slave Trade, militarism and the eighteenth-century psychological principle of the transmutation of pain into pleasure—which was to become a central principle also for Wordsworth—she adopts a more independent approach. In this she is fully matched by John Gutteridge who, in the context of landscape and vision in Coleridge's earlier Conversation Poems, elucidates their textual history from a close editorial study of their revisions, dating and sources. Coleridge's evolving thought is revealed by this method as well as his adaptation of the genre of Conversation Poem into a medium of self-questioning and self-debate. John Gutteridge's essay, therefore, far from being yet another critical commentary on a hackneyed subject, constitues a fresh and illuminating contribution.

It ends with 'This Lime-Tree Bower my Prison', which shows Coleridge moving into his *annus mirabilis,* the products of which are discussed by H. W. Piper in his admirably lucid essay on Coleridge's symbolism. The essay is equally impressive as a wide-ranging critical survey of the principle kinds of symbolism—literary, psychological and mythical—that have been applied to *The Ancient Mariner, Christabel* and 'Kubla Khan'. The survey is followed by a discussion of the views held by Coleridge himself on symbolism in the first half of his life with particular reference to his Unitarian religion and to the principal sources for his imagery. Finally the essay offers a re-interpretation of the symbolic meaning of Coleridge's three major poems, supplemented by the seminal part he played in the development of Romantic symbolism. Echoes of H. W. Piper's earlier researches and formulations on this subject, as expressed in *Active Universe* and in his shorter articles, particularly 'The Two Paradises in "Kubla Khan"', 'The Pantheistic Sources of Coleridge's Earlier Poetry' and 'The Disunity of *Christabel*', can be detected in the latter part of the essay.

A parallel series of echoes can also be detected in the essay by John Beer, whose mythical theory for *The Ancient Mariner* in *Coleridge the Visionary* is itself referred to briefly by H.W. Piper in his discussion of the various schemes that have been put forward in explanation of Coleridge's symbols. John Beer, having lately extended his studies of Romantic imagery from Coleridge and Blake to Wordsworth—as reflected in parts of *Wordsworth and the Human Heart* and *Wordsworth in Time*—explains in his essay, first, how Coleridge adopted and strengthened the eighteenth-century tradition of imagery of fountains, rivers and the sea for emblematic purposes in poetry, and then shows how Wordsworth also gave this fountainous tradition a distinctly 'Romantic' quality with his emphasis on 'fluency and stasis', notably in *The Prelude*. Thus John Beer's essay, which opens with a discussion of the concept of 'influence', arising out of Harold Bloom's *The Anxiety of Influence*, links Wordsworth and Coleridge in the context not so much of their reciprocal influence as of a 'mutually profitable confluence' or 'unity in variety' during their best creative period. The essay is a thoughtful and carefully-phrased contribution to the continuing discussion of the nature of the central concerns of Romanticism associated, as John Beer himself remarks, with the names of M.H. Abrams and Colin Clark.

Finally my own essay closes the collection with a retelling of the genesis, contents, form and historical background of Coleridge's political papers in Malta. The retelling has become necessary for two reasons. First, I have found a set of Malta manuscripts in the Scottish Record Office at Edinburgh relating to Coleridge's first political paper. The set, while fully confirming what I have already written about Coleridge's paper in *Samuel Taylor Coleridge in Malta and Italy* (1969), enables me to present the circumstances and historical background of its composition in fuller detail. The second and more important reason is that since I published *Samuel Taylor Coleridge in Malta and Italy*, a new annotated edition of Coleridge's *Essays on his Own Times* has appeared as volume three of the *Collected Works of Samuel Taylor Coleridge*. This edition, while, in general, drawing on my book as its principal source for

Coleridge in Malta, includes an introduction and notes on his political papers which contain errors of fact and interpretation resulting in misinformation, if not confusion. Moreover, a newspaper report from Malta published in the *Courier* is wrongly attributed to Coleridge, while the genesis, form and purpose of his longest and best Malta paper called 'Observations on Egypt', which I discussed in my book, have been re-interpreted in a manner that I believe to be a serious misreading on several accounts. Even the chronological table relating to Coleridge's return journey from Malta is imperfect, since it represents him as having 'met' Schlegel and Angelica Catalani, the famous Italian singer, in Rome in 1806, whereas he met neither of them there. (A.W. Schlegel, in fact, he was not to meet till 1828 in Germany, and Angelica Catalani he met in London in 1811.) Since these errors, misinterpretations and misattributions, largely arising out of inadequate knowledge of the historical background and of the official papers, appear in an edition intended to be standard, it has seemed proper to me to draw attention to them and to refute the interpretation given to 'Observations on Egypt'. I am grateful to the Scottish Record Office for allowing me to quote from Viscount Melville's papers, deposited in that office.

I also acknowledge with thanks a generous grant from the Postgraduate Studies Committee of the University of Edinburgh for the photocopying of material connected with this collection. As for the notes and references at the end of each essay, I need to explain that, for reasons of space and economy, the place of publications of titles of books is not given except for publications outside the United Kingdom, as can readily be seen in Alexander Kern's essay, which, in addition, retains of course its American spelling.

D.S.

List of Abbreviations

BL	S.T. Coleridge, *Biographia Literaria*, ed. J. Shawcross, 2 vols. (1907) (Oxford 1954 ed. cited)
Br. Lib.	British Library, London
BYRON	*Byron's Letters and Journals*, ed. L.A. Marchand, 10 vols. published (1973 -)
CL	*The Collected Letters of Samuel Taylor Coleridge*, ed. E.L. Griggs, 6 vols. (1956-71)
CN	*The Notebooks of Samuel Taylor Coleridge*, ed. K. Coburn, 3 vols. published (1957 -)
CRD	*Diary, Reminiscences and Correspondence of Henry Crabb Robinson*, ed. T. Sadleir, 3 vols. (1869)
EOT	*Essays on His Own Times*, ed. D.V. Erdman, 3 vols. (1978): vol. iii of *The Collected Works of Samuel Taylor Coleridge*, ed. K. Coburn
Fr.	*The Friend*, ed. B. Rooke, 2 vols. (1969): vol. iv of *The Collected Works of Samuel Taylor Coleridge*, ed. K. Coburn
FRERE	*Works of the Rt. Hon. J.H. Frere*, ed. B. Frere, 3 vols. (1874)
Griggs	E.L. Griggs, 'Ludwig Tieck and Samuel Taylor Coleridge', *Journal of English and Germanic Philology*, liv (April 1955), pp.262-68
HAZLITT	*The Complete Works of William Hazlitt*, ed. P.P. Howe, 21 vols. (1930-34)
LAMB	*The Letters of Charles and Mary Lamb*, ed. E.W. Mars, Jr., 3 vols. published (1975 -)
Pr. (1805)	1805 version of *The Prelude*, from William Wordsworth: *The Prelude: A Parallel Text*, ed. J.C. Maxwell (1971)
PRO	Public Record Office, London
PW	*The Poetical Works of Samuel Taylor Coleridge*, ed. E.H. Coleridge, 2 vols. (1912)
SCOTT	*The Letters of Sir Walter Scott*, ed. Sir H. Grierson, 12 vols. (1932-37)
Sh C	*Coleridge: Shakespearean Criticism*, ed. T.M. Raysor, 2 vols. (1930) (Everyman 1964 ed. cited)
WPW	*The Poetical Works of William Wordsworth*, ed. E. de Selincourt & H. Darbishire, 5 vols. (1940-49)

1

Coleridge, Maturin's *Bertram*, and Drury Lane

by ALETHEA HAYTER

When Coleridge wrote to Byron at the end of March 1815 to ask for help in getting a collected edition of his poems published, Byron not only promised help over that, but also urged Coleridge to write another tragedy for Drury Lane. Byron had helped to get Coleridge's *Remorse* successfully produced there in 1813, and now, as a member of the Sub-Committee of Management of the theatre, he was much involved in the search for promising new plays. The Drury Lane Sub-Committee of Management was set up by the energetic Member of Parliament and brewer Samuel Whitbread when he launched the rebuilt Drury Lane in 1812. The theatre had been destroyed by fire three years earlier, and Whitbread raised the funds to rebuild it by inducing a wide circle of friends and acquaintances to become subscribers by buying £100 shares. The Sub-Committee included representatives of the Royal Family, the House of Lords, the House of Commons and the City of London, and while Byron was on it, Lord Essex, George Lamb, Douglas Kinnaird and Peter Moore were fellow members.[1] They had a sensationally successful new leading actor in Edmund Kean, and they hoped to raise the level of the London theatre by putting on new plays of real literary merit, but these were hard to find. 'You can have no idea what trash there is in the four hundred *fallow* dramas now lying on the shelves of D[rury] L[ane]' wrote Byron later that year. It therefore seemed worth trying to persuade Coleridge to produce another tragedy which might repeat the success of *Remorse*, so Byron wrote 'If I may be permitted, I would suggest that there never was such an opening for tragedy. In Kean, there is an actor worthy of expressing the thoughts of the characters which you have every power of embodying; and I cannot but regret that the part of Ordonio was disposed of before his appearance at Drury-Lane. We have had nothing to be mentioned with "Remorse" for very many years; and I should think that the reception of that play was sufficient to encourage the highest hope of author and audience'.[2]

Coleridge had other literary projects which were much dearer to his heart than writing plays, but if by producing a successful tragedy for Drury Lane he could earn enough money to be able to concentrate, without the distraction of turning out hack work for daily bread, on what he really wanted to write, it would be well worth his while to respond to Byron's encouraging suggestion. He waited over six months before replying, but then he did tell Byron, on 15 October, that he was working on a tragedy which he should be able to deliver by the third week in December.[3] Byron's reply was very gratifying; although he did not want to hurry Coleridge, he was anxious to see the play as soon as possible; no one living was in the same class with Coleridge as a tragic dramatist, and Byron would be proud to have a hand in making this clear to the world. Ten days later, after two more letters from Coleridge promising a whole gamut of dramatic achievements, Byron told Moore that if Coleridge kept his word about producing a tragedy 'Drury Lane will be set up'.[4] If Coleridge had offered Byron a tragedy in December 1815, as promised, instead of sending him nothing at all till the following April, and then a play of a quite different kind instead of the expected tragedy on the *Remorse* formula, Byron and the rest of the Committee would in all probability have welcomed the tragedy and staged it in the early spring of 1816. But by mid-January Coleridge had lost interest in the tragedy (if indeed any part of that had ever got as far as being written down) and was in the middle of writing *Zapolay*, which he himself then considered quite unsuitable for Drury Lane.[5]

Byron and the Committee, while still looking forward to getting the promised tragedy from Coleridge later on, had of course to look elsewhere meanwhile for plays to put on at Drury Lane in the spring. And in mid-December 1815, just when Coleridge's tragedy should have materialised but failed to, Drury Lane had a windfall. Charles Robert Maturin, an Irish parson who so far had published only three moderately successful novels, sent Byron his first play, *Bertram, or the Castle of St. Aldobrand.* It had been written some years earlier, and originally submitted to a Dublin theatre, which rejected it.[6] In 1814 Maturin sent it to Walter Scott, who had reviewed his first novel in the *Quarterly,* and with whom he had been in correspondence for two years, Maturin complaining of his obscure and unfortunate existence, Scott inspiriting him, trying to get him literary work or clerical promotion, and lending him money.[7]

When Scott read *Bertram,* he was considerably impressed, and said so not only to Maturin himself but to Daniel Terry, to whom he wrote that *Bertram* was 'one of those things that will either succeed greatly, or be damned gloriously, for its merits are marked, deep and striking, and its faults of a nature obnoxious to ridicule . . . it is grand and powerful: the language most animated and poetical; and the characters sketched with a masterly enthusiasm'.[8] He sent Maturin two long letters of warm praise and helpful suggestions about possible alterations and cuts in the play, which he then forwarded to the actor John Kemble on Maturin's behalf.[9] However Kemble, after meeting Maturin in Dublin, proved to have 'insuperable objections' to producing the play, which then languished in Maturin's hands till June 1815, when Maturin's hopes were revived by a very encouraging letter from Scott. 'A late occurrence, namely the nomination of Lord Byron to be one of the Committee of management of Drury Lane Theatre, induces me to wish you would again look to the drama. Lord Byron's chief wish in assuming this troublesome and irksome duty is I sincerely believe to assist literary merit. He spoke to me before I left London . . . requesting me to mention any person whom I thought capable of bringing forward a good play. I mentioned the performance which Kemble rejected and its history and I think if it could be brought on with some attention to the criticisms which I ventured to offer, Lord Byron might probably give it a trial at Drury Lane.'[10]

Maturin revised *Bertram*, making the main cut which Scott had advised, and sent it to Byron in early December 1815. Byron received it late one evening, and was so much taken with it that he read it straight through without stopping (it cannot in fact have taken him very long — the printed play only runs to eighty widely-spaced pages) and sent it on that same evening to his fellow-committee-member George Lamb, who also, late as it reached him, could not go to bed till he had finished it.[11] Byron and Lamb both resolved to back the play with the rest of the committee for production at Drury Lane, and on 21 December Byron wrote to Maturin describing *Bertram* as 'a very extraordinary production — of great and singular merit'. He proposed some cuts and alterations, partly to lower the tension at intervals, both for the sake of the physical powers of the actor playing Bertram and also to 'relieve the attention of an audience'.[12]

Byron's admiration of *Bertram*, like Scott's, was genuine and lasting. He continued to be proud of having secured it for Drury Lane, and to regard Maturin as a 'very clever fellow' — personally rather a coxcomb, perhaps, and his later and less meritorious plays showed that he had 'talent — but not much taste'. But *Bertram* was above all, in Byron's view, 'practicable', it would tell, would captivate the audience, in the peculiar conditions of Drury Lane.[13] The rest of the committee shared his opinion, and *Bertram* opened at Drury Lane on 9 May 1816, and ran for twenty-two nights — a long run by the standards of that time — to enthusiastic audiences.

The vast theatre in which *Bertram* was performed was less than four years old. The theatre burnt down in 1809 had been replaced by a massive neo-Classic building by Benjamin Wyatt, which opened on 10 October 1812 with a performance of *Hamlet*. The cavernous interior had four tiers of boxes, as well as the spacious pit and gallery where the audience sat on backless benches. The stage was both wide and deep, allowing for elaborate scenic effects. The auditorium then held no less than three thousand and sixty people, many of whom can have heard and seen very little of what went on on the stage. The theatre was lit by oil lamps and candles (gas lighting was not installed till the year after *Bertram* was performed) and the auditorium remained as brightly lit as the stage throughout the performance, so no subtle gesture or expression by the actors had much chance of being visible to most of the audience.[14]

Coleridge was well aware of the difficulties of getting across to audiences in these huge theatres — he said 'our theatres are fit for nothing — they are too large for acting and too small for a bull-fight'[15] — and he acidly excused meaningless stage movements and effects because 'they afford something to be *seen* by that very large part of a Drury Lane audience who have small chance of *hearing* a word'.[16] It was not that actors had less carrying voices then, but they were not listened to with the silent respectful attention which twentieth-century audiences accord. Even the politer members of the audience in the boxes gossiped to each other, moved about, greeted their friends. Nor was that part of the audience which actually was attending to the performance any more silent. Coleridge records a ludicrous comment, during the performance of *Bertram*, made to him in a 'half-whisper' by his neighbour, and his own loud laugh in reply[17]; and the ruder section of the audience, in pit and gallery, did not restrict themselves to half-whispers. Even if they were not actually rioting about raised seat-prices or theatre alterations, early nineteenth-century audiences yelled their comments on play and actors, hissed and cat-called at any sentiment or performance detail that displeased them, and held up the action of the play by vociferous applause for any well-interpreted speech, convincing stage business or lavish scenic effect that appealed to them. No drama of ideas, no sustained philosophical theme, no subtle imagery, could possibly be put across to an audience in such conditions; even Shakespeare had to be lopped and distorted to be made acceptable to such audiences in such theatres; and the management had to rely primarily on striking scenic effects, and on sensational over-acting by actors of commanding personality and magnetism, to secure and maintain the loyalty of their audiences.

Bertram certainly gave scope for striking scenic effects; it included two tempests, a shipwreck in which the ship is actually seen sinking, a moonlit terrace overlooking a forest, a lavishly-decorated chapel, processions of monks and knights, mobs of banditti, and a dark forest with 'Cavern, Rocks and Precipices above'. The Drury Lane management spared no expense in mounting these scenes; Coleridge, contrasting them with the perfunctory staging accorded to a revival of his own *Remorse* at Drury Lane in 1817, sourly described the 'extreme splendour' of the *Bertram* production 'on which all the colours of the Rainbow were made to play, and one scene (that of the storm) introduced merely as a Picture'. A member of the Drury Lane management said to him, he alleged, that no expense could be too great for Maturin's play, which was nearly as good as Shakespeare, and its success would help to popularize Coleridge's own lesser efforts in the same style.[18] If this remark is faithfully reported (Coleridge himself only vouched for its being substantially correct), his sourness is very comprehensible. The shipwreck effects in *Bertram* seem to have particularly annoyed him, and he made good fun of them in his 'Critique on Bertram': 'the steady, quiet uprightness of the flame of the wax candles which the monks held over the raging billows amid the storm of wind and rain, was really miraculous'.[19]

Far more important to the success of *Bertram* than even these imposing stage effects was the frenetic brilliance with which the leading part was played. It was only two years earlier that Edmund Kean had rocketed to sudden fame with his performance of Shylock at Drury Lane, and he was at the height of his extraordinary powers. This short fiery-eyed sharp-faced man, with his burning impulses and resentments, could express the whole range of emotions and passions — grace and grandeur, pathos and gallantry, sweetness and sarcasm. He found the role of Bertram technically challenging. Bertram, formerly a national hero but ruined by a rival, has become a robber chieftain; returning shipwrecked to his native shore, he learns that his betrothed, Imogine, has married his rival. He then proceeds to seduce her, threatens to kill her child, does kill her husband and — Imogine by now having understandably gone mad and died — ends by killing himself. When the Drury Lane committee sent this play for Kean to approve, before they finally accepted it, Kean saw the role of Bertram — not at first sight a conspicuously amiable figure — as one by which he could increase his reputation. He did not think much of the play, which he described as 'all sound and fury, signifying nothing' (the superstition against quoting *Macbeth* in the theatre evidently did not daunt him) but it would, he thought at first, be easy and a relief after the strain of playing the great Shakespearean roles. At the first rehearsal, however, he began to feel that Imogine, not Bertram, was the most effective part in the play; this put him on his mettle and, congratulating himself on not having Mrs Siddons as Imogine but only a new young actress, Miss Somerville, whom it would be much easier to upstage, he made up his mind to rivet the attention of the audience exclusively on Bertram, by every device in his power.[20]

He succeeded entirely, wringing the last ounce of sublimity, despair, hatred, passionate love, scorn, and fugitive repentance out of every speech and scene, with real tears glistening on his cadaverous cheeks.[21] Even Coleridge exempted Kean's performance from his attack on the play. In a passage in his 'Critique on Bertram' as it first appeared in the *Courier,* which he omitted when reprinting it in *Biographia Literaria,* he said that Kean's interpretation was consistent, gripped the audience's attention, and was the main support and interest of the play, which it perfectly suited. 'We may justifiably contemplate as matter of praise and admiration in his *Bertram,* what I should not hesitate to condemn as extravagance and debasement in *Othello* or *Richard the Third.'*[22] Critics and public were unanimous in praising Kean's passionate performance, above all the scene in which Bertram decides, with no excessive magnanimity, not after all to murder his rival's child, but snatches it up and murmurs over it 'God bless thee, child'. The vibrating tenderness with which he spoke this line never failed to bring the house down, as the pains Kean took over it well deserved. He had practised its intonation by repeating it a hundred times over the head of his own son Charles. It would be interesting to hear the reactions of Charles Kean, then aged five, at being so relentlessly rehearsed over.[23]

While *Bertram* was being rehearsed in the spring of 1816, Coleridge was working on a new play of his own, *Zapolya.* By 16 January he had already completed three acts of it, and by the end of the month it was all but finished, except for two prologues. But at this stage he was very doubtful about sending it to Drury Lane, as it contained three leading female roles and the Drury Lane company did not in his opinion include even one tolerable actress. By March of that year he had decided to send the play to Covent Garden, the only other London theatre licensed to put on 'straight' comedies and tragedies without music; but Covent Garden rejected it in early April, and Coleridge then sent it to Byron on 10 April, at the same time promising also to start again on the tragedy previously promised to Drury Lane.

Byron, however, had other things to think about just then. His wife had left him in January, and by mid-April the terms of their separation had been agreed and signed; seventeen days after Coleridge sent *Zapolya,* Byron left England for ever. The two men had met briefly just before Byron sailed, but the decision about putting on *Zapolya* at Drury Lane rested with other members of the Sub-Committee of Management.

Coleridge's earlier biographers tended to believe that Drury Lane accepted *Bertram* instead of *Zapolya,* but it is now recognized that the dates by themselves are enough to disprove this. *Bertram* was accepted in December 1815 and staged in May 1816; *Zapolya* was not even submitted to Drury Lane till a month before the opening night of *Bertram,* which with its large cast and elaborate stage effects must have been rehearsed and prepared for many weeks before.[25]

In fact for two or three months after Coleridge sent *Zapolya* to Byron, there were good hopes that it would be put on at Drury Lane. Two members of the Committee, Lord Essex and Kinnaird, wanted a shortened and adapted version of it to be presented at Drury Lane at Christmas 1816. All through June and early July 1816, Coleridge still believed that the theatre intended to stage some adaptation of the play at the end of the year. On 8 July he could still write confidently that *Zapolya* would be 'brought out at Drury Lane at or before Christmas'.[26]

We have two accounts of what happened to *Zapolya* at Drury Lane after that, one from Byron and one from Coleridge. Neither account can be accepted at its full face value. Byron, writing in October 1817 after the publication of *Biographia Literaria* with its onslaught on the Drury Lane management, was piqued by what he considered Coleridge's ingratitude. Presumably quoting information given him by Kinnaird, he claimed that Drury Lane had genuinely wanted to do a play by Coleridge, but had to turn down *Zapolya* because it would not be effective on the stage. 'I know that there was every disposition on the part of the S[ub] C[ommittee] to bring forward any production of his' [Coleridge's] 'were it feasible — the play he offered — though poetical — did not appear at all practicable.'[27]

Coleridge, after his letter of 8 July 1816, made no further mention of *Zapolya* and its fate in his letters till February 1817, and his version of its treatment by Drury Lane is spread out in letters from early 1817 to late 1819. By then he had convinced himself that, contrary to what Byron alleged, there had been no disposition on the part of the Sub-Committee or managers of Drury Lane to be helpful about the play. Kinnaird, Coleridge averred, had ridiculed the parts of *Zapolya* which Byron had approved, and had even told Coleridge that Byron habitually over-rated Coleridge's work; and the parts of *Zapolya* that Kinnaird did like, another member of the Committee condemned as bound to make the audience laugh. Coleridge offered to make changes in the text, but Kinnaird was hard to pin down to an appointment to discuss these, and then Kinnaird himself left the Committee. Thomas Dibdin, one of the joint managers of Drury Lane, who had showed some signs of being well disposed to Coleridge's work, was removed from his post; Alexander Rae, the other joint manager, was evasive; no-one at Drury Lane seemed to be responsible for a decision. The only member of the Committee who did discuss *Zapolya* with Coleridge condescendingly told him that after the success of *Bertram*, the public would expect something almost equally Shakespearean, with the implication that *Zapolya* did not come up to this specification. By April 1817, a year after Coleridge had submitted *Zapolya* to Drury Lane, he had, he asserted, still received no decision about it from the theatre.[28]

Even if we discount some of Coleridge's version of events, it seems clear that, though Drury Lane did not take *Bertram* instead of *Zapolya*, the success of *Bertram* established in the minds of the Drury Lane management a criterion of the kind of play their public liked, and that *Zapolya* did not conform to this model. It therefore remains true that *Zapolya*'s rejection was in part due to *Bertram*'s acceptance. Coleridge gives no dates for the conversations with Kinnaird and others at Drury Lane about *Zapolya* which so much offended him, but it seems likely that they took place after 8 July 1816, when he still believed that some version of *Zapolya* would be staged at Drury Lane by Christmas, but before late August 1816 when he started dictating the 'Critique on Bertram' to John Morgan. If he had still had any real hopes of *Zapolya* being staged at Drury Lane, he would hardly have risked publishing, even anonymously, the violent attack on the management of Drury Lane which appeared on 29 August in the *Courier* as the first instalment of the 'Critique on Bertram'.

In his private letters Coleridge alternately admitted and denied, both during and after the publication of the 'Critique on Bertram', that he had written all or part of it,[29] but he finally admitted paternity when he reprinted it a year later in *Biographia Literaria*. He was later most anxious to forestall the implication that his attack on *Bertram*, and on all that it stood for, was motivated by jealousy over the rejection of his own play. 'That man knows little of me (who can affirm with strictest truth that to this hour I know the meaning of the word Envy only by the interpretation given in the Dictionaries) who would look *out* of the Bertram itself for any cause of my abhorrence of that piece.'[30] The sanctimonious phrasing of this disclaimer inclines one to disbelieve it. Coleridge obviously was resentful and jealous, with good reason, when he was told by the Drury Lane management that his own play was not nearly as Shakespearean as Maturin's was. Moreover a wounding critique in the *British Review* of August 1816 had astoundingly compared *Christabel* and *Bertram*, calling the former a 'weak and singularly nonsensical and affected performance' and the latter 'a production of undoubted genius'.[31] A natural resentment that such meretricious stuff should be praised while his own work was neglected and misunderstood may have sharpened the edge of his attack on Maturin's play, but his real interest was in a more general diagnosis, for which Maturin's play was only a symptom, of the vicious and diseased deterioration of public taste for the drama.

The underlying theme of the 'Critique on Bertram' had been

in Coleridge's mind for years. In the preface to the first edition of *Remorse*, published in 1813, he referred to a forthcoming essay on 'Dramatic Poetry, relatively to the present State of the Metropolitan Theatres', and on 8 May 1816, the day before *Bertram* opened at Drury Lane, he said that he had in hand 'the whole outline, and a sheet or so finished' of this essay, which was to be specifically related to the unavoidable and avoidable evils of theatrical representation at Drury Lane and Covent Garden. He felt that this essay, either published separately or in the same volume with *Zapolya*, 'would excite interest among the Frequenters of the Theatre, coming from a successful Dramatist'. At this stage, with *Remorse* behind him and *Zapolya*, as it then seemed, likely to be put on shortly at Drury Lane, he could reasonably describe himself as 'a successful Dramatist'.[32]

The events and preoccupations of the summer of 1816 added two other ingredients to this projected essay. Coleridge had now settled with the Gillmans at Highgate, and was enjoying a period of some recovery in health and some hopes of new dramatic and literary success, soon to be darkened by cruel press criticisms of his work and personality and by the muddles and duplicities of printers and publishers. The first of the two new ingredients which produced the 'Critique on Bertram' was a paragraph about the tendencies of modern drama in a 'Satyrane Letter' which he had published in *The Friend* on 7 December 1809. In early July 1816 he was planning a republication of *The Friend*, and during that month he was going through a borrowed copy (he had none of his own) of the 1812 edition of *The Friend* in book form, with a view to editing it for re-publication. In mid-July he heard the disastrous news that *Biographia Literaria*, then being printed in Bristol, was after all not long enough to fill two volumes and that he would have to produce another 150 pages — 'on *what*, I am left to discover' — to fill up the second volume. 'Satyrane's Letters', including the one printed in *The Friend* on 7 December 1809, were chosen as part of the fill-up material, and the reminder of what he had written in 1809 about the defects of modern drama coalesced with his project for an essay on the problems of London theatres.[33]

The second new ingredient was his revival of a project which had been in his head ever since he went to Germany in 1798, to produce a critical history of German literature. He mentioned this project on 31 August, and linked it with the 'Critique on Bertram' which he had just written. A paragraph in that, on 'the fashionable phrase, the *German* drama', was part of his campaign to 'remove the cloud of Ignorance and Prejudice which to a disgraceful and even inhospitable and ungrateful excess overglooms the mind of the learned Public with regard to German Literature'.[34]

It was unfortunate for poor Maturin that his *Bertram* happened to lie ready to Coleridge's hand as an illustration of the ideas about modern drama which he had already resolved to publish before he ever saw Maturin's play. The last part of the 'Critique' is a detailed analysis of the action of *Bertram,* which Coleridge derides amusingly — Scott's opinion that even its faults would be 'of a nature obnoxious to ridicule' proved unprophetic — but this is only to illustrate the main theme of the essay. Coleridge began his Critique by mocking the taste of the Sub-Committee of Management and the 'proprietary subscribers' of Drury Lane — a passage which lost him Byron's goodwill. He then attacked the phrase 'German drama' as used to describe the modern romantic drama of the school of Kotzebue. True modern German drama was the sober classical style of Lessing and the later Schiller; the so-called 'German drama' owed its origin to English influence on German literature, to the fatal fascination of the earliest English Romantics, of Horace Walpole's *Castle of Otranto*, of Young and Hervey and Richardson, which had stimulated the malign growth of Gothic drama in Germany. The great defect of this type of drama, compared with that of earlier masters, was its want of consistency and intellectual power in the presentation of characters, and this was ultimately due to a deficiency in modern theatre audiences; dramatists, theatrical managers and actors had to debase their offerings to what contemporary audiences would accept.

The key passage in the 'Critique on Bertram' is the one which Coleridge extracted from the 'Satyrane Letter' of 1809. 'Eighteen years ago', he writes in the 'Critique', 'I observed, that the whole secret of the modern Jacobinical drama (which, and not the German, is its appropriate designation) and of all its popularity, consists in the confusion and subversion of the natural order of things in their causes and effects: namely, in the excitement of surprise by representing the qualities of liberality, refined feeling, and a nice sense of honour (those things rather which pass amongst us for such) in persons and in classes where experience teaches us least to expect them: and by rewarding with all the sympathies which are the due of virtue those criminals whom law, reason, and religion have excommunicated from our esteem.'

To claim that he had made this observation eighteen years earlier was disingenuous of Coleridge. He was trying to show that he had been consistent throughout his life in his opposition to 'Jacobinical drama'; to prove this, he needed to suggest that his observations about it had been contained in his original letters from Germany in 1798, eighteen years before the 'Critique on Bertram' was written. But in making this claim Coleridge was shuffling the records; the surviving 1798 letters and notebooks contain no element of the passage on drama in the 1809 'Satyrane Letter' except two brief references in the 1798 Notebook and letters to a comedy, *Le Comte de Waltron,* by Vatron which Coleridge saw performed in Hamburg with much 'frantic and hysterical ranting',[35] a comment which he used as the starting-point for the 1809 *Friend* article. He wrote nothing in 1798 about 'moral and intellectual Jacobinism' in the drama.

It was a pity that Coleridge trailed the red herring of 'Jacobinism' across his hunt after the truth about modern drama. It set Hazlitt baying on his trail, and aroused suspicions about his real motive in writing the 'Critique'. The whole incident of Drury Lane's rejection of *Zapolya* is really irrelevant to the permanent interest of the point Coleridge was making in the 'Critique', and they might never have been linked at all, and finally riveted together by Hazlitt's iron sarcasm, if the hasty gathering-up of material to fill the second volume of *Biographia Literaria* had not brought together in fatal juxtaposition several discrete and unrelated fragments. The concept of Jacobinism in dramatic criticism bitterly irritated Hazlitt when Coleridge applied it to *Bertram* and followed it up, in his Conclusion to *Biographia Literaria,* with complaints about the contemptuous reception of *Zapolya*. There was no essential connection between Coleridge's concept of dramatic 'Jacobinism' in his attack on *Bertram*, and his resentment over unappreciated *Zapolya*, but the fact that the two appeared in close proximity in the last sections of the original edition of *Biographia Literaria* gave Hazlitt an opportunity to renew his campaign against Coleridge's own crypto-Jacobinism, by writing venomously that 'Mr Coleridge ... took such pains, two years ago, to praise himself by depreciating and canting profound German mysticism against Mr Maturin's successful tragedy of *Bertram*, which he proved, being himself in the secret, to be ultra-Jacobinism, and quite different in its philosophical and poetical tendency from his own sweet injured *Zapolya*'.[36]

In any case, 'Jacobinism' was not really a useful description of the kind of audience reaction which Coleridge was trying to define. By 1816 'Jacobinism' had become as blunt a term of abuse as 'Fascism' or 'Marxism' are today, meaning little more than 'the kind of politics, or art, or behaviour, that does not appeal to me'. But Coleridge was proud of having been, as he claimed, the first writer to give a clear definition of Jacobins, as distinct from Republicans, Demagogues or Democrats, and also anxious to show that he had never been a Jacobin himself.[37] The regretful respect, for an ideal which however mistaken and productive of misery was nevertheless a generous one, with which he defined Jacobinism in 1802, has little to do with the execration he bestowed in the 'Critique on Bertram' on 'the spirit of modern Jacobinism', based on envy and callousness, as the cause of the degredation of taste shown by modern theatre audiences.

The really cogent point, to illustrate which he made use of *Bertram*, was that this type of drama excited, and responded to, a wrong and misdirected sympathy in the audience, causing 'all the sympathies which are the due of virtue' to be instead awarded to 'those criminals whom law, reason, and religion have excommunicated from our esteem', and that it did this by 'the confusion and subversion of the natural order of things and their causes and effects', by presenting a series of striking but unrelated actions instead of a consistent character to whom the audience could react consistently. His attack on the villainous ferocity of Bertram and the culpable weakness and inactivity of Imogine, both alike unmotivated by any consistent character development, was echoed by most of the other press criticisms of the play, though Coleridge's criticism was far more unmitigated, more heavily sarcastic, than that of the other critics. Critiques in the *British Review*, the *Monthly Review*, the *Eclectic Review*, all suggested that Maturin had made his criminal hero too sympathetic.[38] No-one seems to have noticed that the fault was mainly Kean's, determined as he was to concentrate the attention and sympathy of the audience on himself.

In fact, if *Bertram* had been staged, and later printed, as it was originally written, Coleridge's attack on Bertram's motiveless and inconsistent villainy would not have been justified, as it certainly was by the final version of the play. Maturin, who was always haunted by the psychological phenomenon of temptation (as he showed at length in his later novel, *Melmoth the Wanderer*) originally intended the character of his Bertram to undergo a fatal change, in the course of the action of the play, as a result of an interview with a supernatural tempter. At the beginning of the play Bertram, though lawless and morose, can legitimately be regarded with some sympathy as a wronged and ruined man, and his wish to revenge himself on his enemy in fair and single combat is conventionally 'honourable'. He then learns that his own betrothed, Imogine, whose memory has been his only consolation in his ruin, has married his rival, and this plunges him into raging despair. In the original play, there was then a scene in which Bertram learned of the existence of the 'dark knight of the forest', a supernatural being whom none return from visiting. Bertram in his new desperation is instantly attracted and, exclaiming

> Contend not with me,
> Horrors to me are kindred and society.
> Or man, or fiend, he hath won the soul of Bertram,

he goes in search of the forest fiend. In the next scene, Bertram is discovered wandering alone in the forest, after having seen the Dark Knight and, in a soliloquy which would have been much the best in the play if it had been allowed to survive, describes his supernatural encounter. The description of the armed figure with its eyeless face and hollow whisper is effectively blood-chilling, and the soliloquy ends with lines that show the development of character that Maturin intended to display in his central figure.

> Forgotten thoughts of evil, still-born mischiefs,
> Foul fertile seeds of passion and of crime,
> That wither'd in my heart's abortive core,
> Rous'd their dark battle at his trumpet-peal . . .
> I am not what I was since I beheld him —
> I was the slave of passion's ebbing sway —
> All is condensed, collected, callous now —
> The groan, the burst, the fiery flash is o'er,
> Down pours the dense and darkening lava-tide,
> Arresting life and stilling all beneath it.[39]

In the light of this speech, Bertram's later villainies become, not more pardonable but at least a consistent development. The obvious comparison, which Scott was later to make, was with *Macbeth*; *Bertram* suffered as much from the removal of all reference to the Dark Knight as *Macbeth* would without the Witches. The physical embodiment on the stage of the psychological process of temptation, or at least a description of such an embodiment — which was all Maturin attempted — seems a perfectly legitimate theatrical device.

However all Maturin's advisers were against it. When he sent *Bertram* to Scott in 1814, Scott strongly counselled him to cut out the 'diabolical agency' as being too difficult to get across to the audience. Four years later, when the truncated play had been successfully produced, Scott admitted that the excised scenes would have given 'probability and consistency' to the story, but still felt that it was right to cut them in performance — the audience would never have stood them.[40] Byron's reaction was the same. 'The "dark Knight" must also be got rid of' he wrote to Maturin when discussing the changes the play would need for production at Drury Lane.[41] 'Got rid of' he was, both in the play as produced and as later printed. Scott had qualms about this; he admired the 'Dark Knight' passages, and asked Maturin to let him have a copy of them to stick into his own copy of the printed play,[42] and he later printed them in a review of Maturin's novel *Women: or Pour et Contre* in the *Edinburgh Review,* thus ensuring their survival.[43] As he said to Maturin when asking for the copy, 'I always missed the dark mysterious machinery of the black Knight whose influence and agency gave to the atrocities of Bertram an appearance of involuntary impulse which serves to reconcile the feelings of sympathy with which we cannot help regarding him with the horror that his actions are calculated to inspire'. This acute comment is an effective answer to Coleridge's point in the 'Critique' about misdirected sympathies, and confirms that the real gravamen of Coleridge's attack was upon the audience, whose refusal to accord any thoughtful attention convinced men like Scott and Byron that it was useless to try and put across to them any psychological subtleties.

The 'Critique on Bertram' was published in the *Courier* on 29 August and 7, 9, 10 and 11 September 1816, but it was not till it was reprinted as a fill-up for Volume II of *Biographia Literaria* in July 1817 that it was known for certain to be by Coleridge, and became more widely circulated and angrily resented. Maturin's feelings were much hurt, and he meditated replying to Coleridge's attack in a preface to the novel *Women* which he published in 1818. He sent the draft of his preface to Scott, who wisely advised him against printing it. 'Coleridge's work has been little read or heard of, and has made no general impression whatever, certainly no impression unfavourable to you or your play.' Literary controversies almost always did the injured party, as well as the injurer, more harm than good in the public esteem, and in any case Coleridge, a 'disappointed and wayward man', a 'genius struggling with bad habits and difficult circumstances', had been handled roughly himself by the critics and deserved some forbearance on that score. Maturin at once took Scott's advice; he burnt the draft preface five minutes after reading Scott's letter.[44]

Byron also, though for different reasons, decided not to reply to Coleridge's assault in the 'Critique' on the Drury Lane Sub-Committee of Management, though he found it offensive, 'not very grateful nor graceful on the part of the worthy auto-biographer . . . He is a shabby fellow — and I wash my hands of, and after him'. His reason for not replying to the attack was that he had 'obligated' Coleridge, that is, both given him money and persuaded Murray to publish his work and Drury Lane to put on *Remorse*. A reply would therefore seem like a public reproach for ingratitude, which Byron considered beneath him.[45]

Hazlitt, whom Coleridge had 'obligated' in the past quite as much as Byron had obligated Coleridge, was even less grateful to Coleridge than Coleridge was to Byron. He attacked the 'Critique on Bertram' violently and repeatedly. His own opinion of *Bertram*, given in a review in the *Examiner* on 19 May 1816, had been only moderately enthusiastic, mainly because of the very defect of which Coleridge subsequently complained. The fault of the play, said Hazlitt, was 'a want of that necessary connection between what happens, what is said, and what is done . . . the passion described does not arise naturally out of the previous circumstances, nor lead necessarily to the consequences that follow'.[46] But once the 'Critique on Bertram' had appeared in *Biographia Literaria*, Hazlitt seized on it as a stick to beat Coleridge with. In February 1818 he castigated Coleridge in *The Yellow Dwarf* for calling *Bertram* Jacobinical in order to rescue his own works from the imputation of past Jacobinism.[47] In April 1820 in the *London Magazine* he suggested that 'the charge of sophistry and paradox, and dangerous morality, to startle the audiences, in lieu of more legitimate methods of exciting their sympathy, which he' [Coleridge] 'brings against the author of Bertram' could fairly be retorted on Coleridge's own head; Hazlitt instanced a speech of Ordonio's in *Remorse*, justifying fratricide, as an example of such unworthy methods of audience-startling.[48]

It would altogether have been more prudent of Coleridge to have left both *Bertram* and 'Jacobinical drama' alone when he made his worthwhile protest about contemporary theatre audiences and their debasing influence on the drama. In the 1809 'Satyrane Letter' he had already included an imaginary dialogue between himself and a 'spokesman' of the crowd', a typical member of a theatre audience, in which the latter made it clear that as a plain citizen he was only interested, when he went to the theatre, in how the plot turned out. He did not care for plays about kings and queens and pagan heroes, but preferred 'valiant tars, high-spirited half-pay officers' and so on, people with ordinary feelings and experiences just like his own. He wanted these characters to display only such painless sacrifices and well-sounding sentiments as might flatter and please, but not disturb, the audience. They were to exhibit only the conventional virtues of profuse and indiscriminate liberality, athletic life-saving, and bold brow-beating of lords and baronets, while anyone represented as genuinely a moralist had to be shown up eventually as a hypocrite.[49] In the 'Critique on Bertram' Coleridge followed up this satire on the public's taste by violently chastising the 'depravation of the public mind' exhibited by the audiences at *Bertram* who received with thunders of applause the appearance of 'a human being supposed to have come reeking from the consummation of this complex foulness and baseness'; that is, Bertram's appearance at the opening of the fourth act when he has just seduced Imogine. Imogine, Coleridge indignantly remarks, is 'every-where . . . made the object of interest and sympathy . . . And did a British audience endure all this? — They received it with plaudits'.

Scott's attitude to these scenes sounds less prudish; he told Maturin that a friend of his 'demurs somewhat to the criminal intercourse taking place during the course of action' but he himself did not object; all 'means to excite pity and terror which are not otherwise offensive to real delicacy' are legitimate, he considered.[50] Most of the critics, however, agreed with Coleridge and with Scott's demurring friend in condemning the 'vicious and abominable morality' of this incident in the play,[51] and so did even an ordinary member of the audience, a 'plain elderly man' sitting next to Coleridge who 'with a very serious face, that at once expressed surprise and aversion, touched my elbow, and, pointing to the actor, said to me in a half whisper — "Do you see that little fellow there? he has just been committing adultery!"'.[52] Coleridge's neighbour showed more correctly directed sympathies than the rest of the audience who greeted Kean with thunderous applause, but not a more sophisticated critical approach to the drama. The essence of the situation that Coleridge was attacking was that a huge theatre like Drury Lane could only be made to pay if it catered for an undiscriminating public, but that under the peculiar London theatre-licensing laws then in force, there was nowhere else, except the equally enormous Covent Garden, where a serious play could be shown. Coleridge was prepared to admit that plays like *Zapolya* might be 'unfit for the present state of our immense theatres',[53] but until 1843 the patents of these two theatres gave them a monopoly of presenting legitimate drama in London. There was nothing new about the contest between what dramatists thought audiences ought to like, and what the majority of the audience actually did like; it is implicit in Hamlet's address to the players, and it is still with us today. But an intellectual play-goer of today who does not care for musical comedy at Drury Lane or Her Majesty's can go and find what suits him better at the Royal Court or the Round House, or even at the National Theatre or the Aldwych, where subsidization enables the managements sometimes to give the general public what it is thought to need, not what is does actually like best. But no Royal Court existed in Coleridge's day where *Zapolya* could be put on; there were no Government subsidies to the vast legitimate drama theatres, which would have enabled them to pay less regard to the vast legitimate drama theatres, which would have enabled them to pay less regard to the lowest common denominator of their customers' taste; and the story of the *Bertram* imbroglio leaves us sympathizing equally with Coleridge for attacking the harmful restrictions of the London theatre of his day, and with Scott and Byron for facing the reality of the situation and trying to get the best out of it.

REFERENCES

1 B. Dobbs, *Drury Lane: Three Centuries of the Theatre Royal 1663-1971* (1972).
2 **BYRON**, iv. 318-19, 285.
3 *CL*, iv. 589, 598.
4 **BYRON**, iv. 318-19, 322.
5 *CL*, iv. 617-18.
6 N. Idman, *C. R. Maturin* (Helsingfors, 1923), 100-1.
7 **SCOTT**, xii. 338-48.
8 Idman, 101.
9 **SCOTT**, xii. 349-55.
10 **SCOTT**, xii. 354-55.
11 S. Smiles, *A Publisher and his Friends* (1891), i. 288.
12 **BYRON**, iv. 336-37.
13 **BYRON**, v. 79, 201, 203, 237-38, 267.
14 Dobbs, 124-25.

15 Dobbs, 135.
16 *BL,* ii. 205.
17 *BL,* ii. 202.
18 *CL,* iv. 720.
19 *BL,* ii. 194.
20 B. W. Procter, *The Life of Edmund Kean* (1835), ii. 158-61.
21 F. W. Hawkins, *The Life of Edmund Kean* (1869), i. 372.
22 *EOT,* ii. 438-40.
23 Procter, ii. 158-61.
24 *CL,* iv. 617-18, 620, 625, 627, 628n[1].
25 *CL,* iv. 664n[2].
26 *CL,* iv. 628n[1], 644, 650.
27 **BYRON**, v. 267.
28 *CL,* iv. 704-5, 752, 720-21, 971.
29 *CL,* iv. 664, 670, 720.
30 *CL,* iv. 720.
31 *British Review,* August 1816, viii. 80.
32 *CL,* iv. 637-38; *PW,* ii. 815.
33 *CL,* iv. 650, 669, 660, 661.
34 *CL,* iv. 663-64.
35 *CN,* i. 337 f. 7[v]; *CL,* i. 437.
36 **HAZLITT**, xix, 206-10.
37 *BL,* ii. 164, 180; *EOT,* ii. 367-73; *Fr.,* i. 220-22.
38 Idman, 116.
39 *Edinburgh Review,* June-September 1818, xxx. 254-56.
40 *Edinburgh Review,* xxx. 254-56.
41 **BYRON**, iv. 336-37.
42 **SCOTT**, xii. 356-58.
43 *Edinburgh Review,* xxx. 254-56.
44 **SCOTT**, v. 95-8 and n[1].
45 **BYRON**, v. 267.
46 **HAZLITT**, v. 304-8.
47 **HAZLITT**, xix. 206-10.
48 **HAZLITT**, xviii. 309-10.
49 *BL,* ii. 160-64; *Fr., ii. 218-20.*
50 **SCOTT**, xii. 352-53.
51 Idman, 116.
52 *BL,* ii. 202.
53 *BL,* ii. 212.

2

The Impertinent Barber of Baghdad: Coleridge as Comic Figure in Hazlitt's Essays

by GEOFFREY CARNALL

The complexity of Hazlitt's feelings towards Coleridge is evident. He never lost his sense of exhilarated gratitude for what he owed to the poet who had helped him find a language to express himself. He never forgave him for his political apostasy. He could never reconcile himself to the apparent paucity of the achievement of this 'great but useless thinker'. These feelings co-exist turbulently in much of what Hazlitt wrote about Coleridge, although one or other is usually uppermost at any given moment. In the stormy years of the Regency, it is the apostate who figures most conspicuously. In the somewhat mellower frame of mind that he achieved after 1820, the response is more magnanimous, notably in the fine essay devoted to Coleridge in *The Spirit of the Age*. But whether the feeling that predominates is positive or negative, Coleridge almost always elicits from Hazlitt a strong reaction in which he takes a good deal of pleasure.

Hazlitt had a genius for eloquent denunciation which, although some have found it deplorable, has given many readers enjoyment. 'Your only good damner' was Keats's tribute on one occasion, and on another he identifies the sense of intense vitality apparent in Hazlitt's rhetoric, 'the force and innate power with which it yeasts and works up itself. . . . He hath a demon, as he himself says of Lord Byron.' Keats keenly appreciated the zest with which Hazlitt developed that 'sentence of a page long, out of the feelings of one's whole life': it was, he said, 'a Whale's back in the Sea of Prose'.[1] Thus, although Hazlitt's diatribes against the 'apostate poets' Coleridge, Southey, and Wordsworth are often ferocious, he evidently delights in his own ferocity. His animation is enhanced by the very outrage he felt at the change in people who had meant so much to him at a crucial stage of his own life, for the outrage contains a lively element of appreciation for their past state.

Hazlitt was always ready to confess that Coleridge was the only person he ever knew who 'answered to the idea of a man of genius'.

> He talked on for ever; and you wished him to talk on for ever. His thoughts did not seem to come with labour and effort; but as if the wings of his imagination lifted him from off his feet. His voice rolled on the ear like the pealing organ, and its sound alone was the music of thought. His mind was clothed with wings; and raised on them, he lifted philosophy to heaven.[2]

What though this vision, recalling the cherubims who guarded the ark of the covenant, had ended in 'swallowing doses of oblivion and in writing paragraphs for the *Courier*'?[3] It was the fate of genius to be fitful and irregular. As Hazlitt put it in the essay in *The Plain Speaker* 'On the Qualifications Necessary to Success in Life',

> The man of perhaps the greatest ability now living is the one who has not only done the least, but who is actually incapable of ever doing any thing worthy of him—unless he had a hundred hands to write with, and a hundred mouths to utter all that it hath entered into his heart to conceive, and centuries before him to embody the endless volume of his waking dreams.[4]

William Duff had explained the matter satisfactorily half a century earlier in his *Essay on Original Genius* (1767): the very immensity of the conceptions in the mind of genius was apt to make them unmanageable.

John Kinnaird, in his admirable recent study of Hazlitt, has shown just how powerful Coleridge's appeal to the Unitarian minister's son must have been in 1798. 'All the discords that we have traced in Hazlitt's education,' he says, 'were now suddenly, if only for a brief interlude, to vanish.'[5] The stresses he had experienced in growing away from his father's beliefs and developing his own secularised version of them, dedicated to the advancement of a democratic revolution, were forgotten in the spectacle of this philosophical reformer in the pulpit Hazlitt had renounced, uttering an eloquent declamation against war. If the spectacle proved to be a transient one, Hazlitt felt bound to admit that it could hardly have been otherwise, for the leading actor had not had the good fortune to have been brought up as a dissenter. An essay on 'court-influence' contributed to the *Yellow Dwarf* in 1818 testifies to the difficulty of venturing to oppose the 'torrent of opinion setting in upon him from the throne and absorbing by degrees every thing in its vortex—undermining every principle of independence, and obliterating every trace of liberty'.[6] In arguing thus, Hazlitt chose to ignore the extent to which in 1818 there was a 'torrent' of popular opinion as well as of court opinion: but the point here is that Hazlitt's partisan analysis encouraged him to sympathise with Coleridge's position. The stubborn radical certainly did not feel himself to be a sublime figure defying the forces of corruption, Gray's Bard declaiming against Edward's alien armies. He was more like John Martin's Sadak in search of the Waters of Oblivion, having at best a precarious foothold in a paralysingly hostile landscape. To differ from the public 'is like arguing against the motion of the world with which we are carried along: its influence is as powerful and as imperceptible'.[7] Even the most potent civil virtue was not altogether reliable. There is a wry aside in this connection in Hazlitt's *Life of Napoleon* when he is considering Napoleon's policy in Switzerland, and arguing that its object was to master Austria rather than Switzerland itself. The Swiss, says Hazlitt, had no reason to oppose the French, and if William Tell himself had come to life again, he would hardly have sided with Switzerland's old oppressors, '(though there is no saying.)'[8] The brief phrase is startling in its bitter acquiescence in sin. And if even William Tell couldn't be counted on, how should a man like Coleridge, morbidly dependent on the sympathy of others, withstand the insidious influence of established authority?

On occasion, it is true, Hazlitt can be blatantly hysterical, as in the 'apologue' which closes the article on 'the connexion between toad-eaters and tyrants', where Coleridge, Southey, and Wordsworth are imagined

> following in the train of the Pope and the Inquisition and the Bourbons, and worshipping the mark of the Beast, with the emblem of the human heart thrown beneath their feet, which they trampled and spit upon![9]

But even at this period, Hazlitt is capable of a more adequate response to Coleridge. This is apparent even in the attack which Herschel Baker singles out as particularly unpleasant, the anticipatory review of the *Lay Sermon* in the *Examiner* for 8 September 1816. Although one can only endorse Professor Baker's complaint that the article was 'grotesquely unfair to a great and greatly troubled man',[10] the fact remains that while each particular accusation is hurtful and derogatory, the effect of the whole series is to create a sense of chaotic energy which can only be categorised as sublime:

> All his notions are floating and unfixed, like what is feigned of the first forms of things flying about in search of bodies to attach themselves to; but *his* ideas seek to avoid all contact with solid substances. Innumerable evanescent thoughts dance before him, and dazzle his sight, like insects in the evening sun. Truth is to him a ceaseless round of contradictions: he lives in the belief of a perpetual lie, and in affecting to think what he pretends to say. His mind is in a constant estate of flux and reflux: he is like the Sea-horse in the Ocean; he is the Man in the Moon, the Wandering Jew. . . . [11]

In its original form, the passage moves towards its climax with a sentence which Lamb thought a 'horrible licence': 'Mr. Shandy would have settled the question at once:—"You have little or no nose, Sir."'[12] The sentence was deleted when Hazlitt reprinted the article in *Political Essays*, and it does come in rather abruptly. He makes use of the same observation with a greater tact in 'My First Acquaintance with Poets', where the underlying purpose of the allusion to Sterne's novel is clarified:

> His mouth was gross, voluptuous, open, eloquent; his chin good-humoured and round; but his nose, the rudder of the face, the index of the will, was small, feeble, nothing—like what he has done.[13]

This is unkind, even brutal: but it is an essential part of an identification with Tristram Shandy that is far from being predominantly negative. Tristram's *Life and Opinions* present a splendid set of variations on the theme of the magnificence and futility of human enterprises. Although Tristram's unhappy accident with his nose is only one of a series of misfortunes condemning him to a lifetime of inadequacy, his case is neither more or less distressing than that of his father, his uncle, or the parish bull. *Tristram Shandy* is an elaborate emblem of the absurdity of the human condition; but it also contains, as Hazlitt remarked (thinking of My Uncle Toby), 'one of the finest compliments ever paid to human nature'.[14] Coleridge's notions may have been floating and unfixed, but that was a condition of their peculiar amplitude. 'Hardly a speculation has been left on record from the earliest time,' Hazlitt says in *The Spirit of the Age*, 'but it is loosely folded up in Mr. Coleridge's memory, like a rich, but somewhat tattered piece of tapestry.'[15]

It is in the same part of *The Spirit of the Age* that Coleridge reminds Hazlitt of two Shakespearian figures: the fallen Mark Antony, dissolving like the ever-varying forms of the evening clouds:

> That which is now a horse, even with a thought
> The rack dislimns, and makes it indistinct
> As water is in water;[16]

and also that other flawed but alluring character, Sir John Falstaff: Coleridge's understanding, says Hazlitt, is 'fertile, subtle, expansive, "quick, forgetive, apprehensive", beyond all living precedent'. The allusion to Falstaff's encomium on the good effects of 'sherris-sack'[17] underlines the wilfulness of Coleridge's virtuosity, but associates it too with the positive qualities which Hazlitt attributed to the fat knight:

> Falstaff's wit is an emanation of a fine constitution; an exuberance of good-humour and good-nature; an overflowing of his love of laughter and good-fellowship; a giving vent to his heart's ease, and over-contentment with himself and others.[18]

Falstaff, Antony, and the world of Tristram Shandy are 'loosely folded up' in Hazlitt's memory in association with Coleridge, and the effect is to heighten an impression of copious vitality.

An even dizzier succession of allusions occurs in a contribution to the *Yellow Dwarf* (21 February 1818). After explaining how Coleridge's capacious mind has room for all opinions, both those which he believes and those which he does not, Hazlitt concludes:

> You can no more know where to have him than an otter. You might as well hedge the cuckoo. You see him now squat like a toad at the ear of the *Courier*; and oh! that we could rouse him up once more into an archangel's shape.[19]

We pass from Mistress Quickly to Lear's Fool, and from thence to Milton's Satan:

> Him thus intent *Ithuriel* with his Spear
> Touch'd lightly; for no falshood can endure
> Touch of Celestial temper, but returns
> Of force to its own likeness: up he starts
> Discoverd and surpriz'd. As when a spark
> Lights on a heap of nitrous Powder, laid
> Fit for the Tun some Magazin to store
> Against a rumord Warr, the Smuttie graine
> With sudden blaze diffus'd, inflames the Aire:
> So started up in his own shape the Fiend.[20]

Hazlitt makes an improbable Ithuriel, but there is plenty of gunpowder in his composition to give a convincing force to the idea of rousing Coleridge into 'his own shape'.

Hazlitt's mercurial vigour is particularly evident in the wounding review of *The Statesman's Manual* published in the *Examiner* for 29 December 1816. He makes great play with Coleridge's tentative comparison between current ministerial policies and the events recorded in the First Book of Kings after the death of Solomon, when the new king spoke to his people roughly, threatening to chastise them 'with scorpions'. Coleridge did not himself enlarge on the possible parallels. 'I tread on glowing embers,' he remarked, with an embarrassment which tickled his reviewer considerably. Nothing, obviously, would satisfy readers of the *Examiner* but the full, unexpurgated text from the Bible, which Hazlitt obligingly supplies, thus proving that *that* portion of the statesman's manual, at least, gives no endorsement to policies of authoritarian repression. Before entering upon this congenial task, he compares Coleridge's abrupt withdrawal from the argument to the behaviour of

> the impertinent barber of Baghdad, who being sent for to shave the prince, spent the whole morning in preparing his razors, took the height of the sun with an astrolabe, sung the song of Zimri, and danced the dance of Zamtout, and concluded by declining to perform the operation at all, because the day was unfavourable to its success.[21]

The reference is, of course, to the Tailor's story in the *Arabian Nights*, and the parallel is a happy one. The barber is not only a man who talks rather than acts (though to his own mind he is a weighty personage, not given to idle talk), he also has large pretensions to polymathy. In addition to his skill as a barber, he claims to be

> an experienced physician, a very profound chymist, an infallible astrologue, a finished grammarian, a complete orator, a subtle logician, a mathematician perfectly well versed in geometry, arithmetic, astronomy, and all the divisions of algebra: an historian fully master of all the kingdoms of the universe: besides, I know all parts of philosophy: I have all the traditions upon my fingers ends. I am poet, I am architect; nay, what is it I am not? There is nothing in nature hidden from me.[22]

This generous endowment serves chiefly, so far as the young man is concerned, to thwart his assignation with the daughter of the Cadi. Hazlitt would have had no difficulty in making the application to a writer who was 'the Dog in the Manger of literature, an intellectual Mar-Plot, who will neither let any body else come to a conclusion, nor come to one himself'.[23]

Citing the tale from memory, Hazlitt makes one curious slip. The 'song of Zimri' is perhaps a misremembering of the song and dance of Sali, the boiled-pease-seller, one of the barber's friends. Presumably the Biblical name crept in because Hazlitt was thinking of Dryden's portrait of the Duke of Buckingham as Zimri in *Absalom and Achitophel*:

> A man so various that he seemed to be
> Not one, but all mankind's epitome:
> Stiff in opinions, always in the wrong,

> Was every thing by starts and nothing long;
> But in the course of one revolving moon
> Was chymist, fiddler, statesman and buffoon . . .[24]

The parallel is not exact, but as far as it goes it reinforces that sense of irrespressible energy that appealed equally to Dryden and to Hazlitt.

Hazlitt mentions the story of the Impertinent Barber again when he comes to discuss wit and humour in the first of his *Lectures on the English Comic Writers* (1819). It carries, he says, 'the principle of callous indifference in a jest as far as it can go'. This is an important illustration of Hazlitt's theory of laughter, which he relates to keeping disagreeable consequences of unexpected and incongruous experiences out of sight. Sudden transitions, baulked expectations, seem to 'give additional liveliness and gaiety to the animal spirits'.[25] The *Arabian Nights* are the product of a society dominated by an arbitrary and despotic power which naturally engenders monstrous and disjointed dreams and fictions, and this makes them 'an inexhaustible mine of comic humour and invention'. They display 'an heroic contempt for the untoward accidents and petty vexations of human life. It is the gaiety of despair . . .' Hazlitt finds the serious stories in the same collection correspondingly distasteful, and notes that in this he was at odds with most readers and in particular with the author of *The Ancient Mariner*, 'who must be allowed to be a judge of such matters' (if not, one almost hears Hazlitt adding, of modern politics). Coleridge had his own explanation for this distaste: 'if I did not like them, it was because I did not dream'.[26]

Hazlitt perhaps recalls this characteristic piece of subtle philosophical conjecture on Coleridge's part because he believed that Coleridge and his friends dreamed too much. One of his complaints against the Lake Poets — paradoxically in view of their political conversion — was that they had failed to relinquish the impossible dreams of a perfectible human nature that had possessed them in their radical youth. In a passage in Hazlitt's review of *The Excursion*, to which Mr Kinnaird has rightly drawn particular attention, he regretfully dismisses Wordsworth's vision of the triumph of humanity as unrealistic:

> It is a consummation which cannot happen till the nature of
> things is changed, till the many become as united as the *one*, till
> romantic generosity shall be as common as gross selfishness, till
> reason shall have acquired the obstinate blindness of prejudice,
> till the love of power and of change shall no longer goad man on
> to restless action . . .[27]

A similar disagreement lies behind the argument between
Coleridge and Hazlitt about whether it was possible for a child
to have 'a naturally wicked disposition'.[28] Coleridge's
reluctance to detect wilfulness in a squalling infant is of a piece
with what Hazlitt saw as his unduly optimistic view of other
kinds of human misbehaviour, and it made him peculiarly
vulnerable to the deceits of the wily Duessa of Legitimacy.

Hazlitt tells the story of the Apostate Poets in an outrageous
parable written for the *Yellow Dwarf*, describing their encounter
with an old masked bawd who claimed to have just escaped
being robbed and ravished by revolutionary violence. Even
after she has 'pulled off her mask of Legitimacy', they are so
charmed by her paint and patches or her gold and trinkets that
they

> put a grave face upon the matter, make it a point of conscience, a
> match for life—*for better or worse*, stick to their filthy bargain, go to
> bed, and by lying quiet and keeping close, would fain persuade
> the people out of doors that all is well, while they are fumbling at
> the regeneration of mankind out of an old rotten carcase, and
> threatening us, as the legitimate consequence of their impotent
> and obscene attempts, with the spawn of Bible and Missionary
> Societies, Schools for All, and a little aiery of children, with a
> whole brood of hornbooks and catechisms.[29]

This has all the gross energy of a Gillray cartoon, with the
transformed child-actors out of *Hamlet* providing a fine closing
touch of fanciful grotesquerie, and the hornbooks and
catechisms taking on an animation that is almost surrealistic. It
tells one a great deal more about Hazlitt than it does about
Coleridge, but it also helps to explain Coleridge's abiding
fascination for Hazlitt, even when viewed with such contempt.
Like the Impertinent Barber, Coleridge continued eloquently,
inventively, and irrepressibly consistent in his role as
comprehensive and useless genius; and however unwelcome to

Hazlitt this might be in some respects, at least it manifests that *keeping* in comic character which he finds peculiarly delightful.[30]

REFERENCES

1 See *Letters of John Keats,* ed. H.E. Rollins (Cambridge, Mass., 1958), to B.R. Haydon, 21 March 1818, i. 252; to G. and G. Keats, 13 March 1819, ii. 76; to L. Hunt, 10 May 1817, i. 138.
2 **HAZLITT,** v. 167.
3 *ibid.,* xi. 34.
4 *ibid.,* xii. 198-99.
5 J. Kinnaird, *William Hazlitt: Critic of Power* (New York, 1978), 43.
6 **HAZLITT,** vii. 236.
7 *ibid.*
8 *ibid.,* xiv. 198.
9 *ibid.,* vii. 152.
10 Herschel Baker, *William Hazlitt* (Cambridge, Mass., 1962), 355-56.
11 **HAZLITT,** vii. 117.
12 *ibid.,* vii. 381n.
13 *ibid.,* xvii. 109.
14 *ibid.,* vi. 121.
15 *ibid.,* xi. 29.
16 *ibid.* See *Antony and Cleopatra,* IV. xiv. 9-11.
17 *2 Henry IV,* IV. iii. 85 et seq.
18 **HAZLITT,** iv. 278.
19 *ibid.,* xix. 210.
20 *Paradise Lost,* iv. 810-19.
21 **HAZLITT,** vii. 122.
22 *Arabian Nights' Entertainments,* 14th ed. of English translation of the French version by Antoine Galland (Edinburgh, 1772), ii. 49.
23 **HAZLITT,** vii. 115.
24 lines 545-50.
25 **HAZLITT,** vi. 6.
26 *ibid.,* vi. 13-14.
27 *ibid.,* iv. 119.
28 *ibid.,* xii. 347.
29 *ibid.,* xix. 204-5.
30 *ibid.,* vi. 11.

3

Two Extraordinary Men: Scott and Coleridge

by ERIC ANDERSON

'That extraordinary man Coleridge' — Scott's *Journal*, p. 462.

'Perhaps the most extraordinary Man, assuredly the most extraordinary *Writer*, of his Age.'

Coleridge's *Letters*, no. 1230.

Scott and Coleridge were the principal guests at a dinner given by William Sotheby in April 1828. When the ladies had left the table, the remark that Coleridge did not believe in the existence of Homer occasioned an impromptu lecture, amusingly chronicled by James Fenimore Cooper who was among those present:

> It was not a discourse, but a dissertation. Scarcely anyone spoke besides Mr. Coleridge, with the exception of a brief occasional remark from Mr. Sotheby, who held the contrary opinion; and I might say no one *could* speak. At moments he was surprisingly eloquent, though a little discursive, and the whole time he appeared to be perfectly the master of his subject and of his language. As near as I could judge, he was rather more than an hour in *possession of the floor*, almost without interruption. His utterance was slow, every sentence being distinctly given, and his pronunciation accurate. There seemed to be a constant struggling between an affluence of words and an affluence of ideas, without either hesitation or repetition. His voice was strong and clear, but not pitched above the usual key of conversation. The only peculiarity about it was a slightly

observable burring of the r-r-rs, but scarcely more than what the
language properly requires.

Once or twice, when Mr. Sotheby would attempt to say a word
on his side of the question, he was permitted to utter just enough
to give a leading idea, but no argument, when the reasoning was
taken out of his mouth by the essayist, and continued, pro and
con, with the same redundant and eloquent fluency. I was less
struck by the logic than by the beauty of the language, and the
poetry of his images. Of the theme, in a learned sense, I knew too
little to pretend to any verbal or critical knowledge, but he
naturally endeavoured to fortify his argument by the application
of his principles to familiar things; and here, I think, he often
failed. In fact, the exhibition was much more wonderful than
convincing.[1]

The company had no doubt hoped to hear Scott in his
celebrated vein of anecdote and reminiscence, but there was no
chance of hearing him or anyone else. 'Scott sat, immovable as a
statue, with his little gray eyes looking inward and outward,
and evidently considering the whole as an exhibition, rather
than an argument; although he occasionally muttered,
"Eloquent!" "Wonderful!" "Very extraordinary!".'[2] From the
entry in his *Journal* it appears that Scott was actually more
amused by the discomfiture of his friend John Morritt, who took
the other view of the Homeric question and whose impatience
on this occasion 'must have cost him an extra sixpence worth of
snuff'.[3] Although the noise from the hall indicated the arrival of
other guests, 'Mr. Coleridge lectured on, through it all, for half
an hour longer'. When Sotheby finally rose, the house was full
of guests assembled to see Scott, and the two great men can
have had no chance of further conversation, for Scott (says
Cooper) 'walked deliberately into a maze of petticoats, and . . .
let them play with his mane as much as they pleased'.[4] Scott
and Coleridge did not meet again. This last encounter neatly
symbolizes their relationship, for although the two men were in
the ascendant at the same time, they never became intimate.
They met, to some extent they admired each other, and they
parted.

They met at most perhaps half a dozen times. Writing in
1811, Coleridge said he had met Scott 'twice or thrice in
company'.[5] He had also visited the Tower of London with him

in 1807, when young Hartley Coleridge remembered that 'the economy of the bard' (that is, Coleridge) did not allow them to see the crown jewels, but that 'Mr. Scott had evident pride in showing me the claymores and bucklers taken from the loyalists at Culloden'.[6] On another occasion, meeting at Sotheby's table in the company of Humphry Davy, Dr Howley and 'a grand congregation of lions',[7] Scott and Coleridge became allies in debate. Ignorant of the author, Scott recited and commended the poem called 'Fire, Famine and Slaughter' which he had recently read. The company was minded to disagree with his praise of it. Coleridge gave a heated defence of the poem and finally confessed that it was his own.

On several other occasions which might have been propitious to friendship, Scott and Coleridge failed to meet. Coleridge must have hoped to see Scott during his visit to Edinburgh in 1803; he went to his house in Castle Street ('divinely situated—it looks up a street, a new magnificent Street, full upon the Rock & the Castle, with its zig-zag Walls like Painters' Lightning'[8]) but he found that Scott was in his country quarters at Lasswade. They might have met in 1807 when Scott intended a visit to Wordsworth at Coleorton in March, but instead had to speed on to London. In 1820, when Scott was again in London, Coleridge's neighbour, Matthews the actor, knowing that he intended to call on him the next day, suggested that Coleridge should join them. Coleridge's scruples prevented him from accepting:

> I took it very kind of him; but to obtrude myself on Walter Scott, nolentem volentem, and within a furlong of my own abode, as he knows (for Mr Frere told him my address) was a liberty, I had no right to take: and tho' it would have highly gratified me to have conversed with a Brother-bard, & to have renewed on the mental retina the image of perhaps the most extraordinary Man, assuredly the most extraordinary *Writer*, of his Age, yet I dared not purchase the gratification at so high a price, as that of risking the respect, which, I trust, has not hitherto been forfeited by . . . S.T. Coleridge.[9]

The letter reflects the awe Coleridge felt for Scott, but also reveals how little he understood the sort of life Scott led. He was in London for the conferment of his baronetcy, to sit to

Chantrey for his bust and to Lawrence for a portrait to hang at Windsor. It was an exhausting as well as an exhilarating visit. 'If I had three heads like Cerberus I could eat three dinners with them every day' he told Constable, his publisher, 'and am fairly in a way to be smothered with kindness.'[10] 'I find I cannot bear late hours and great society so well as formerly,' he wrote to Ballantyne; 'but yet it is a fine thing to hear politics talked of by Ministers of State and War discussed by the Duke of Wellington.'[11] It is small wonder that he did not think to seek out Coleridge with whom he had 'no habits of friendship and scarce those of acquaintance'.[12]

In any event politics had always interested Scott more than literary conversation. He saw himself as a bluff good-humoured fellow, mixing 'with people of business and sometimes with politicians', and he had little patience with 'the imaginary consequence of literary people who walk with their noses in the air'.[13] Although there is always some element of self-depreciation when Scott speaks of his art, it is evident that his preference for men of action who were useful to him as a novelist was genuine. Had circumstances allowed Scott and Coleridge to know each other better, it is still not likely, therefore, that they would have become close friends. As it is, they remained acquaintances. The striking thing is, that in an age where literary assassination was in vogue, these two very different men, neither fully capable of understanding the other, nonetheless kept alive a warm regard for each other's abilities and often spoke in each other's praise. They were alike in their generosity of spirit.

Scott, for instance (perhaps with more generosity than judgement) gave Coleridge an honourable mention in his *Essay on the Drama*.[14] A note added to *The Abbot* in 1830 is a somewhat ponderous compliment to the 'beautiful and tantalizing fragment of Christabel',[15] and Coleridge is again commended in a note to *St. Ronan's Well*.[16] There is no reason to think that Scott's private and public utterances were much at variance. Lockhart recalls that during his first visit to Abbotsford in 1818 the conversation turned to Coleridge who was said to be translating *Faust*. Scott, who was enthusiastic about *Wallenstein*, expressed his usual regret that Coleridge could not manage his gifts 'so as to bring out anything of his own on a large scale at all worthy of his genius', and enthused over the idea that he 'might easily make a sort of fame for himself as a poetical translator'.[17] Coleridge's prose did not appeal to him. He owned a second edition of *Biographia Literaria,* but, at least by February 1818 when he wrote to Maturin about Coleridge, he had not read it,[18] and on his final journey to the Mediterranean he confided to Mrs Davy that he thought the great part of Coleridge's prose writing very little better than nonsense.[19] Of his poetry, however, he thought highly. Basil Hall heard him read *Christabel* to the company at Abbotsford at the end of 1824 'with a wonderful pathos and variety of expression'[20]; he included 'Genevieve' in his *English Minstrelsy* (1809) and describes the poem, in a letter of 1814, as 'among the most beautiful in the English language'.[21]

We know, too, that Scott tried on occasion to be of practical help to Coleridge. His name comes tenth among the early subscribers to *The Friend* listed in Coleridge's notebooks[22]; he sent his 'trifling subscription'[23] in 1810 and the volume is on the library shelves at Abbotsford.[24] From letters to Southey (with whom Scott was better acquainted) it appears that he had hoped to be of more substantial use, even to the extent of finding a publisher for the paper. His 'high quarrel with Constable and Co.'[25] over the conduct of the *Edinburgh Review,* and the establishment, with Scott's support, of the rival *Quarterly,* left him for the time being without any interest in that direction, but he promised at least to encourage Ballantyne the bookseller to send a 'handsome order'.[26] His interest in Coleridge's welfare continued, for some years later he intervened, as described elsewhere in this volume,[27] to put an end to the literary quarrel between Coleridge and Maturin; and in 1821, when his advice was asked about the appointment of Royal Associates of the Royal Society of Literature, Scott named Coleridge and (ironically) Maturin as the only two men of undeniable merit who needed the pensions of £100 a year.[28] Scott felt that Coleridge 'had some room to be spited at the World', and was sorry for him 'as a man of genius struggling with bad habits and difficult circumstances'.[29]

Coleridge's liking for Scott was warmer than Scott's regard for Coleridge. 'Those who hold that a Man's nature is shewn in his Countenance would not need the confident assurance, which all his Friends & Acquaintance so unanimously give, that he is of the most frank and generous disposition, incapable of trick or concealment'[30] was Coleridge's account of the impression which Scott made on him during their fleeting acquaintance in company in London. It confirms what he told J.P. Collier that 'he personally liked'[31] Scott. He was flattered to be told by a bookseller that Byron and Scott had both told him that 'taking him all in all, Mr C. is the greatest man, we have'[32] (although since Scott nowhere records such an opinion, the unnamed bookseller, probably John Murray, may have misrepresented him); and when he thought of publishing a select collection of his poems in 1823, omitting all but his best work, it was to the judgement of Samuel Rogers and Scott that he would willingly have left the final choice.[33]

Later his feelings for Scott became tinged with envy. It has to be remembered that Scott, as he himself put it, 'had the crown'[34]; that he made, as well as lost, a fortune by his writing, and that, first as poet and then as novelist, he towered in reputation and popular esteem over his great contemporaries. Conscious of his own originality and of his superiority as a poet, and seldom free from financial worries, Coleridge could not but compare Scott's worldly success with his own poverty and obscurity. 'I certainly should be glad to have the fifth part of Scott's reputation — but if I know myself — even this not for its own sake, but as the means of obtaining that frugal competence which would emancipate me', he wrote in the letter to Frere which ends 'O that I had but three hundred a year'.[35] When, a month later, he heard that Scott was ruined, he enjoyed a moment of triumph:

> when I think of the wretched trash, that the Lust of Gain induced him to publish for the last three or four years, which must have been *manufactured* for the greater part, even my feelings assist in hardening me. I should indeed be sorry if any ultimate success had attended the attempt to unite the Poet and the Worldling. — Heaven knows! I have enough to feel for without wasting my Sympathy on a Scotchman suffering the penalty of his Scotchery.[36]

It is a human if not a particularly admirable response to the fall of a popular idol. Two causes of offence may have sharpened his pen on this occasion. A year or two earlier C.R. Leslie had produced an illustration for the 1823 edition of *The Antiquary* in which the ludicrous German Dousterswivel bears a considerable resemblance to Coleridge.[37] From what we know of the pressures under which Scott worked, he may well have been unaware of Leslie's discourteous joke, but Coleridge would reasonably assume that he knew and approved. More importantly the failure of *Christabel* when it was finally published in 1816 continued to rankle; and nearly ten years later the abuse heaped on it by the *Edinburgh Review* and the failure of the *Quarterly* to review it at all, are again mentioned in a letter to John Coleridge: 'Sir W. Scott *might* have served me if he had at [that] time said only *one half* of what he has since avowed, in large companies — as at Sir G. Beaumont's, Mr Rogers's, Mr Sotheby's, &c'.[38] Disappointment revived in his mind the old allegations that in *The Lay of the Last Minstrel* Scott had plagiarized *Christabel,* and to that he partly attributed its poor reception. For these reasons he felt by 1827 that he had 'little reason to hold myself obliged to him'.[39] These feelings did not survive Scott's death, and Coleridge delighted in his friendship with Sophia, Scott's favourite daughter, and her husband, John Gibson Lockhart.[40]

As a critic of Scott, Coleridge is very good indeed. Much of what he had to say about Scott ran counter to the popular view at the time but it is now the received opinion in almost every detail. For Scott's poetry he had little time. His detailed criticism of *The Lady of the Lake,* contained partly in his notebooks[41] and partly in a frank and amusing letter to Wordsworth, leaves it without much claim to serious consideration:

> The movement of the Poem . . . is between a sleeping Canter and a Marketwoman's trot — but it is endless — I seem never to have made any way . . . In short, what I felt in Marmion I feel still more in the Lady of the Lake — viz. that a man accustomed to cast words in metre and familiar with descriptive Poets & Tourists, himself a Picturesque Tourist, must be troubled with a mental Strangury, if he could not lift up his leg six times at six different Corners, and each time p— a canto'.[42]

In a notebook, in preparation for a review he never wrote,[43] he criticizes Scott's commonplace metaphor and 'dislocation of the words for purpose of rhyme and metre'[44], and dismisses his diction as 'a language which claims to be poetical for no better reason, than that it would be intolerable in conversation or prose'.[45] He prophesied to Thomas Allsop that 'Not twenty lines of Scott's poetry will ever reach posterity; it has relation to nothing'.[46] Elsewhere Coleridge wrestled with the problem posed by the general acclaim with which Scott's poems were greeted, and solved it by drawing a distinction between the poetry which is judged by 'Fashion', by 'the Taste of the Age', and by 'The Ideal of Human Nature'. The third kind is the poetry which endures. Scott he places under Fashion and concludes that 'without the aid of this, i.e. Fashion, there is no instance of any vast *run* & *rush* of Popularity'.[47]

Of Scott's novels, by contrast, Coleridge was fond. He told Allsop in April 1820 that he had 'read the far greater part of his Novels twice, & several three times over, with undiminished pleasure and interest'. With the exception of *Ivanhoe* and *The Bride of Lammermoor*, he admired the Waverley Novels both for their reflection of past ages and for 'the *permanent* nature of the Interest, which they excite'. He disliked the *'false Effect'* of 'the use of the Scotch Dialect' and 'Ossianic Mock-Highland Motley Heroic', but marvelled at 'the number of characters *so good* produced by one man & in so rapid a succession'. Anticipating the best later criticism, he sees the grand theme of Scott's best work as its enduring interest:

> the contest between the Loyalists & their opponents can never be *obsolete,* for it is the contest between the two great moving Principles of social Humanity — religious adherence to the Past and the Ancient, the Desire & the admiration of Permanence, on the one hand; and the Passion for increase of Knowledge, for Truth as the offspring of Reason, in short, the mighty Instincts of *Progression* and *Free-agency,* on the other.[48]

If we add to this his remarks on plot and prose-style in a letter written eight years later —

> but assuredly, Polish of Style, and that sort of Prose which is in fact only another kind of Poetry . . . this is not Sir Walter's Excellence. He needs Sea-room — space for development of character by Dialogue, &c, &c— and even in his most successful Works the *Tale* is always the worst part — clumsily evolved & made up of incidents that are purely accidental[49]—

we have in brief the outline of all the most perceptive criticism of Scott the novelist. By contrast the marginalia in Coleridge's set of the Waverley Novels[50] are disappointing. Some deal amusingly with improbabilities of plot or character and infelicities of style. Other passages throw less light on the author than on the annotator, who picks out from the novels texts for brief excursions of his own on religious, moral and social matters.

It is to Coleridge's credit that he was not tempted into the sort of literary quarrel with Scott which would have titillated the literary world. He refused to accuse Scott of plagiarism when 'at least half a dozen'[51] of his friends professed to see close resemblances of style and manner between *The Lay of the Last Minstrel* (published in 1805) and the as yet unpublished *Christabel*. His first reaction, which is both creditable to him and substantially correct, was of disbelief; but he was in no hurry to open *The Lay*. Writing to Josiah Wedgewood in late June 1807, a full eighteen months after the poem's first appearance, he still refers to it as 'a work which I have not read'.[52] By late November he had read it; and wrote to Dorothy Wordsworth that he 'could not detect either in manner, matter, or metre, a single trace of dishonourable or avoidable Resemblance to the Christabel',[53] and to Southey that, although he 'did not over-hugely admire' it, he 'saw no likeness whatsoever to the Christabel, much less any improper resemblance'.[54] A later letter describes *The Lay* as the production of someone so 'Habitually conversant with the antiquities of his Country . . . passionately fond of natural Scenery, abundant in local Anecdote, and besides learned in all the antique Scrolls of Faery Land' that 'His Poems are evidently the indigenous Products of his Mind & Habits'.[55] Thus acquitted by Coleridge himself, Scott scarcely needs Sir Herbert Grierson's defence of his 'heartier and clumsier' rhythms,[56] or Edgar Johnson's claim that Scott exaggerated his metrical debt to Coleridge 'with characteristic generosity'.[57]

Utterly unlike each other as the two poems are, there is in fact some metrical similarity and one line which Scott caught up from Coleridge. This came about because *Christabel* was begun in 1797 and was well-known in literary circles long before it was first published in 1816. Scott's account[58] of its influence on him is that John Stoddart recited it to him at Lasswade before he had begun work on *The Lay* (almost certainly in 1802, not, as Scott says, in 1800)[59]. Scott made no secret of his admiration for the poem then or afterwards, and indeed introduced Byron to it in the hope that it would encourage him to recommend *Zapolya* to the management at Drury Lane. Griggs hints that Scott might have admitted his debt more speedily, instead of delaying until stung into action by Medwin's report of Byron's opinion that but for Coleridge 'perhaps "The Lay of the Last Minstrel" would never have been thought of'.[60] Scott, however, would have been surprised to be accused of plagiarism. He *had* exploited the metre of *Christabel* for his own purposes; but as Southey said, it was not designedly, simply that 'the echo was in his ear'.[61]

The diversity of the Romantic Movement is well illustrated by the acquaintanceship of Scott and Coleridge, so apparently similar in their interests and yet opposites in so many ways. Both were fascinated by the supernatural: it is at the heart of Scott's goblin tale of *The Lay* and of *Guy Mannering,* and in his final years he collected together many of his favourite tales in his *Demonology and Witchcraft.* His use of the supernatural is, however, far removed from *The Ancient Mariner* or *Christabel.* To Scott, the supernatural is material to be worked into a story for the purpose of the plot. However it may suit him to invest his characters with belief in the supernatural (and as Coleridge points out, Scott is unwilling even to concede sincerity to the astrologer in *Quentin Durward* whom he calls a 'cheat and impostor')[62] he seldom leaves the reader long in doubt about his own views. These are rational and sceptical. Scott was attracted by tales of mystery and witchcraft, because he loved anecdote of any kind and especially anecdotes of the Scottish peasantry, but he was careful to distance himself, like the Augustan that he was, from enthusiastic belief and unexplained mystery.

On the other hand his imagination was fired, as Coleridge's was not (for all his evocation of mediaeval times in *Christabel*) by the details of great events and objects from the past. The armoury at Abbotsford is not just a nineteenth-century gentleman's collection of curiosities; it is a reflection of the passion for the past which inspired his best work. At times he is led astray by his obsession with details of dress and accoutrements, but at his best there emerges from the antiquarian details the people who lived and breathed in a former age and truths about human behaviour which transcend any age. He taught the world that history was about real men and women, but his starting point was often antiquarian. Coleridge was so far from sharing these interests that he barely understood them:

> Dear Sir Walter and myself were exact, but harmonious, opposites in this: that every old ruin, hill, river, or tree called up in his mind a host of historical or biographical associations . . . whereas, for myself, notwithstanding Dr. Johnson, I believe I should walk over the plain of Marathon without taking more interest in it than in any other plain of similar features.[63]

They were not twin spirits, and their influence on each other was slight. But each recognized the extraordinary quality of the other—Coleridge the achievement of 'Dear Sir Walter' as a novelist, and Scott the fragmentary brilliance of 'that eccentric but admirable poet, Coleridge'.[64]

REFERENCES

1 J.F. Cooper, *Gleanings in Europe*, ed. R.E. Spiller (1930), ii.162.
2 *ibid.*
3 Scott's *Journal*, ed. W.E.K. Anderson (1972), 462.
4 J.F. Cooper, *op. cit.*, ii.162.
5 *CL*, iii.355.
6 *Poems by Hartley Coleridge*, ed. Derwent Coleridge, 2nd ed. (1851), i.ccxxii.
7 J.B. Lockhart, *Life of Scott*, 2nd ed. (1851), iii.185.
8 *CL*, ii.989.
9 *ibid.*, v.38.
10 **SCOTT,** vi.158.
11 *ibid.*, vi.160.
12 *ibid.*, v.97.
13 Scott's *Journal*, 6.
14 Scott's *Miscellaneous Prose Works* (1848), vi.387.

15 Note VIII.
16 Note II.
17 *Life of Scott*, v.379-80.
18 **SCOTT,** v.97. See also Alethea Hayter's essay, p.33.
19 Scott's *Journal*, 690n[4].
20 *Life of Scott*, vii.291.
21 **SCOTT,** iii.400. For 'Genevieve' see p.78 n[6].
22 *CN*, iii.3471.
23 **SCOTT,** ii.342.
24 *Abbotsford Library Catalogue*, comp. J.G. Cochrane (1838), 340.
25 **SCOTT,** ii.151.
26 *ibid.*, ii.160.
27 Page 33.
28 **SCOTT,** vi.397-405.
29 *ibid.*, v.97.
30 *CL*, iii.355.
31 *Sh C.*, (1930 ed., publ. Constable), ii. 44.
32 *CL*, iv.736.
33 *ibid.*, v.283.
34 Scott's *Journal*, 393.
35 *CL*, vi.541-42.
36 *ibid.*, vi.562.
37 *ibid.*, v.422.
38 *ibid.*, v.437.
39 *ibid.*, vi.699.
40 See Marion Lochhead's essay, particularly pp.72-4, 77.
41 *CN*, iii.3970.
42 *CL*, iii.291-92.
43 *CN*, iii.3952 f.72^v.
44 *ibid.*, iii.3970.
45 *ibid.*, ii.2599 f.89.
46 T. Allsop, *Letters, Conversations and Recollections of S.T. Coleridge* (1864), 104.
47 *CN*, iii.4301.
48 *CL*, v.33-5.
49 *ibid.*, vi.778.
50 T. Raysor, *Coleridge's Miscellaneous Criticism* (1936), 321-38.
51 *CL*, ii.1191.
52 *ibid.*, iii.22.
53 *ibid.*, iii.39.
54 *ibid.*, iii.42.
55 *ibid.*, iii.360-61.
56 H.C. Grierson, *Sir Walter Scott, Bart.* (1938), 81.
57 E. Johnson, *Sir Walter Scott, The Great Unknown* (1970), i.338.
58 Scott's *Poetical Works* (1832), vi.23-7.
59 *CL.*, iii.356n.
60 *ibid.*; T. Medwin, *Conversations of Lord Byron* (1824), 203.
61 *Life and Correspondence of Robert Southey*, ed. C.C. Southey (1849-50), ii.316.

62 T. Raysor, *op.cit.*, 337.
63 *Table Talk and Omniana of S.T. Coleridge,* ed. H.N. Coleridge (1917), 260.
    See also *CN*, i.2026 f.6.
64 **SCOTT,** i.146.

4

Coleridge and
John Gibson Lockhart

by MARION LOCHHEAD

Coleridge among English writers is in the front rank at once as poet, as critic and as philosopher. The combination of poetic sympathy with logical subtlety gives unsurpassed value to his work.

Considered merely in a literary point of view the work is execrable. That he is a man of genius is evident, but he is not a man of strong intelligence nor of powerful talents . . . The truth is that Mr Coleridge is but an obscure name in English literature . . . . We cannot see in what way the state of literature would have been different had he been cut off in childhood, or had he never been born; for except a few wild and fanciful ballads, he has produced nothing worth remembering.

If there be any man of grand and original genius alive in Europe at this moment, such a man is Mr Coleridge . . . He is perhaps the most splendid versifier of our age, he is certainly, to my ear, without exception the most musical.

This trio of quotations has, for theme, the same man and, in particular, the same book: Samuel Taylor Coleridge and his *Biographia Literaria,* that unique blend of memoir, criticism, philosophy, and controversy. The first comes from the article in the *Dictionary of National Biography* by Leslie Stephen, the second from the review in *Blackwood's Magazine* of October 1817, written by Christopher North — whose real name was John Wilson; the third is from *Peter's Letters to His Kinsfolk,* published in 1819 by Blackwood, and written by young John Gibson Lockhart, disguised as Dr Peter Morris, a middle-aged Welshman travelling in Scotland.

Dr Morris declared that the bitter attack by *Maga* (as *Blackwood's Magazine* was familiarly called) was 'a total departure from the principles of the Magazine, and almost, I think, a specimen of the worst kind of spirit which the Magazine professed to be fighting against in the *Edinburgh Review*'. For this Dr Morris was 'at a loss to discover—not an apology—but a motive'.[1]

The rebuke must have stung, for Lockhart, *in propria persona*, was one of *Blackwood's* chief contributors, and a close friend of Wilson. His own first biographer, Andrew Lang, pronounced the attack on Coleridge to be 'an example not only of the violence but of the incalculable waywardness of the Magazine',[2] which was Tory, as Coleridge himself was by this time. As such, it was opposed to the Whiggery of the *Edinburgh Review*. An attack upon a political adversary might have been violent but would not have been wayward. Lang called it also 'the evil article'.[3]

This was, indeed, one of the most savage periods in the history of literary criticism, a continuation of the enmity between Jacobite and Hanoverian or between hostile clans. Blackwood's men and Jeffrey's of the *Edinburgh Review* might not lurk, armed with dirk or dagger, in Edinburgh's wynds and closes, but they effectively kept up the old spirit.

Dr Morris was not uncritical, but his criticism was stimulating and perceptive, bringing out the beauty as well as the flaws in Coleridge's work.

> A certain rambling, discursive style of writing, and a habit of mixing up, with ideas of great originality, the products of extensive observation and meditation, others of a very fantastic and mystical sort, borrowed from Fichte and the other German philosophers, with whose works he is familiar—these things have been sufficient to prevent his prose writings from becoming popular beyond a certain narrow class of readers, who, when they see marks of great power, can never be persuaded to treat lightly the works in which these appear, with whatever less attractive matter they may chance to be intermingled. Yet even his prose writings are at this moment furnishing most valuable

materials to people who know, better than the author himself does, the art of writing for the British public; and it is impossible that they should continue to be much longer neglected as they now are. But the poetry of Coleridge, in order to be understood perfectly and admired profoundly, requires no peculiar habits of mind beyond those which all intelligent readers of poetry ought to have, and must have.[4]

Referring to Wordsworth's Preface to *Lyrical Ballads* and to the 'psychological system' which lay at the root of his poetry, and which Coleridge had adopted with something like reverence, Dr Morris commended the latter for having none the less 'abstained from bringing his psychological notions forward in the same open and un-courting way' as Wordsworth. (An excellent word: *un-courting*.) Coleridge had not adopted Wordsworth's 'peculiar notions regarding poetic diction'.

Then came the tribute, already quoted, to 'the most splendid versifier . . . the most musical', which continued:

> Nothing can surpass the majestic richness of words which he heaps round his images—images which are neither glaring in themselves, nor set forth in any glaring framework of incident, but which are always affecting to the verge of tears, because they have all been formed and nourished in the recesses of one of the most deeply musing spirits that ever breathed forth its inspirations in the majestic language of England.[5]

In Coleridge's love poetry there was a quality that Byron could not attain: more reverence for women,

> far deeper insight into the true grandeur of their gentleness. I do not think there is any poet in the world who ever touched so truly the mystery of the passion as he has done in *Genevieve*.[6]

It was altogether bewildering that a critic, writing for *Blackwood's*, should so lose dignity and reverence as to 'heap new ridicule upon the character of a great genius who had already been made the butt' of so much mockery.

There could not have been a defence more valiant or more valued. Coleridge expressed his gratitude in a letter he wrote, in November 1819, to this Dr Peter Morris, of whom he knew nothing beyond his authorship; and who might indeed, he thought, be not one writer but two comrades in literature writing as one. This idea he put to his friend, Thomas Allsop, to whom he said that *Peter's Letters*

> seem to have originated in a sort of familiar conversation between two clever men, who have said, "Let us write a book that will sell; you write this, and I will write that," and in a sort of laughing humour set to work. This was the way that Southey and myself wrote many things together.[7]

In his letter to Dr Morris Coleridge wrote:

> If I have but little appetite for literary applause, I have not, however, cheated myself into mistaking a weak stomach for strength of mind.

There was, however, a kind of applause, of praise, of sympathy which was at once objective and life-giving; it brought forth true judgement and stimulus.

> To *Praise,* that springs from such a root, to the buds and blossoms of such a judgement, God forbid that I should be otherwise than alive.

It was a necessary support without which 'the hopes and purposes of genius sink back on the heart like a sigh on the tightened chest of a sick man'. Coleridge had had a 'rare and transient possession' of such sympathy; and had felt its absence or withdrawal the more keenly.

> What then should we think of those who feel the full worth of such a tribute in their own case, yet withhold it in that of others? Such is *Atticus*.[8]

And *Atticus* was believed to be Wordsworth, who was better at receiving than at bestowing praise. For *Atticus*, Coleridge continued, not without bitterness, and certainly with pungency, 'the admiration of his writings is not merely his gauge of men's *taste*—he reads it as the index of their *moral* character'. He was a *balancer* in judgement, and 'with the same comfortless discretion does he communicate to the author his opinions, grounded on the specimens of an unfinished work'.

'Comfortless discretion' is an excellent phrase for a quality often found in critics by their victims.

Then Coleridge rounded off his complaint with a typical

psychological observation not unmixed with painful personal experience:

> There are men richly gifted, who yet after each successive effort of composition, lose the inward courage that should enable them to decide rightly on the degree of their success, and who seek the judgement of an admired friend with a timid and almost girlish bashfulness. On such a temper, and in such a mood, this chilly, doubting qualifying *wiseness* may check and inhibit the infant buds of power for months—nay, should the hapless wight continue so long under the spray, for the whole summer of his life![9]

There had already been a note of bitterness in Coleridge's exposition of his own principles of criticism in *Biographia Literaria:*

> I know nothing that surpasses the vileness of deciding on the merits of a poet or painter, (not by characteristic defects; for where there is genius, *these* always point to his characteristic *beauties;* but) by accidental failures or faulty passages; except the impudence of defending it, as the proper duty and most instructive part, of criticism.

There should be principles of criticism; reviewers should refer to 'fixed canons of criticism' instead of indulging in 'arbitrary dictation and petulant sneers'. Readers of intelligence and good judgement would rightly 'pronounce it arrogance in them thus to announce themselves to men of letters, as the guides of their taste and judgement'. To dwell upon *defects* was no help to the possible reader; to point to the beauties of any work was to inform and stimulate.[10]

There was no suggestion in this Letter to Peter Morris (whom Coleridge did not yet know to be Lockhart) that it be kept private, and Lockhart wrote to Christopher North (apparently treating him as editor of *Blackwood's*):

> I trust there is no impropriety in my sending to you for your magazine . . . a very characteristic letter of one whom I well know you agree with me in honouring among the highest. You will laugh, as I did, about some little mistakes into which our illustrious and excellent friend has fallen; above all, that highly absurd one about your humble servant's *personality.* On no account, however, omit one word of the letter, and I will be

answerable to Coleridge for the making public thereof . . .

Peter Morris.[11]

The assumption that Christopher North honoured Coleridge 'among the highest' is a distillation of irony and impudence with a touch of mystification. Peter Morris may have seemed unaware of the identity of that reviewer in *Blackwood's* but Lockhart must have known, and doubtless North-Wilson knew that he knew.

The publication of the letter brought acute embarrassment to Coleridge. In December 1820 he wrote to Lockhart:

> . . . Some weeks after the appearance of my Letter to you, I heard that both my Sons had been vexed and distressed at the circumstance, on the ground that so many persons would know that it alluded in part to Wordsworth—that it would widen the breach or rather convert a coolness into a breach—but chiefly that it was so distressing to them, & still more to their Mother & Sister at Keswick.—I was vexed myself at the circumstance, sorely vexed; but *only with myself*. Not you—how could I? but myself I did blame inwardly for sending off a Letter in the first sketch, written in the first warmth of feeling, & the *general* contents of which indeed I remembered but not the particular sentences, nor how far they enforced the interpretation that had been made, more or less strongly.[12]

The realisation almost overwhelmed him, and at the height of his vexation a visitor (he thought it was Charles Lamb) added his reproaches:

> I answered, or muttered rather, impatiently—a foolish, vexatious business—that there was nothing in the Letter that my own feelings did not bear out and justify—however I was vexed at it—& had not the heart to see what I had written—& turned off the subject—But as to telling anyone that it was a *confidential Letter to a Friend* — what nonsense a man may chuse to *infer*, I cannot say — but that it should have been said by me, or fairly inferable from my words, is out of the Question.[13]

Coleridge emphasised his own ignorance, at the time of writing the letter, of the identity of Dr Morris—'whom I rather supposed to be two Persons—and this too expressed in the Letter itself—! this a confidential Letter? It is too absurd'. But it was not too absurd to be used as a charge against

Lockhart. Coleridge continued:

> Merciful Heaven! Had I had the most distant anticipation, the slightest suspicion, of either my name or your's being brought forward to the Public on the circumstance, I should have hastened to have first taken the whole on myself, and then to have reproached the friend, if a Friend as in the case of Charles Lamb, with having even *intended* to make bad worse, and bring me once more before the Public Bar, as if for the mere wanton purpose of forcing an open breach between me and Wordsworth's friends and family.[14]

The absolution of Lockhart was here complete and generous. We, for our part, may find it difficult to absolve him from irresponsible indiscretion: one of the faults of his intellectually reckless youth, for which he was now to pay heavily.

Lockhart had a bitter enemy in one John Scott, a journalist, who, writing in the *London* (or, as it was sometimes called from its publisher, *Baldwin's*) *Magazine*, accused Lockhart of being the editor of *Blackwood's* and of concealing that fact, and of having himself written that virulent attack upon Coleridge. Scott, moreover, now found Lockhart guilty of a breach of confidence in publishing the Letter to Dr Peter Morris. The accusations continued to mount up. For a complexity of reasons, Lockhart's oldest and most devoted friend, John Christie, was drawn into the affair which ended in a duel between him and Scott. Christie fired into the air, was ordered by both seconds to fire again, and this time fatally wounded Scott. Christie fled to the continent, returned to stand trial and was discharged. It was a pitiful business, hard to understand now; of all the protagonists, Christie emerges with the cleanest record. Some may see in this episode a turning point in Lockhart's life: *catharsis; metanoia*.[15]

Apart from this tragedy the sequel to the correspondence was a long and happy friendship, both personal and professional, between Lockhart and Coleridge. There was a reconciliation, also, between Coleridge and William Blackwood, founder of the firm and editor of the Magazine. The poet wrote to the publisher, after meeting William Davies, the firm's representative in London. The letter is post-marked: Highgate, 12 April 1819.

> . . . I do indeed feel myself much obliged to you for having made me acquainted with a man of such genuine worth and so much sound unostentatious good Sense. Besides, I am always glad to have any of my prejudices counteracted or overset; . . . and I honestly confess, that my experience had tinged my opinions concerning *the Trade* with rather a sombre die. God forbid that I should at any time or under any provocations have been guilty of so unchristian a thought as to doubt that a Bookseller might be a truly good and honourable man; but still (I am ashamed to say) my belief was much stronger in the Posse than the Esse thereof. Perhaps, your experience of *Authors* has been tit for tat with mine of *your* Brotherhood.[16]

Blackwood had suggested Coleridge's contributing some 'scrips and scraps' to the Magazine, and Coleridge did eventually send him a poem, 'Fancy in Nubibus', and a 'Character of Sir Thomas Brown[e] as a Writer', which appeared in *Blackwood's* in November 1819;[17] but he had no opinion of either scraps of writing or scraps of payment. Writing for *Blackwood's* must be a major work to which he would give 'two thirds of my time' and 'the utmost of my powers in my most genial moods'.[18]

He suggested 'a sort of Letter or Essay on the Desiderata of a Magazine': a subject he had already treated with liveliness, even pungency in *Biographia Literaria*.[19] (Had, one wonders, Mr Blackwood himself read those passages?) Further, he would suggest contributing a monthly article which would be 'as far as my comparative Talents and Genius render it possible', equivalent to the leader in the *Edinburgh Review* and the *Quarterly Review*. He would also be willing to act as London editor for *Blackwood's*, and make the Magazine known abroad through his correspondence with 'Foreign Literati'.[20]

For all these services—what would Mr Blackwood pay? After many unhappy experiences with 'the Trade', Coleridge had learned, like every good professional man of letters, to put a proper value on payment.

Mr Blackwood replied cautiously but not uncordially:

> With regard to the payment, you may rest assured it will be liberal. I have it not in my power to say more than ten pounds per sheet; but as I mentioned to you, the Editor has it in his power to add to this allowance according to the value of the articles.

He had been surprised to learn, from Davies, that Coleridge had

> listened to the calumnies and falsehoods of a disappointed party, who have vainly attempted to run down the Magazine. That there were some articles in the early numbers which displayed rather too much of a personal tone [a nice *meiosis*] I will not attempt to deny; but these bear a very small proportion to the great mass of able and clever papers which are free from this fault.[21]

Relations were now friendly, and Coleridge wrote to his friend, William Mudford, in November 1819, that a connection might be formed

> on the condition that the Magazine is to be conducted henceforward first, pure from private slander and personal malignity; 2nd., on principles the direct opposite to those which have been hitherto supported by the Edinburgh Review, moral, political and religious.[22]

The connection was duly formed, although it was not so near a partnership as Coleridge had suggested, and the Magazine was henceforth among his most genial critics, chiefly through Lockhart who, some time later, in 1821, told Blackwood:

> Coleridge is evidently mad and unintelligible, but I venture to say you will never repent giving him sixteen pages a month.[23]

In October 1819 Lockhart wrote, in *Blackwood's*, one of the articles in a series on 'The Lake School of Poetry' which he devoted to Coleridge. He condemned malign criticism—'those unfair, and indeed wicked arts' by which superficial readers were 'so easily swayed'. Coleridge was indeed eccentric, with much in his poetry that was fantastic. This element was easy to represent, or misrepresent, as 'senseless and absurd'. It was pitiful to see 'how the grandest mysteries of the meditative soul lie at the mercy of surface-skimming ridicule'. It was like 'seeing the most solemn gestures of human dignity mimicked into grotesque absurdity by monkeys'.

(Reading this, it seems almost incredible that the man who wrote with such sympathy and righteous indignation should also have written the notorious review of Keats.)

The sad effect of those mocking criticisms had been to

make Coleridge throw aside almost all regard for the associations of the multitude, and to think that nothing could be so worthy of a great genius, so unworthily despised, as to reject in his subsequent compositions every standard save that of his private whims!

A poet should at least wish to please the public, and Coleridge had paid dearly for having ignored this desire, yet after all

> the native power of his genius has still been able to scatter some of its image upon all his performances . . . he has written a few poems which are, though short, in conception so original, and in execution so exquisite, that they cannot fail to render the name of Coleridge co-extensive with the language in which he has written, and to associate it for ever in the minds of all feeling and intelligent men, with those of the few chosen spirits that have touched, in so many ages of the world, the purest and most delicious chords of lyrical enchantment.

This was in tune with the praise given by Peter Morris, and like that tribute it was enhanced by the slight astringency of criticism which might have been expected from a man older than the poet, rather than from a younger. Lockhart, born in 1794, was twenty-two years Coleridge's junior.

His youth and early manhood made an orderly pattern. He was the son of a minister of the Church of Scotland, a cadet of one of the oldest families in Lanarkshire. From Glasgow High School he had gone to Glasgow University, then, with a Snell Exhibition, to Oxford, where he took a First in Classics, and found time, besides, to read widely, and to learn German and Spanish. After coming down, he travelled in Germany, and wrote, for the newly founded *Blackwood's Magazine*, a series of travel articles. This knowledge of German was to prove another link of intellectual sympathy with Coleridge.

Besides *Peter's Letters* he wrote, while still in his twenties, four novels: *Valerius; Reginald Dalton; Matthew Wald;* and *Adam Blair*—this last, a minor classic; and some delightful poetry, some comic, some—in the *Spanish Ballads*—romantic. In 1820 he made his profoundly happy marriage with Sophia, elder daughter of Sir Walter Scott; in 1825 they moved to London when Lockhart became editor of John Murray's *Quarterly Review*, from which he was to retire only two years before his death in 1854.

In his *Blackwood* days Lockhart gave a good deal of offence and scandal by his satire, his often merciless criticism, his sheer intellectual impudence; in society his reserve, deepened by deafness, gave an impression of arrogance. In time, he mellowed, greatly helped by Sophia. Yet even in those days he could, as we have seen, be generous and perceptive in criticism. In private and domestic life he was a most loving husband and father, a devoted son and brother, a loyal friend; and what is too rare in the respectable, law-abiding Scot, he was tolerant and compassionate towards those failures and vagrants whom he happened to like. Loving a jest, he looked benignly upon jesters even when they wandered from sobriety, stability and other virtues. This was notable in his friendship with the brilliant Irishman William Maginn, and with Theodore Hook, that prince of *improvisatori*, of whom more will be told presently.

This sympathy, one of Lockhart's most endearing qualities, warmed his friendship with Coleridge whose life and fortunes had, at the time of their meeting, been erratic and unstable to the point of tragedy, the more poignant for his warm-hearted character and his creative power. This brilliance had been darkened by ill health, domestic unhappiness, and opium. What for most men would have been a new and successful career in public service—the period in Malta (1804-1806) as secretary to our plenipotentiary, Sir Alexander Ball—had become a sad fantasy, almost a nightmare through his addiction to the drug.

Coleridge's schooldays in Christ's Hospital, London, had brought him a lifelong friend, in Charles Lamb, and a major intellectual influence in the headmaster, James Boyer. The latter had made a classical scholar of him, and had added to his Latin and Greek a sound knowledge of English poetry. His portrait of this master is one of the most attractive passages in *Biographia Literaria*.[24] This, for some inexplicable reason, some perversity, brought upon him the mockery of that *Blackwood* review.[25]

From school Coleridge had gone, with an Exhibition, to

Cambridge, but without taking a degree; then had come a brief, fantastic episode of military service. A year in Germany (1798-99) had given him the knowledge of German poetry and philosophy which deeply influenced his own thought, and had brought fruition in his translation of Schiller's *Wallenstein*. This was praised by Lockhart in *Blackwood's*, in 1823, pronouncing it 'by far the best translation of a foreign tragic drama which our English literature possesses'. Coleridge could claim to be 'in the very first rank of poetical translators'.[26]

In those years of light and shade Coleridge's friendship with Wordsworth, once happy and inspiring, had been broken, or at least shaken. He had produced, for a time, his own periodical, *The Friend*, followed by the drama *Remorse*, the two *Lay Sermons* and various articles. He had written copiously, sometimes obscurely, and sometimes, as Lockhart declared, divinely.

As the two men came more and more to know each other, Lockhart's affection and admiration increased. In 1824 he wrote to Christopher North from London:

> I have seen a host of lions, among them Hook, Canning, and Coleridge, the last being worth all the rest, and 500 more such into the bargain. Ebony should merely keep him in his house for a summer, with Johnny Dow in a cupboard, and he would drive the windmills before him.[27]

(*Ebony* was their nickname for Blackwood, and Johnny Dow was a shorthand writer. Had modern inventions occurred earlier, there would have been a tape-recorder. And Coleridge would have been a superb broadcaster.)

At this period, Coleridge was living at Highgate, in the house of James Gillman, his good friend and doctor. His marriage was broken, though he still kept in touch with his sons, Hartley and Derwent. The kind Gillmans took him to the sea. This was becoming a popular habit. The Sussex and the Kentish coast towns were frequented by families, among them the Lockharts. In the summer of 1833 the Gillmans with Coleridge, and Sophia with her children Walter and Charlotte, were staying at Ramsgate. Lockhart came down at intervals, by steamboat.

Coleridge wrote to Lockhart:

> ... It would be doing poor Justice to say, that I thank you for the *pleasure*, which the introduction to your Wife and Children has

given me; for I feel that it has done my heart good, and that in my remembrance of Mrs Lockhart, I shall have one more affection to be glad of. God bless her, and you, and your's.[28]

In the same month of July he wrote to his friend James Green of 'receivings and returnings of Visits, specially from the Lockharts (Mrs L., Sir Walter Scott's favorite Daughter, is truly an interesting and love-compelling woman)'.[29] He wrote to Sophia herself:

> I have persuaded Mr and Mrs Gillman to let their joint *wishes* overcome *her* fears, i.e. to gratify themselves by accepting your & Mr Lockhart's kind invitation for tomorrow. All that Mr Gillman dare venture on, in the way of eating, is a Lamb Chop— & you know, that my powers in the same line are not much more extensive.[30]

About a week later, he wrote again, offering to escort Sophia, the two children, and her cousin Anne Scott, to the Jewish Synagogue—'which not Jewish but Christian Ignorance has named the Temple'. The Minister, Mr Mayer, would show them all that could be shown. Then, if they would care to see 'their ceremonial service on Friday evening', he would gladly escort them:

> I happen to be a favorite among the Descendants of Abraham; and Mr Montefiore, the Munificent Founder of this Synagogue, has expressed a strong Wish to be introduced to the Author of THE FRIEND.[31]

Coleridge had shown sympathy with persecuted Jews in Germany and in Malta.[32] He had a warm friendship with a Jewish neighbour at Highgate; and he had published in *The Friend* 'Specimens of Rabbinical Wisdom'.[33]

His letter to Sophia was signed—'With an old man's Love & Blessing to Walter and his Sister'. In yet another he wrote: 'May God bless you, Mrs Lockhart, and your Husband, and Walter & Charlotte—this is the fervent uplifting of the Heart and Spirit of an Old Man who is glad to have seen and known you'.[34]

A little later, he escorted Anne Scott on a journey from Ramsgate to Canterbury. Anne wrote an enthralled account of his conversation, and Lockhart made fun of this, to Anne's painful embarrassment. Coleridge wrote to her in benevolent reassurance:

> ... Permit me, dear Miss Scott, to repeat, that your having any other concern in the representation, excepting as having unconsciously suggested the Date, Scene, and Dramatis Personae to our good Friend's Comic Muse, or at the utmost some slight Hint for the Opening of the Plot—a Hook, as it were, for the story to hang from—never occurred to me even among the possibilities of this world. It would have stood in too violent a contrast with the impression, I had retained, of your character and whole frame of mind.[35]

He added the doubtful compliment that women were 'too veracious creatures' fully to enjoy a joke. 'A certain degree of obtuseness in this respect I have ever considered among the characteristic traits, nay *charms*, of Womanhood.'

The friendship between Coleridge and Lockhart blended with that which both of them enjoyed with Theodore Hook: one of the most extraordinary figures of near-genius and almost incredible eccentricity to be found in a century that was far from devoid of eccentrics.

Hook was born in 1788, the son of an organist and composer whose talent he inherited and developed. There are two vivid and sympathetic accounts of him: one by Richard Garnett, in the *Dictionary of National Biography,* the other, by Lockhart, in the *Quarterly Review* of May 1843, two years after Hook's death.

A writer of much energy and versatility, Hook produced a quantity of novels under the general title of *Sayings and Doings;* for a time he edited *John Bull* in which he defended George IV and attacked Queen Caroline. He had, in Garnett's words, 'a reckless humour and praeternatural faculty of improvisation' as a writer, and still more as a pianist, composing both words and music as he played. Garnett, indeed, calls him 'the most brilliant *improvisatore,* whether with a pen or at the piano, which this country has seen'.

The word *improvisatore* links him with Coleridge who had more than a touch of that quality in him; who improvised freely in his light poetry and showed his awareness of that character in one of his later poems entitled precisely 'The Improvisatore'.[36]

This quality is the very essence of an incident related by Lockhart as climax to his Memoir of Hook in the *Quarterly Review*.[37] The Memoir itself has been praised by Andrew Lang as worthy of the author of the great *Life of Sir Walter Scott*.[38] It is written with affectionate insight, with humour, indeed with gusto. In his estimate of Hook as novelist, Lockhart compared him with Dickens whose presentation of low life Hook matched with descriptions of middle- and upper-class society. Of his improvising brilliance as pianist he declared that 'England never had a really successful performer in this way except Theodore Hook'.

Lockhart then recalled — with Dickensian exuberance—a party at 'a gay young bachelor's villa near Highgate, when the other lion was one of a very different breed, Mr. Coleridge'.[39] The bachelor was Frederick Mansell Reynolds, editor of *The Keepsake* to which Coleridge had contributed.[40]

> Much claret had been shed before the "Ancient Mariner" proclaimed that he could swallow no more of anything, unless it were punch. The materials were forthwith produced—the bowl was planted before the poet, and as he proceeded in his concoction, Hook, unbidden, took his place at the piano. He burst into a bacchanal of egregious luxury, every line of which had reference to the author of the "Lay Sermons" and the "Aids to Reflection". The room was becoming excessively hot—the first specimen of the new compound was handed to Hook who paused to quaff it, and then, exclaiming that he was stifled, flung his glass through the window. Coleridge rose with the aspect of a benignant patriarch, and demolished another pane—the example was followed generally—the window was a sieve in an instant—the kind host was farthest from the mark, and his goblet made havoc of the chandelier. The roar of laughter was drowned in Theodore's resumption of his song—and window and chandelier and the peculiar shot of each individual destroyer had exquisitely apt, in many cases, witty, commemoration.

Lockhart ended his narrative with a recollection of walking home with Coleridge and another guest, when he [Coleridge] delivered 'a most excellent lecture on the distinction between talent and genius, and declared that Hook was as true a genius as Dante—*that* was his example'.

From Coleridge drunk to Coleridge sober is but a step. His poetic thought is consistent, and although we, in sobriety, may deprecate the elevation of Hook to the side of Dante, we may read, with profit, the definitions of talent and genius in *Biographia Literaria*[41] and in *The Friend*.[42]

Another account of this famous party was given, in his *Autobiography*,[43] by William Jerdan, a contemporary journalist and critic. This is quoted by Lucyle Werkmeister in an article in the *Philological Quarterly*.[44]

Jerdan's story differs in some details from Lockhart's, and he adds one or two effective touches—as in his description of Hook:

> I never saw Hook, often as I have seen him in his hours of exuberant humour, in such glorious "fooling" as on this occasion. From his entrance to his departure his countenance beamed with overflowing mirth, and his wonderful talent seemed to be more than commonly excited by the company of Coleridge.

Jerdan further enriches the description of the broken window and chandelier with a sequel:

> The last of the limited glasses was mounted upon the bottom of a reversed wine-tumbler, and to the infinite risk of the latter, he [Coleridge] was induced to shy at the former with a silver fork, till after three or four throws, he succeeded in smashing it into fragments, to be tossed into the basket with its perished brethren.

He recalled a letter to himself from Lockhart which described 'the roseate face of Coleridge, lit up with animation, his large grey eye beaming, his white hair floating, and his whole frame radiating, as it were, with intense interest'.

One is irresistibly drawn, by this description of the poet, to quote his own magic lines from 'Kubla Khan'.

> Beware! Beware!
> His flashing eyes, his floating hair!
> Weave a circle round him thrice,
> And close your eyes with holy dread,
> For he on honey-dew hath fed,
> And drunk the milk of Paradise.[45]

Just as Coleridge the poet had long been honoured by

Lockhart, so another aspect of his genius was celebrated by him in a review of the posthumously published *Specimens of the Table Talk of Samuel Taylor Coleridge* in the *Quarterly Review* of February 1835.[46] In this, Lockhart declared that while Coleridge was utterly unlike Dr Johnson in every other way, he was undoubtedly his successor 'as the great literary talker of England'. Had Coleridge only had the good fortune to meet another Boswell, we might have had 'many goodly volumes' of his rich talk. For what we were given in those *Specimens* we must be grateful, especially for 'the numerous fragments of delicious criticism of Shakespeare'. Coleridge could be a stern and a prejudiced critic, but he could also be, and more often was 'shrewd and subtle', expressing himself in a 'most genial and generous tone'.

Lockhart himself is here at his most 'genial and generous', and his most compassionate. He referred to the failures and miseries of Coleridge's life (in particular, to the withdrawal, by the Whig government of Lord Grey, of the annuity granted him as an Associate of the Royal Society of Literature) but remarked that, as the poet himself had not complained, we might

> spare ourselves the pain of any further comments on the dark and melancholy circumstances in which this great light of his time and country, this beautiful poet, this exquisite metaphysician, this universal scholar and profound theologian was permitted to pass so many of his years.

Lockhart could reach nobility in his praise and valediction. It is the more fitting that Coleridge should have spoken his own farewell to this good friend in a poem (one of the many versions of 'Epitaph') which he enclosed in his last letter to Lockhart, in November 1833, asking him to give it to that 'love-compelling woman', Sophia. The letter ended 'with affectionate respect to Mrs Lockhart, and my blessing on Walter & his Sister'. The poem, headed by his initials—'better known . . . than . . . the name itself' — reads:

> Stop, Christian Passer-by! stop, Child of God!
> And read with gentle heart. Beneath this sod
> A Poet lies: or that which once seem'd He.
> O lift one thought in prayer for S.T.C.
> That he who many a year with toil of Breath

Found Death in Life, may here find Life in Death.
Mercy for Praise, to be forgiven for Fame,
He ask'd, and hop'd through Christ. Do Thou the Same.[47]

REFERENCES

1 *Peter's Letters to His Kinsfolk* (1819), ii. 218.
2 A. Lang, *Life and Letters of J.G. Lockhart* (1897), i. 148.
3 *ibid.*, i. 220.
4 *Peter's Letters to His Kinsfolk*, ii. 218.
5 *ibid.*, ii. 220.
6 *ibid.*, ii. 221. 'Genevieve' is now more commonly known as 'Love' (*PW*, i. 330-35).
7. *CL*, v. 127n[2].
8 *ibid.*, iv. 966.
9 *ibid.*, iv. 967.
10 *BL*, i. 43-4.
11 *CL*, v. 124n.
12 *ibid.*, v. 127.
13 *ibid.*
14 *ibid.*, v. 128.
15 *ibid.*, v. 124n, 128n[1]; A. Lang, *op. cit.*, i. 255 et seq.; M. Lochhead, *John Gibson Lockhart* (1954), 82 et seq.
16 *CL*, iv. 931.
17 *ibid.*, iv. 976n[2].
18 *ibid.*, iv. 931.
19 *ibid.*, iv. 932; *BL*, chs. i-ii, xxi.
20 *CL*, v. 932.
21 *ibid.*, v. 933n[2].
22 *ibid.*, v. 928.
23 M. Oliphant, *Annals of a Publishing House: William Blackwood and His Sons* (1897), i. 218.
24 i.4-6.
25 *Blackwood's Magazine*, vi (October 1817), 4.
26 *ibid.*, xiv (1823), 377.
27 Mrs Gordon, *'Christopher North', A Memoir of John Wilson* (1862), ii. 70. See also *CL*, v. 361 and n[4].
28 *CL*, vi. 942.
29 *ibid.*, vi. 947.
30 *ibid.*, vi. 942.
31 *ibid.*, vi. 943.
32 *ibid.*, i. 473; v. l; *CN*, ii. 2594, 2646, 2668.
33 *CL*, iv. 656 and n[3], 701; *Fr.*, i. 370-73; ii. 170-71.
34 *CL*, vi. 944.

35 *ibid.*, vi. 957 and n[1], 958.
36 *PW*, i. 462-68.
37 *Quarterly Review*, Lxxii (May 1843), 65-6.
38 A. Lang, *op. cit.*, ii. 265-70.
39 *Quarterly Review*, Lxxii (May 1843), 65.
40 *CL*, vi. 753-54, 756nn[1-2].
41 Ch. iv. 59-60; ch. xi. 53.
42 No. 5, 14 September 1809, 73-4.
43 W. Jerdan, *Autobiography* (1852-53), iv. 230-6; *Men I have Known* (1866), 121-22, 128-30.
44 xl (January 1961), 104-11.
45 *PW*, i. 298, lines 49-54. See *ibid.*, ii. 974 for an epigram by Coleridge prompted by Hook.
46 vol. Liii. 79-83.
47 *CL*, vi. 973.

5

Coleridge and John Hookham Frere's Translations of Aristophanes

by MARGO VON ROMBERG

Nowadays, John Hookham Frere is known—if he is known at all—as the author of *Whistlecraft*, the humorous poem the metre of which Byron used for *Beppo* and *Don Juan*. This is a pity, as his translations of Aristophanes can still be ranked among the best in the English language, not only for the craftsmanship and brilliance of the actual translation but for the entertaining and informative running commentary added by Frere, which was intended, Shavian fashion, to help the reader visualise the plays as dramatic performances. When he began his translations some time around 1815-16, Frere was breaking new ground, for until then Aristophanes had suffered neglect in England. In 1812 a reprint of four eighteenth-century translations was published, giving the *Quarterly Review* an opportunity to lament that 'the works of Aristophanes have been so much more talked of than read, and so much more read than understood'.[1] By the time Frere's translations of four plays appeared in print in 1839-40, metrical translations of one or more plays by four other men had been published, and the leading magazines had even found space for Aristophanes in their columns.[2] One reason for this increased popularity is certainly to be found in the work of the Schlegels, which did much to rehabilitate the Greek comic poet. But Frere's translations excited interest even while they were in manuscript, and their non-appearance in print perhaps

80

encouraged others to try and fill the gap.[3] Coleridge was one of the earliest and most enthusiastic admirers of Frere's work, and exercised an influence on the history of the translations even after his death.

Frere had shown a talent for translation early in life. His rendering of an Anglo-Saxon poem, written at Eton, was published in Ellis's *Specimens of the Early English Poets* (1790). In 1808 Southey thought highly enough of Frere's translations from *Poema del Cid* to include them in an appendix to his own *Chronicle of the Cid*. In the course of his life, Frere translated from several languages, including Greek, Latin, Hebrew, German, Spanish, Italian and French.[4] By his own account, his translations from Aristophanes began almost by accident:

> It happened, owing to circumstances in which the public can have no interest, that some passages longer than usual were translated from Aristophanes; but the possibility of producing an adequate translation of an entire play never would have entered his mind but from the example of his friend Mr W. Hamilton, who had himself completed a translation of almost the whole of Aristophanes.[5]

The casual origin of the translations explains why Frere did not translate one play from beginning to end before starting another one, but instead translated piecemeal over a number of years. The work was probably begun in 1815, and by mid-1816 Frere had translated parts of the *Knights* and the *Frogs*.

He had also renewed his acquaintance with Coleridge, whom he had known at Cambridge, and whose translation of *Piccolomini* he had admired.[6] The exact time and place of their meeting is not certain. Frere himself said that he had been anxious to meet the author of 'some verses in a newspaper signed S.T.C.', but did not in fact make his acquaintance until, fifteen years later, he introduced himself to Coleridge 'after one of his lectures'.[7] This is not particularly helpful, especially as Coleridge did not lecture at all in 1815-16, and his lectures in 1814 were at Bristol, where Frere is not likely to have been. The sudden burst of enthusiasm for Frere in Coleridge's letters in mid-1816 suggests that their friendship really began at that time. Perhaps they met once again in Murray's famous drawing-room, where Frere was a regular visitor. Coleridge was at this time in touch with Murray in the hope that Murray might publish his work.[8] Griggs suggests[9] that Frere was to Coleridge what Wordsworth had once been. Certainly, there was strong mutual admiration. Frere thought highly of Coleridge's 'learning, and critical as well as poetical powers'; Coleridge admired Frere's talent as a translator, poet and critic, and also looked up to him as the English gentleman *par excellence*.[10]

The catalyst of this new friendship was undoubtedly Frere's translations from the *Knights* and the *Frogs* which he showed to Coleridge. Writing to Murray on 8 May 1816, Coleridge was full of praise for Frere's 'Taste' and 'Genius', praise which was accorded 'not lightly but after long & most impartial meditation on the difficulties of translating the Parabases of Aristophanes, and on the quantity and quality of the inventive and discriminative Powers manifested in the unexampled Conquest of them all'.[11] The *parabasis*, which is a unique feature of Aristophanic comedy, is that part of the play in which the Chorus, breaking the dramatic illusion of the plot, addresses the audience directly on behalf of the poet, giving his opinions on anything of current interest. Its metrical structure follows a fairly regular but complex pattern, which would offer quite a challenge to the verse-translator. Since prosody was one of Coleridge's lifelong interests, he was particularly attracted by Frere's talent for finding suitable metrical equivalents in translating from the Greek. The *parabasis* in question must have been from the *Knights,* for on 2 July 1816, in a letter apparently delayed because Frere had been indisposed, Coleridge again praised Frere's 'Taste' as well as his 'inventive and constructive power', which Coleridge saw 'in the one Imitation of the Parabasis from the Knights of Aristophanes'.[12]

Meanwhile the translation of the *Frogs* had advanced far enough for lines 1-837 to be printed on five sheets of paper watermarked 1814 and 1815, copies being circulated privately.[13] At the beginning of July 1816 Coleridge had seen some of the sheets and looked forward to seeing more. Writing to Murray, he again praised Frere's work:

Most unfeignedly can I declare, that I am unable to decide,

whether the *admiration*, which their *excellence* inspires, or the wonder, which the knowledge of the countless *difficulties* so happily overcome never ceases to excite in my mind during the re-perusal & collation of them with the original Greek, be the greater![14]

Such was his admiration that in December 1816 he wrote to Frere's brother George, hoping that he might obtain Frere's permission to use four lines of the translation, alongside the original, as a motto for one of the essays in the *rifacciamento* of *The Friend*—'with or without his name as he may prescribe'. The quotation duly appeared, above Frere's name, and with an acknowledgement from Coleridge expressing the conviction that, if the translations were to be published in full, they would 'open out sources of metrical and rhythmical wealth' in the English language.[15]

Coleridge's interest in the metre and rhythm of Frere's translation can also be seen in two notebook entries made by Coleridge at about this time. Into one notebook he transcribed the first 209 lines of Frere's *Frogs*, leaving the following pages blank, as if intending to transcribe more; and into another he transcribed lines 1-4, 10-11, 214, 483-501, 502-3 and 578-80 of the same play.[16] Kathleen Coburn suggests that both entries were written on the same day, although it is impossible to tell why Coleridge used two notebooks. The lines transcribed in the latter notebook entry seem to have been specially chosen for their metrical interest, with Coleridge jotting down the scansion (or occasionally Frere's accentuation marks) for some of them. Coleridge headed the longest section (lines 483-501) 'Compensation of the Spondaic'. The original Greek passage is entirely in spondees, except for one anapaest to accommodate a proper name, and it was chanted by the Chorus of Initiates as they solemnly marched round the *orchestra*. Frere's translation, as Coleridge noted, does come remarkably close to the original in rhythm.

The transcription of the dialogue of lines 1-209, while also offering scope for an examination of Frere's versification, may have had another main purpose. Coleridge's transcript of the dialogue is substantially the same as the published 1839 text. Frere's side-notes, commentary and stage directions are either condensed or omitted by Coleridge. Kathleen Coburn suggests that Coleridge might have provided the notes at the request of Frere, who then worked them up and added them to the printed version. This seems unlikely, as this part of the play was already in print, and although side-notes might easily be added to the pages set, the commentary and stage-directions could not possibly have been added without a major dislocation of the type. If Frere was anxious years later to avoid unnecessary expense, as well as inconvenience for his printer, there is no reason why he should not have been equally concerned in 1816.[17] In June 1817 Coleridge mentioned that he had been 'revising and correcting some notes on Aristophanes at the request of the Commentator'.[18] This proves that Frere was anxious to obtain suggestions from Coleridge for inclusion in his commentary, but it does not necessarily refer to this part of the translation, which seems to have been already complete. Kathleen Coburn's alternative suggestion, that Coleridge made the transcript out of enthusiasm for Frere's work, is supported by Coleridge's own heading for his notebook-entry: '*Model* of *Transfer* of Genius from a dead to a living *Language*'. He might even at this time have been thinking of writing the review of Frere's translations which he mentioned to Murray in August 1820.[19]

Frere spent most of 1818 in Tunbridge, apparently working hard on his translations while his wife, Lady Errol, recovered from an illness. He certainly translated a scene from the *Birds,* possibly translated more of the *Knights,* and probably continued the *Frogs* from where he had left off. On 29 May 1818 he told Murray that he had translated about a third of two other plays which Murray had never seen, but was 'in no hurry either to finish or publish them'.[20] He may have taken his work seriously, as Eichler has suggested,[21] but it was the seriousness of a craftsman who takes pleasure in good workmanship, rather than that of a writer ambitious for literary renown.

In August 1818 Murray bought a half share in *Blackwood's Magazine,* and acted as agent in London, sending several articles to Edinburgh for inclusion in the magazine. But the continuing scurrility of the editors, resulting in a writ against them by Hazlitt, made Murray warn them that several prominent people, including Frere, could only be persuaded to contribute articles if the personal attacks in the magazine were to cease.[22] Lockhart and Wilson replied in a lengthy emollient letter, which ended by showing particular interest in Frere's translations:

> I regret particularly the non arrival of Freres Aristophanes. As that has already been handed about, I sh[oul]d think you m[igh]t still venture on sending it & hope you will. You may have an opp[ortunit]y of sending Mr Frere the last No. & the next perhaps in neither of which anything to offend him can be found. We are very anxious however, to have the Translation for next M[on]th, *if possible*. I pledge myself personally that is shall be accompenied w[i]th observations & criticisms such as will remove all idea of its being handed to us by Mr Frere by way of an Advertisement.[23]

The translation duly arrived and was published in the January 1819 issue of *Blackwood's Magazine,* with a short introduction by Lockhart. Frere is not mentioned by name, but the veiled reference to his tranlations from *El Cid* would leave few readers in doubt about the author's identity.[24] The translation is of lines 838-1235 of the *Frogs*, and includes part of the contest between Aeschylus and Euripides, justly described by Lockhart (p. 422) as 'the most untranslateable passage in the most untranslateable of books'. There are numberous variant readings when compared with the 1839 text, and Frere's usual side-notes and commentary are missing. Soon after this, Murray terminated his connection with *Blackwood's Magazine,* thus making it unlikely that further extracts from Frere's translation would appear in it.[25]

Meanwhile, the friendship between Coleridge and Frere continued on excellent terms. In 1817, Coleridge introduced Ludwig Tieck to Frere, Tieck's planned translation of Shakespeare giving them an interest in common. In return, Frere took great interest in Coleridge's literary work, offered assistance for Coleridge's son Derwent if he went to Cambridge, and in 1818 paid for a shorthand writer to record Coleridge's lectures on philosophy.[26] We may be sure that Frere's translations, and the general theory of translation, would be regular topics of conversation when they met. Frere's opinions on translation are contained in his review of Thomas Mitchell's translation of the *Acharnians* and *Knights,* but Coleridge has left nothing of any real length, published or otherwise, which discusses the theory of translation. We must therefore glean what we can from a few passing references to the subject.

Three phrases form the basis of Coleridge's theory: 'imitation', 'alter et idem', and 'theory of compensation and equivalence of effect'. Before discussing them, it would be helpful to give a brief outline of the theory of translation in the early years of the nineteenth century. Almost inevitably, the theory was still based on Dryden's distinction of 'metaphrase', 'paraphrase' and 'imitation'. 'Imitation', in Dryden's sense (but not in Coleridge's), permitted such freedom on the part of the translator that the result could not really be considered a proper translation, and may therefore be disregarded. Of the two other terms, 'metaphrase' meant a close word-for-word 'servile' translation, which Dryden and later critics found to retain the letter at the expense of the spirit of the original, and thus to be virtually lifeless. 'Paraphrase', while not altogether abandoning close translation, was more concerned with transposing the original author's 'spirit' and giving readers a better idea of his characteristic style, and was therefore always open to considerable freedom of interpretation. In the eighteenth century such freedom became excessive; but by the beginning of the nineteenth century a reaction had set in, and the preferred poetic translation at the time of Coleridge and Frere was as close to the letter of the original as was compatible with the retention of its 'spirit', and with the impression that one was reading an original composition.[27]

Coleridge regularly used 'imitation' to refer to Frere's verse translations.[28] What he meant by this term, as applied to translation, was much the same as Dryden's 'paraphrase', just as his term 'copy' approximated to Dryden's 'metaphrase'. Coleridge himself provided the clue to this in his letter of 2 July 1816, in which he substantiated his praise of Frere's 'imitations' by referring Frere to the first two chapters of the second volume of *Biographia Literaria* (Chapters XIV-XV), the proof sheets of which he enclosed with his letter. Frere would have found the most relevant passage in Coleridge's definition of the poet's power, which 'reveals itself in the balance or reconciliation of opposite or discordant qualities: of sameness, with difference; of the general, with the concrete; the idea, with the image; the individual, with the representative; the sense of novelty and freshness, with old and familiar objects'.[29] This definition, which Fruman[30] traces to Schelling's definition of art as 'harmony of the subjective and objective', has an obvious application to translation, since the translator's problem is how to give an exact rendering of the original, while also adding enough of himself to ensure that the translation lives as a work of art in its own right. This principle of translation was first expressed by John Denham in his preface to *The Destruction of Troy*,[31] and regularly repeated or paraphrased thereafter.

The principle of reconciliation of opposites was directly linked with 'imitation' in Coleridge's essay 'On Poesy or Art', which Shawcross dates as no earlier than 1818, and which might therefore reflect something of Coleridge's conversations with Frere, as well as his reading of Schelling:

> In all imitation two elements must coexist, and not only coexist, but must be perceived as coexisting. These two constituent elements are likeness and unlikeness, or sameness and difference, and in all genuine creations of art there must be a union of these disparates. The artist may take his point of view where he pleases, provided that the desired effect be perceptibly produced,—that there be likeness in the difference, difference in the likeness, and a reconcilement of both in one.[32]

The idea of combined 'sameness and difference' is repeated in the Latin phrase 'alter et idem', twice applied by Coleridge to translations which he was praising: in 1816 he described Voss's German translations of Homer and Virgil as 'truly marvellous Translations—alter et idem'; and in 1827 he told Sotheby that his translation of Virgil's *Georgics* was 'the best Translation of *any* Work that exists in our Language and the nearest to the ideal *Alter et Idem*'.[33]

Coleridge's adoption of a Latin phrase is curious and seems to derive from his interest in metaphysics. He apparently first used the phrase in a letter dated 14 April 1816 in which he referred to 'a Deus alter et Idem' as the primal creative force in the metaphysical universe of Plato and Philo Judaeus, upon which all things are modelled. He then stressed the application of the term *eikon* ('likeness') to this creative force, as distinct from the terms *eidolon* and *idea* ('phantom' and 'outward appearance') which apply respectively to corporeal and mental copies.[34] It is significant that this letter was written at about the same time as he became acquainted with Frere.

In his letter to Sotheby, Coleridge also referred to 'the only two legitimate kinds of poetic translation' which carried 'the transfusion of the Spirit and Individuality of a Poet, each in it's kind, to the highest point of Perfection'. These two kinds of translation are mentioned again in another letter to Sotheby, in which Coleridge described his plans for an article on Sotheby's *Georgics* to be contributed to Blanco White's *London Review,* which would include 'the question of metres, and the two modes of translation, the identical and the equivalent'.[35] Coleridge is clearly thinking of translation in accordance with Dryden's definition (identical = idem = metaphrase; equivalent = alter = paraphrase), and like Dryden, visualises the best translation as a combination of the two.

Coleridge's interest in Prosody, as has already been shown, found practical application in his study of Frere's translation of the *Frogs*. The idea that it might be possible to adapt classical metres in order to extend and enrich English versification was a mirage that glittered before him all his life, and which may be traced in numerous notebook entries. He even suggested that the best English translation of Homer would be 'a metrical Romance', and envisaged *Christabel* translated into a Greek choral metre taken from *Prometheus Vinctus*.[36] The phrase 'compensation and equivalence of effect', which does not seem to pre-date his acquaintance with Frere,[37] is at least partly concerned with metrical equivalence. He first used it in his letter to Murray in August 1820, in which he said that he and his son Hartley had been working on an essay on 'Metre, Metres, & [the] possibility of transferring, by compensation & equivalence of effect, the measures of the Greek Dramatists to the English Language'. This essay he proposed to offer to the *Quarterly Review* as a review of Frere's 'Aristophanics', should they ever be published.[38]

In some form or other, it was apparently still lying around years later, to be rewritten as the review of Sotheby's *Georgics* mentioned above, for Coleridge told Sotheby on 13 July 1829 that he soon hoped to 'have brought together as a part of my Critique some remarks on translation on the principle of Compensation, proportional to the differences in the Genius of the two Languages'. Unfortunately the *London Review* was short-lived, and Coleridge's essay (if, indeed, it had progressed any further than a few notes on paper and some ideas in Coleridge's head), was never published.[39] His only other reference to this particular theory, in a letter to Wordsworth, suggests a wider application of the principle. Wordsworth had submitted his translation of the *Aeneid* I-III to Coleridge for his comments in April 1824. In reply, Coleridge said that Wordsworth was wasting his time, for, in translating Virgil, there was 'no medium between a prose version and one on the avowed principle of *compensation* in the widest sense, that is, manner, genius, total effect'.[40] When applied as widely as this, the 'principle of compensation and equivalence of effect' is simply a restatement of the principle of 'sameness and difference' in an imitation.

Frere's theory of translation, expressed in his article reviewing Mitchell's translations from Aristophanes, shows clear links with Coleridge's theory.[41] Frere believed that 'the object of poetic and dramatic art' was to show people their faults, but in such a way that the author does not seem to be directly criticising anyone. This was to be achieved by a mixture of truth and unreality:

> Either the persons must be obviously fictitious, as in fable, or the events must be impossible, as in the Aristophanic comedy; or supposing the events to be combined with probability, the language and sentiments must be removed from the reality of ordinary life, as is the case in tragedy, and (to a certain degree) in our own old regular comedy of the seventeenth century, the comedy of Jonson and Fletcher. Thus, absolute Reality is to be avoided as too directly offensive; but absolute Unreality is equally objectionable; it is vague, feeble, and applies to nothing. The two opposites must be combined. Where the events are coherent and possible, the language must be ideal—Where the fiction is wild and extravagant, its extravagance must be compensated by a reality in the language. (pp. 478-79)

A translation of Aristophanes, to be successful, must therefore be written in English equivalent to the colloquial language of the original, and not (as Mitchell had done) in the archaic English of Renaissance comedy.

Having thus echoed Coleridge's principle of reconciliation of opposites, Frere went on to discuss the need for the translator to work according to a principle of generalization. This meant that the translator should avoid idioms and allusions belonging to a particular time and place, which would remind the reader that he was reading a translation, and translate such phrases according to 'the general spirit of the original author' (p.483). The translator of Aristophanes should be aided by Aristophanes' natural tendency, which he shared with Shakespeare, to compose in 'a spirit of generalization, in which the local and peculiar allusions served but as types and abstracts of universal and permanent forms' (p.484). Frere's source must again be Coleridge, whose insistence on generalization and the avoidance of 'accidentality' was a central point in *Biographia Literaria* and the Shakespeare lectures.[42] But it is possible that the applicability of his theories to translation did not occur to Coleridge until he began discussing the subject with Frere in 1816, and that the fuller definition of 'imitation' in 'On Poesy or Art' owed a little to the stimulus of his conversations with Frere, as well as to his reading of Schelling.

In the summer of 1820 Frere decided to go abroad for the sake of his wife's health, and they eventually settled in Malta. He continued sporadically to translate Aristophanes. In January 1823 he sent his translation of the *Knights* to his brother George in London, and late in the following year he was able to promise him a copy of the completed translation of the *Acharnians*. At the same time he was working on the *Birds,* of which he had done about 1200 lines. All this work was interrupted by his year-long visit to England beginning September 1825, but was resumed on his return to Malta and almost finished by March 1828.[43]

There is no record of any correspondence between Frere and Coleridge at this time, but since Coleridge was on good terms with George Frere, we may assume that he was kept *au fait* with the progress of Frere's translations. Soon after returning to England, Frere resumed his acquaintance with Coleridge, who dined with him on 24 December 1825,[44] and saw him several times thereafter, usually at Highgate, where, on his first call,

Frere recited to an enthusiastic Coleridge 'several sublime passages of a religious and Philosophic Poem'.[45] This poem, which has remained unknown to Coleridge scholars, is possibly the fragment with unmistakable echoes of Coleridgean metaphysics included in Frere's *Works,* ii.333-5.

It must also have been during Frere's visit to England that Coleridge received 'the Manuscript volume lettered, Arist: Manuscript—Birds, Acharnians, Knights', which Coleridge bequeathed to the Gillmans in his will. According to Frere, he had 'lent' the manuscript to Coleridge, but Coleridge seems to have been in no doubt that the manuscript had been 'presented' to him.[46] Coleridge's book-borrowing habits were notorious. In July 1816 he had even felt it necessary to defend himself against the charge of not returning borrowed books before he asked Frere if he could help him to obtain certain volumes he was anxious to read.[47] It is therefore rather ironic that Frere himself should become another victim, albeit not an aggrieved one, of Coleridge's absent-mindedness.

Frere also did what he could to help his impecunious friend. He had, for example, made good his promise to subsidise Derwent Coleridge at Cambridge.[48] He also tried— unsuccessfully, as it turned out—to obtain a sinecure of £200 per annum for Coleridge.[49] And, if we can believe what Coleridge himself confided to his nephew Edward Coleridge, he had suggested that Coleridge was to receive any profits on the sale of the 'Aristophanics' when they were eventually published.[50] Perhaps Coleridge received this suggestion together with the manuscript of Frere's translations, and this, rather than his book-borrowing habits, might explain why he thought the manuscript was now his.

Back in Malta, Frere continued to work on his translations. By 11 September 1829 he had completed the *Frogs,* 'as far as they are capable of being translated', and was asking his brother Bartle to oversee the printing of the play for him in London. In 1830 he envisaged having 500 copies printed, but without his name on the title-page. Unfortunately his wife was now dying, and although Frere sent a transcript of the *Frogs* to Bartle, he had neither time nor inclination to finish the notes or write a preface, without which he did not wish his *Frogs* to be distributed. At Frere's request, Bartle copied out the 1300 lines of the translation of the *Birds* that Frere had left behind in England (this might have been the manuscript in Coleridge's possession, or possibly another copy), and sent them out to Malta, where they arrived soon after Lady Errol's death, and helped to take Frere's mind off his bereavement.[51]

There was now a delay of some years, during which—instead of writing the promised preface and notes—Frere diverted himself by learning Hebrew and translating the Greek elegiac poet Theognis. In April 1837 he was still apologising to Bartle for his procrastination, and might have delayed still longer if George Cornewall Lewis, who had come to Malta in the office of Commissioner, had not offered to superintend the printing of Frere's translations at the Government Printing Office. By contrast, the next few years were a bustle of activity, with Frere sending the last corrected proofs of the *Frogs* to Bartle in London, and keeping his brother informed about the progress of the printing of the *Acharnians*, *Birds* and *Knights* in Malta.[52]

Frere knew, of course, about Coleridge's death in 1834, and about the contents of Coleridge's will. In keeping with his generous nature, Frere did not complain about Coleridge's apparent expropriation of his manuscript, but instead proceeded to confirm Coleridge's presumption that he [Coleridge] was to benefit from the sale of the translation. Writing to Bartle on 11 July 1839, Frere stated that half of the edition was to be sold for the benefit of the Gillmans, in accordance with his interpretation of the request made by Coleridge in his will, 'that some of the transcripts which I had lent to him might be allowed to remain with Mr. [Gillman]'.[53] Frere, being unwilling to involve himself in commercial transactions, suggested to the Gillmans that the publisher and bookseller William Pickering would undertake the sale for them, but, apart from sending approximately 160 copies direct to Pickering, took no further part in the business himself. Other copies of the three plays were shipped to Bartle, who was also given instructions about distributing copies among Frere's friends and acquaintances. As the *Frogs* had been printed in London, it was not included in the arrangement with Pickering, and does not seem to have been put on sale at all. In 1843 Frere asked Bartle to find out from Pickering 'whether Mrs. [Gillman] has profited by the sale of the Aristophanes'. By this roundabout method he could ensure that his benevolent wishes had been fulfilled, without causing any embarrassment.[54]

George Cornewall Lewis reviewed the translations in the *Classical Museum* in 1843, and, as they were not generally available, his review consisted almost entirely of long extracts from all four plays.[55] Unfortunately, for all the excellence of the translations, a review in a periodical of such limited popularity was not likely to generate much public interest. Mary Russell Mitford tried in her turn to rescue the translations from oblivion by including a specimen in her *Recollections of a Literary Life*. She told a correspondent in 1852 that, although she possessed copies of Frere's *Knights* and *Birds,* she had particularly wanted to quote from his *Frogs,* and being unable to obtain a copy of the play anywhere, she had been obliged to make use of the scene printed in *Blackwood's Magazine* in 1819. Her hope, however, was that by including this scene in her own book, she would hasten the appearance of the collected edition of Frere's works, which she had been told was in the course of preparation.[56] Procrastination must have been a trait of the Frere family, for the edition she referred to did not appear for another twenty years, some forty years too late for Coleridge to fulfil his proposal to review the 'Aristophanics'.

NOTES AND REFERENCES

1 *QR,* ix (1813), 139-40.
2 F.M.K. Foster, *English Translations from the Greek. A Bibliographical Survey* (New York, 1918), lists these translations on pp. 21-2, although he gives the date of Mitchell's translation incorrectly as 1819 instead of 1820. His entry for Frere's translations is also completely wrong. Complete translations of the *Clouds* and *Plutus* appeared in *Blackwood's Magazine,* xxxviii (1835), 516-46, 763-89. See also note 3. *Fraser's Magazine* published a parody of Aristophanes in vol. xiv (1836), 286-97, and a series of articles on Aristophanes in vols. xv (1837), xviii (1838), xix (1839) and xx (1839).
3 An article by James Christie entitled 'Review of Mordaunt's *Eirene* of Aristophanes' appeared in *Blackwood's Magazine,* xxiii (1828), 551-61. According to Christie, this translation of Aristophanes *Peace* was dedicated to the translator's 'friend and schoolfellow, Mr J. Hookham Frere, whom he follows in whimsicality and pleasantry'. An exhaustive search has failed to uncover any trace of either the supposed translation or its author (H. Mordaunt, Esq. M.A.). Christie's elaborate hoax is the most remarkable example of interest in Frere's work.

4 See **FRERE,** i. 175; ii.337-425.

5 *ibid.*, i.297n[2]. Mr W. Hamilton is perhaps Sir William Hamilton (1788-1856), the metaphysician.

6 See *CL*, ii.1091; *CN*, i.1656; iii.4331n; **FRERE,** i.49. Their earlier acquaintance had not been exactly friendly. Frere had attacked Coleridge and his friends in the *Anti-Jacobin* (1798). See **FRERE,** ii.157.

7 **FRERE,** i.248-49.

8 S. Smiles, *A Publisher and His Friends* (1891), i.266; *CL*, iv.650n[1].

9 *CL*, v.xxxvii.

10 **FRERE,** i.248. Coleridge often referred to Frere as *ho kalokagathos ho philokalos*, which might be roughly translated as 'the perfect gentleman'. See, for example, *CL*, vi. 734-35; and Coleridge's will, *ibid.*, vi.999.

11 *CL*, iv.637.

12 *ibid.*, 647.

13 *ibid.*, 649n[1]; *National Union Catalog Pre-1956 Imprints*, xx.574.

14 *CL*, iv.649.

15 *ibid.*, 696; *Fr.*, i.18.

16 *CN*, iii.4331-332 and nn.

17 **FRERE,** i.220, 229, 233.

18 *CL*, iv.735.

19 *ibid.*, v.93. See further on p.88.

20 **FRERE,** i.174, 180, 194; Smiles, *op. cit.*, ii.25.

21 A. Eichler, *John Hookham Frere. Sein Leben und Seine Werke. Sein Einfluss auf Lord Byron* (Vienna and Leipzig, 1905), 52.

22 Smiles, *op. cit.*, *i.480-86*. Cf. Margaret Oliphant, *Annals of a Publishing House* (1897), i.162-68.

23 This letter was reprinted almost in full by Margaret Oliphant, *op. cit.*, i.164-67, but without the paragraph referring to Frere, which is quoted here by kind permission of the Trustees of the National Library of Scotland from MS.4003, f.139.

24 'Specimen of an Unpublished Translation of Aristophanes', *Blackwood's Magazine*, iv (1819), 421-29.

25 Smiles, *op.cit.*, i.494-95.

26 *CL*. iv.744-6, 777, 917, 951n[2].

27 The fullest outline of Dryden's theory of translation is in his *Preface to Ovid's Epistles* (1680). See J. Dryden, *Of Dramatic Poesy and Other Critical Essays*, ed. G. Watson (1962), i.262-73. Eighteenth-century theory is discussed by J.W. Draper, 'The Theory of Translation in the Eighteenth Century', *Neophilologus*, vi (1921), 241-54. The views expressed by A.F. Tytler, *Essay on the Principles of Translation*, 3rd ed., rev. and enlarged (1813), were generally accepted in his time, although a little old-fashioned. Criticism of Tytler's views can be found in C.A. Elton's preface to *Specimens of the Classic Poets* (1814), i.xv-xxxiii.

28 *CL*, iv.647; v.93; *Fr.*, i.18.

29 *BL*, ii.12.

30 N. Fruman, *Coleridge, the Damaged Archangel* (1972), 184-88.

31 'Poetry is of so subtle a spirit that, in pouring out of one language into

another, it will all evaporate; and, if a new spirit be not added in the transfusion, there will remain nothing but a *caput mortuum*.' See Dryden, *op. cit.*, i.270n[2], 271. Cf. Sir Walter Scott's version in his *Life of John Dryden, The Works of John Dryden* (1808), i.516. See also n. 37 below.

32 *BL*, ii.256. For earlier examples of Coleridge's favourite distinction of 'imitation' and 'copy', see *CN*, ii.2211, 2274; *Sh C*, i. 177 & n[2], 181, 197; ii.53, 123; and *BL*, ii.30.

33 *CL*, iv.655; vi.692.

34 *ibid.*, iv.632-33. Platonic theory is well suited to the discussion of translation, which is a copy of a copy of the Ideal Poem. Cf. also Scott, *op. cit.*, i.514, and T. Webb, *The Violet in the Crucible. Shelley and Translation* (1976), 27-8.

35 *CL*, vi.771.

36 *ibid.*, iv.655; *CN*, ii.2900.

37 Coleridge had first used the simple term 'compensation' in his preface to the first edition of *The Death of Wallenstein* (1800), in a context which suggests that he was familiar with Denham's remarks on translation, but had not yet formulated his own theories. See *PW*, ii.725.

38 *CL*, v.93.

39 *ibid.*, vi.798. Coleridge's notes on metre in British Library, Egerton MS 2800 ff. 54-7, might be the 'remarks' in question, although they are very general in character.

40 *CL*, v.347n[1], 353-54.

41 'Mitchell's Translation of Aristophanes', *QR*, xxiii (1820), 474-510. See especially pp. 478-84.

42 *BL*, ii.33, 101, 107, 159; *Sh C*, i.53; ii.33, 160.

43 **FRERE**, i.188, 192-94, 205.

44 *CL*, v.529.

45 *ibid.*, vi.534, 537-38, 542; *The Table Talk and Omniana of S.T. Coleridge*, ed. T. Ashe (1884), 257.

46 **FRERE**, i.296; *CL*, vi.999.

47 *CL*, iv.655-56. For Coleridge's book-borrowing habits, see Fruman, *op. cit.*, 445-46n[40].

48 *CL*, v.37n[2], 193.

49 *ibid.*, vi.539n[3].

50 *ibid.*, vi.559.

51 **FRERE**, i.208, 220-29.

52 *ibid.*, i.237-38, 275-95. See also Eichler, *op. cit.*, 61-3.

53 **FRERE**, i.296; *CL*, vi.999.

54 **FRERE**, i.299-315, 322-23. An unpublished letter from Frere to Pickering postmarked 11 September 1839 (National Library of Scotland MS 3304) informs Pickering of two shipments containing 92 and 71 copies respectively of all three plays.

55 'Mr Frere's Translation of Aristophanes', *Classical Museum*, i (1844), 238-66.

56 Mary Russell Mitford, *Recollections of a Literary Life* (1852), iii. 149-72, includes extracts from Frere's *Whistlecraft* and *Frogs*. See also her unpublished letter dated 'Novr. 22nd 1852', National Library of Scotland MS 3304.

6

Coleridge's Friendship with Ludwig Tieck

by KATHLEEN WHEELER

> The thought of you has been with me continually, our
> conversations, your friendliness . . . I have since then read your
> books with the greatest joy and delight and have learned much.
> One of the greatest pleasures of my life would be to see you again,
> indeed, to live near you and become something to you. For it
> happens all too rarely that men who belong together find each
> other. Where indeed does one meet with such noble humanity,
> such breadth of erudition, such a reflectiveness unified with wit
> and a great poetic talent, as in you?[1]

Although Tieck's pronouncements on Coleridge were not
always as unequivocably enthusiastic as this sample, and
although he disagreed with Coleridge over issues which were
central to their views about literature, this letter extract
nevertheless well expresses the admiration which both men felt
for one another. Coleridge was no less appreciative of Tieck,
when he wrote to John Hookham Frere:

> We have had for some weeks in England one of the most
> celebrated German Literati, who as a Poet and philosophic
> Critic is by a large and zealous party deemed second only to
> Goethe. . . I have both seen enough of the Man and read enough
> of his Works to feel no hesitation in expressing myself in the
> highest terms concerning his Genius and multiform
> Acquirements . . . he [is] a sound Scholar as well as a man of

exquisite taste . . . It is much at my heart, that a Scholar and Poet
of such high and deservedly high Reputation on the Continent
(for it is not confined to his own Country) and so good a man to
boot (to which I may safely add, a polished Gentleman) should
receive the marks of respect due to him from the Country and
countrymen of Shakespeare.[2]

Although Coleridge met Tieck for the first time in 1806 at
Rome, he may have been familiar with his poetry somewhat
earlier.[3] For during his stay in Germany in 1798-99, he made
the acquaintance of a Professor Heyne, a literary figure who
might have brought Coleridge's knowledge of German
literature up to date. As Alois Brandl has explained:

> Tieck and the two Schlegels, the pioneers of German
> Romanticism, were with [Heyne] at school. He became known to
> Coleridge through his work on Virgil while Coleridge resided in
> Stowey; perhaps his reputation played a part in Coleridge's
> desire to go to Göttingen to study . . . . Coleridge went to him
> soon after matriculating, on the 16th of February, 1799, in order
> to obtain a library card.[4]

Brandl later referred to Heyne as the 'tonangebende Professor
daselbst', or the fashionable professor in Göttingen, and
Coleridge mentioned that 'Heyne has honoured me so far, that
he has given me the Right, which properly only the Professors
have, of sending to the Library for an indefinite number of
Books, in *my own* name'.[5] While this link with the new
movement of German Romanticism (which was still in its
infancy) and with Tieck is a mere thread, it seems almost
prophetic of the direction which Coleridge's thought was to
take over the coming twenty years before his next extended
contact with these 'pioneers' in 1817.

Shortly after his return from Germany, Coleridge began the
translation of Schiller's *Wallenstein* in December 1799, which
was to gain him the praise of Tieck, Frere, and Scott amongst
others.[6] Coleridge reported in a letter to William Godwin of
February 1823:

> I . . . am gratified by Lady Caroline Lamb's admiration of the
> Wallenstein—in the merits of which I must conclude myself to
> have some Share, since the celebrated German Poet &
> philosophic Critic, Ludovicus Tieck assured me that familiar as

he was with the German play, he could never read my Wallenstein but as an Original—nor did he hestitate to declare that in *diction* and *metre* it was decidedly superior to Schiller's: and that it had the not ordinary good fortune of Mr Pitt's applause, in addition to Mr Canning's & Mr John H. Frere's.[7]

The excellence of Coleridge's *Wallenstein* translation seems to have been a matter of general agreement in the nineteenth century, as Brandl's remark suggests:

> Today Coleridge is the recognised authority for 'Wallenstein", as in Germany Schlegel and Tieck are for Shakespeare.[8]

In 1806 Coleridge had the opportunity to renew his contact with the German literati while in Rome (from Malta) in the home of Wilhelm von Humboldt.[9] It was apparently on this occasion that he first made the acquaintance of Ludwig Tieck. Some years later he wrote to Southey:

> Mr Tieck is the Gentleman who was so kind to me at Rome . . . as a Poet, Critic, and Moralist, he stands (in *reputation*) next to Goethe—I believe, that this reputation will be *fame*.[10]

At this first meeting Coleridge and Tieck were supposed to have discussed Shakespeare, and were supposed to have come up against the disagreement which characterized all later discussions—the ascription by Tieck of several doubtful plays to Shakespeare.[11] Since the turn of the century Tieck had planned a work on Shakespeare which was to be an extensive critical analysis, translation, and biographical-historical account, a project which he worked on throughout his life.

Coleridge too would have brought to these discussions a wealth of erudition and mature thought. That he had profoundly admired Shakespeare and had been interested in him from a critic's point of view is clear from the notebooks and letters as far back as 1796-97, which show him reading and taking notes on the plays and sonnets throughout this period.[12] As early as 1803 he had already decided to write a systematic account of Shakespeare. He referred on five different occasions between June 1803 and February 1804 to this plan, which he described as part of 'a great Book of Criticism respecting Poetry and Prose'.[13] How ambitious and systematic this work was to have been can be appreciated from his letter to Sir George

Beaumont of February 1804, explaining that he planned a set of essays, the first to be on Shakespeare, and in the last, 'to establish in the utmost depths, to which I can delve, the characteristics of Good & Bad Poetry—& the intimate Connection of Taste & Morals'. (This last comment almost sounds like a programme for the Lectures of 1808):

> In explaining what I shall do with Shakespere I explain the nature of the other five. Each scene of each play I read, as if it were the whole of Shakespere's Works—the sole thing extant. I ask myself what are the characteristics—the Diction, the Cadences, and Metre, the character, the passion, the moral or metaphysical Inherencies, & fitness for theatric effect, and in what sort of Theatres—... and when I have gone thro' the whole, I then shall collect my papers, & observe, how often such & such Expressions recur/ & thus shall not only know what the Characteristics of Shakespere's Plays are, but likewise what proportion they bear to each other. Then, not carelessly tho' of course with far less care I shall read thro' the old Plays, just before Shakespeare's Time, Sir Phillip Sidney's Arcadia—Ben Johnson [sic], Beaumont & Fletcher, & Massinger/ in the same way—so as to see & to be able to prove what of Shakespere belonged to his Age, & was common to all the first-rate men of that true Saeculum aureum of English Poetry, and what is his own, & his only—Thus I shall both exhibit the characteristics of the Plays—and of the mind—of Shakespere—and of almost every character at greater or less Length a philosophical Analysis & Justification, in the spirit of that analysis of the character of Hamlet, with which you were much pleased ...[14]

Several entries during this period also reveal that Coleridge had already not only thought out a philosophical analysis of Hamlet, but had hit upon some of the central tenets of his Shakespeare criticism to be made public many years later. In November 1801 he spoke of the relation of the particular to the universal as the 'philosophy of Poetry'.[15] He was fond of crediting Shakespeare with this capacity for '"involuting" the universal in the individual'. He also habitually referred to Shakespeare as the proof that a great poet must also be a profound philosopher.[16] In an entry of 1810 he referred in Greek to Shakespeare as the 'myriad-minded one', and other phrases describe him as the 'great-voiced herald of the truth' and 'complex and multiform in the variously versatile wisdom', a phrase which suggests Coleridge's 'unity in multeity'.[17] An entry of a few months later expresses the important idea of the integration of judgement with imagination in Shakespeare, which was a formulation of Coleridge's rejection of the notion that Shakespeare was a 'wild genius' without skill and intelligence:

> Great Injury that has resulted from the supposed Incompatibility of one talent with another/Judgment with Imagination, & Taste—Good Sense with strong feeling &c—if it be false, as assuredly it is, the opinion has deprived us of a test which every man might apply—Locke's opinions of Blackmore, Hume of Milton & Shakespere/&c[18]

In a letter to Sotheby of July 1802, Coleridge gave a concise account of Shakespeare's genius and achievement, and anticipated important later insights when he said,

> It is easy to cloathe Imaginary Beings with our own Thoughts & Feelings; but to send ourselves out of ourselves, to *think* ourselves in to the Thoughts and Feelings of Beings in circumstances wholly & strangely different from our own . . . who has atchieved it? Perhaps only Shakespere.[19]

Somewhat later he immersed himself in the Sonnets as a sequel to this criticism of the plays.[20] These various early lucubrations would have informed Coleridge's conversations with Tieck at their first meeting in 1806.

Coleridge confessed that at the time of the 1806 meeting he did not realize Tieck's 'eminence as a poet'.[21] But he must have begun to read some of his poetry soon after, for between January and March of 1806 he jotted down in a notebook a translation or adaptation of a poem of Tieck's entitled 'Herbstlied'.[22] The poem would have appealed to Coleridge from several perspectives, the most obvious being the use of the image of the singing bird as a metaphor for imagination.[23] And it contains the synthesis of light and sound which was to fascinate Coleridge in later years, and which was a topic of discussion in a letter to Tieck some twelve years afterwards.[24] This synthesis of music and light seems to be an image expressive of the integration of thought and feeling, which was a central idea for both Tieck and Coleridge, as was the seasonal metaphor, which expresses the fears of loss of love and imagination, while in stanza IV the cycle is overcome in the affirmation of a perpetual spring.[25]

By 1814 Coleridge was considering a translation of Goethe's *Faust* for John Murray, to which he intended to affix an introductory essay. His awareness of Tieck's importance as a poet is obvious from a description of the contents:

> In my Essay I meant to have given a full tho' comprest critical account of the 4 Stages of German Poetry from Hans Sachs to Tiek and Schlegel, who with Goethe are the living Stars, that are now culminant on the German Parnassus.[26]

He also intended to try to justify the supposed faults of Goethe's *Faust*, and compared this intention with his justification of Shakespeare and, particularly, of *Hamlet*. He may well have tried to influence Tieck in favour of *Faust* in 1817, for Crabb Robinson later reported on Tieck's objections to the work.[27]

Shortly before Tieck arrived for his 1817 visit to England, Crabb Robinson introduced Coleridge to J.H. Green, who shared Coleridge's enthusiasm for German literature. It was at Green's home that Coleridge renewed his acquaintance with Tieck.[28] Tieck had come to England to collect materials for his 'Buch über Shakespeare', and found in Coleridge once again a congenial spirit for his interest in Shakespeare. Since he had last met Tieck in 1806, Coleridge had given several courses of lectures on Shakespeare, in 1811-12, at the Surrey Institution in 1812-13, and at Bristol in the autumn of 1813.

Both Tieck and Karl Solger disagreed with August Wilhelm von Schlegel on several important Shakespearean matters, and Coleridge was closer to Tieck and Solger on these disputed issues. Solger wrote to a friend that Tieck's views on Shakespeare were profound and revealed important conclusions for the whole of dramatic poetry, 'very different from Schlegel's views, which we both condemned'.[29] One of Tieck's main coincidences with Coleridge was that he saw Shakespeare not in radical contrast and distinction from the other poets of his age, but as a model for poets. In the following passage Tieck expressed views similar to Coleridge's.[30] He wrote to Solger:

> Shakespeare is only the focal point of the English theatre and the new art. If one does not know exactly the nature of previous

101

theatres, Shakespeare remains a puzzle, and one most easily characterizes him by those things which he has in common with all the others. One must study his period and the following periods if one is finally to be fully convinced that he is for us the key to our world and our situation. Unfortunately he remains only a curiosity to many. Who has recognized in him the inner harmony and the true law by which he must be our eternal model, or this deepest truth, which through itself becomes poetry? When I come to this point, expression often fails me; to no one can the fact be given from without, which one must experience and raise within himself. But to make room;— thereby, in regarding all of Shakespeare's plays as a single work, much is clarified by this alone.[31]

Schlegel's notion that Shakespeare should be related to the other poets of his age as a kind of anomaly or special case was thus rejected by Tieck as well as by Coleridge. Another important difference from Schlegel is the nature and consequence of the distinction between the classical and the modern. Tieck, Solger and Friedrich Schlegel all seemed to insist that Greek and modern drama, though opposites in a sense, followed essentially the same laws. Tieck and the others unified these two antithetical forms through irony, in the high, German romantic sense of the word.[32] Coleridge agreed with Schlegel that the two types were opposites, but he seems to have gone further and insisted that they were 'true opposites', that is, reconciled in essence; in this he agreed with Lessing as well as with Tieck and Solger:

> [Shakespeare's apparent irregularities] were deviations only from the *accidents* of the Greek tragedy . . . [Lessing] proved that in all the essentials of art, no less than in the truth of nature, the plays of Shakespeare were incomparably more coincident with the principes of Aristotle than the productions of Corneille and Racine . . . [33]

Tieck explained that very early in his work on Shakespeare he had begun to sense that it was a quality of self-consciousness which made Shakespeare's genius what it was. He spoke of the 'tension' in the language, manifested by ambiguity, double-meanings, pun and wit, metaphor, and symbol.[34] Moreover, Tieck spoke of the relation of the individual to the universal, very much as Coleridge did, and in the same breath captured the nature of Shakespeare's genius as Coleridge had characterized it:

> I am so much more an individual the more I can lose myself in the all: it is not really a losing, since we only understand and feel a thing in so far as we are that thing.[35]

Tieck also agreed with Coleridge when he discussed the relation of intention and judgement to instinct or inspiration. He explained that genius 'works according to dark, inner laws; its artistic drive is its law, and precisely because of this it is Genius'.[36] Coleridge, like Tieck and Schlegel, had often insisted upon the idea that imagination works according to its own laws, not subject to conscious volition, though nevertheless unified with the consciousness. Genius for Coleridge was a law deeper than consciousness, but it worked through and in the conscious mind of the artist. Coleridge, in a passage partly drawn from Schlegel, explained:

> No work of true genius dare want its appropriate form; neither indeed is there any danger of this. As it must not, so neither can it, be lawless! For it is even this that constitutes it genius—the power of acting creatively under laws of its own origination . . . even such is the appropriate excellence of her chosen poet, of our own Shakespeare, himself a nature humanized, a genial understanding directing self-consciously a power and an implicit wisdom deeper than consciousness.[37]

Coleridge wrote to his friend Frere in the highest terms of praise for Tieck's achievements and especially for his understanding of English literature. He concluded his panegyric with these lines:

> For the last 15 years or more [Tieck] has devoted the larger portion of his Time and Thought to a great Work on Shakespear, in 3 large Volumes Octavo—he has communicated to me the plan & contents of the whole and tho' the hypothetical part perplexes me at present, spite of or rather perhaps in consequence of the numerous and striking facts that he adduces in support of it (viz. that Shakespear was the Author not only of the three parts of Henry VI, but even of the rejected Plays) yet as a compleat Work of Biography and sound criticism extending over the whole poetic literature, manners, etc. of the reigns of

Elizabeth and James, it appears to me unique.[38]

Tieck also confirmed Coleridge's resistance to his ascription of the doubtful plays to Shakespeare, and described Coleridge as saying that this ascription 'contradicts everything that has ever been thought or written about Shakespeare in England'.[39] Crabb Robinson further reported:

> [Tieck] says he has learned a great deal from Coleridge, who has glorious conceptions about Shakespeare (*herrliche Ideen*). Coleridge's conversation he very much admires, and thinks it superior to any of his writings. But he says there is much high poetry in 'Christabel'.[40]

We can only wish that Robinson had reported more exactly the nature of these 'herrliche Ideen' about Shakespeare (since Tieck would have been familiar enough with A.W. von Schlegel's criticism to have detected borrowings by Coleridge).

Some years after Coleridge's death, Tieck is known to have spoken highly of his Shakespearean criticism to a Herr von Ense, and shortly before this he discussed Coleridge with Carlyle.[41] But Tieck's admiration for Coleridge can best be appreciated from his long letter to Coleridge six months after he returned to Germany from his English tour. In this letter he desired that Coleridge seriously consider a matter which they had already discussed in England, that Coleridge should collaborate with Tieck in his work on Shakespeare. Tieck planned an English edition of the 'Buch über Shakespeare' which was to differ in substantial ways from the German edition,[42] and Coleridge was to be responsible for making the necessary 'kritische und philosophische' alterations:

> The situation of this book is very different in our two countries. The Germans I can assume to be acquainted with much philosophical and critical insight, some principles about beauty and art, matters with which the Englishman is entirely unfamiliar, or else which would seem to him to be the worst form of heresy. On the other hand every Englishman who is interested in old English poetry knows a thousand things, things which to him are ordinary, common knowledge, but of which the most educated German knows not even a hint . . . You see then that if you want to join yourself to my work as a friendly, illuminating star, you will have a double assignment: 1) to add some

explanatory material which I need not say to the Germans, and 2) to remove or shorten that which is current knowledge to the English reader.[43]

This difference between the English and German editions recalls a remark of Crabb Robinson's in 1811, after he had attended a lecture of Coleridge's with a German friend:

> Coleridge's mind is much more German than English. My friend has pointed out striking analogies between Coleridge and German writers whom Coleridge has never seen.[44]

Robinson also noted:

> Coleridge's fourth lecture. It was on the nature of comedy—about Aristophanes, &c. The mode of treating the subject very German, and of course much too abstract for his audience.[45]

Tieck's comment to Coleridge on *Biographia Literaria* refers more explicitly to this alleged lack of communication between Coleridge's German, philosophizing spirit and the English mind. Tieck wrote:

> Your Biographia Literaria utterly enchanted me, instructed me, and amused me; I should think, however, that for the greater number of English readers it is too weighty and profound.[46]

At the time of this assessment, Tieck seems to have read every major work of Coleridge's which had been published, for he discussed these writings in his letter to Coleridge:

> And now, my dear Friend, allow me a still more urgent request: finish your excellent poem Christabel, which I have already read four or five times with renewed pleasure, and which I continue to admire for its language, descriptions, and verse. Work, write still more poetry, for your countrymen and for all our joy, especially for mine. How beautiful is the 'Mariner', how splendid so many pages in the collection [*Sibylline Leaves*], which I read with genuine edification, as I also read the 'Sermons' .... With regard to the tragedy 'Remorse', your own estimation of it seems correct, except that it is too modest; the language is really outstanding and truly tragic—it has the old majesty and strength and never loses itself in that shallow sentimentality and empty phrasing, which characterizes almost all of our new tragedians. I would prefer however to name the whole a dramatised Novella,

rather than a tragedy . . . . Plan, plot should not in my opinion ever become intrigue.[47]

Tieck's comment that Coleridge never degenerates into 'shallow sentimentality' suggests that he viewed Coleridge's style as truly 'ironic' in the high German Romantic sense. Sentimentality was a sign that the artist was not in control of his material and was unable to gain the necessary objective distance of a detached, reflective, and self-conscious spectator of the process of his own composition. Although in the following extract Coleridge disagrees with Tieck in respect of the example under discussion, he seems to take for granted the distinction between sentimentality and self-consciousness:

> I have just looked into Kleist's first play—it seemed to me harsh and branny, and the freedom from sentimentality, for which our friend Tieck gives him so much credit, too evidently a matter of purpose, and forethought—industrious omission not absence by nature and consequence of the some thing instead.[48]

Tieck's (and Karl Solger's) criticism of Byron is a reminder of the chasm which separates the English notion of 'irony' from the German conception, a difference which the Germans express by their distinction between 'common and high irony'. It also explains the resistance met with in linking Coleridge to these German Ironists, for whom satire and sarcasm are only superficial, unnecessary elements, and to whom irony is not 'mockery, persiflage, or derision, or anything similar to these; it is rather the most profound earnestness, which at the same time is bound up with wit and true joviality'.[49] Tieck's friend Solger was also repelled by Byron's 'egotism and his turbulent, gloomy, and self-flirtatious Nature'.[50] Tieck's religious views may have affected to some extent his attitude towards Byron, as is suggested by his criticism, in his letter to Coleridge, of Byron's scorn for the 'most sacred':

> I have now read Byron's works through with eagerness, and though the style is grandiose, nevertheless they are highly distasteful. What he lacks is restraint . . . he despises the most sacred in his gloomy fierceness. He knows humility as little as he knows faith and love, but so much more exactly does he know the evil spirit of man.[51]

Tieck had apparently objected to Goethe's Prologue to *Faust* on religious grounds as well. Coleridge had also been ambivalent towards *Faust* in earlier years, though his later pronouncements became unequivocably favourable.[52]

Although the discussions with Coleridge during Tieck's visit in 1817 may have once again centred on Shakespeare, as in 1806, other topics were also of interest, such as the German mystic Tauler, Boehme (who was a crucial point of departure for the thought of both Tieck and Coleridge), Spanish divines, and Giordano Bruno.[53] Solger must also have formed an important topic of conversation, in view of Green's departure for Berlin to study with him, and in view of Coleridge's request to Thomas Boosey for Solger's *Erwin*, and for 'all the works, you may have of LUDWIG TIECK'.[54] Tieck's requests to his own German book supplier upon his return on behalf of Coleridge are an indication of the other topics which they must have discussed. He asked for everything of Fichte's, Schubert, Solger's works, Wolf and Böckh, and the complete works of Boehme. He was anxious to obtain these books for Coleridge, for 'this friend gave me all his things to take with me'.[55] In addition, Tieck seems to have awakened Coleridge's interest in his young friend Wackenröder and in Goethe's *Zur Farbenlehre*, for Coleridge wrote to Tieck in 1817 to 'learn the specific Objections of the Mathematicians to Goethe's Farbenlehre, as far as it is an attack on *the assumptions* of Newton'.[56]

After Shakespeare, the most fascinating topic of discussion for Tieck and Coleridge may have been animal magnetism, in which Coleridge had been interested for nearly two decades. An interest in Mesmerism had arisen in London during his schooldays at Christ's Hospital[57], and had so deeply affected Coleridge's imagination that it became immortalized in the serpent eye of Geraldine in *Christabel*, the glittering eye of the Mariner, and the flashing eye of 'Kubla Khan'. The idea of animal magnetism may have had a more general and pervasive effect upon the atmosphere of these poems than is often realised, with the rhythms and imagery which tend to create a mood of enthralment similar to hypnotism.[58] While in Gemany, Coleridge's fascination for this phenomenon had been dealt a crushing blow by the lecturer J.F. Blumenbach, who was a complete sceptic about animal magnetism.[59] In an 1809

107

number of *The Friend*, Coleridge had referred disparagingly to the topic, but in the spring of 1817, when he read Blumenbach's recantation of his scepticism, he wrote, in a margin of a passage on Blumenbach in *The Friend*, 'This is a condemnation, which I must retract'.[60] His well-known interpolated passage in 'The Eolian Harp' in *Sibylline Leaves* (1817) was a public gesture of reinstating animal magnetism.[61]

In early June, while conversing with Tieck, Coleridge anxiously requested Tieck's opinion of the magnetism phenomenon. Tieck was clearly favourable and was able to give Coleridge numerous instances seen by himself, since he was in intimate contact with one of the most active magnetizers, K.C. Wolfart.[62] Shortly after these discussions with Tieck, Coleridge was proposing to write an article on the subject, and a short manuscript was the result.[63] His interest in animal magnetism continued throughout his life, in a variety of forms, in connection with single and double touch, a warmth sense, and unifying energy.[64] The Victorians were fascinated by it, and it partly survives today in the form of hypnotism.

From these wide-ranging discussions, Coleridge gained a much broader view of Tieck as an intellectual. Until Tieck's 1817 visit, Coleridge had apparently not been familiar with anything more than Tieck's poetry, and he tried to procure his entire works while Tieck was still in England. But he only succeeded in obtaining *William Lovell* (1795-96) and Wackenröder's *Phantasien*, edited by Tieck. Tieck apparently later sent his works to Coleridge. But Coleridge's estimation of Tieck's prose is in contrast to his high appreciation of the poetry and conversation. For he commented to Green in December 1817:

> I do not *very much* like the Sternbald of our Friend [Tieck's *Franz Sternbalds Wanderungen*, 1798]—it is too like an imitation of Heinse's Ardinghello, and if the Scen[e in] the Painter's Garden at Rome is less licencious than the correspondent Abomination in the former Work, it is likewise duller—in short, it is a lewd day-dream, in which the Dreamer at once *yawns and itches*.[65]

He had quite a different impression of Tieck's *Phantasus*, however, as a marginal note written in a translation of stories by Tieck indicates:

A Translation of the whole of the Phantasus (in 3 vol.) by a man of Genius, would indeed be a benefaction to English literature. S.T.C.

Another note written on the tale 'Lovecharm' is also of interest:

There are splendid passages in the original but as a whole, it is very inferior to the other Tales and Dramas of the Phantasus— the work in which Tieck's Genius reached its zenith. S.T.C.[66]

Coleridge's esteem for Tieck is also reflected in the fact that he compared Tieck to his other most valued friends, such as Frere and Wordsworth. He desired to introduce Tieck to Frere, because 'their pursuits have been so similar—& to convince Mr Tieck, that [Frere] is *the* Man among us, in whom Taste at it's maximum has vitalised itself into productive power— Genius'.[67] According to Coleridge, Tieck was impressed with Frere's translation of the *Frogs,* and in the same letter he stated that Tieck's 'literary Career bears a striking resemblance to Wordsworth's'.[68] In a letter to Southey a few weeks later, he expanded upon this and remarked.

Mr Tieck has had to run, and has run, as nearly the same Career in Germany, as Yourself, and Wordsworth & (by the Spray of being known to be intimate with you) your's sincerely, S.T. Coleridge.[69]

Sixteen years after Tieck's visit to England, he wrote to Coleridge of the 'unforgettable hours' at Highgate, and added:

. . . the Lay-Sermons, Christabel, Biographia Literaria, I read again and again with especial feeling.[70]

Finally, upon hearing of Coleridge's death, Tieck was reported by Crabb Robinson to have spoken 'of Coleridge with high admiration and heard of his death with great apparent sorrow'.[71] It can only be a great loss that the conversations of these two extraordinary minds were not somehow more fully preserved, and that the encounters of such congenial intellects were restricted to two brief visits.

NOTES & REFERENCES

1 From a letter of Tieck to Coleridge in Griggs, 265. My translations throughout.

2 *CL,* iv.744-46.

3 *CN,* i.ll28n (1802) suggests use of Schiller's *Musenalmanach* (1796-99), in which some of Tieck's poetry was published. See *CN,* i.2791.

4 A. Brandl, *Samuel Taylor Coleridge und die englische Romantik* (Berlin, 1886), 253-54.

5 *CL,* i.475 and see 472, 477.

6 See **FRERE,** i.49, and J.G. Lockhart, *Life of Sir Walter Scott,* Everyman ed. (1937), 344. For Tieck see below.

7 *CL,* v. 269 and n.

8 Brandl, *op. cit.,* 280. Tieck's views on the disputed plays are not generally accepted.

9 See D. Sultana, *S.T. Coleridge in Malta and Italy* (1969), 386ff.

10 *CL,* iv. 754.

11 Brandl, *op. cit.,* 309.

12 See e.g., *CL,* i. 444, 391, 386, and *CN,* i. 127 and 215. Coleridge looked to Shakespeare as a model, with Schiller, for his own play *Osorio* (*CL,* i. 304).

13 *CL,* ii. 960, and see 951, 955, and *CN,* i. 1646 for variations on the plan.

14 *CL,* ii. 1054. Note the reference to a discussion of *Hamlet.*

15 *CN,* i. 943. See *BL,* ii. 159, 187 and *Fr.,* i. 457.

16 See *CL,* ii. 810.

17 *CN,* i. 1070; cf. *CL,* iii. 528; *Fr.,* i. 453 and *BL,* ii. 13n.

18 *CN,* i. 1255 and n. Cf. *BL,* , Chs. xiv-xv, esp. ii. 12-13. Note that Coleridge refers here to the English tradition of Shakespeare criticism.

19 *CL,* ii. 810.

20 See *CN,* ii. 2428. This entry, dated 1805, may belong to an earlier date.

21 *CRD,* i. 305.

22 *CN,* ii. 2791, January-March 1806. E.H. Coleridge's version in *PW,* ii. 1108-9 was substantially revised from the notebook entry. The published version, 'Glycine's Song', *PW,* ii. 919, lacks the charm of the notebook entry.

23 See, e.g., *CN,* iii. 3314 on the bird-harp.

24 *CL,* iv. 750-1; cf. 11.26-33 added to the text of 'The Eolian Harp', *PW,* 1828. These lines were first added to the *errata* page of *Sibylline Leaves* (1817). See pp. 157-58 of this volume (John Gutteridge's article).

25 Cf. the last verse paragraph of 'Frost at Midnight' for a similar transcendence of the cycle: 'Therefore all seasons shall be sweet to thee' (1.65). See *CL,* i. 610, 615, 658 and *CN,* i. 1575, 1577 for sources of the 'column of light' image.

26 *CL,* iii. 528.

27 See *CL,* iii. 523-28 and *CRD,* ii. 59.

28 See *CL,* iv. 738-39. Green was so impressed by Tieck's discussions of Solger that he left that summer for Berlin to study with him.

29 *Solger's Nachgelassene Schriften und Briefwechsel,* ed. Tieck and von Raumer (Leipzig, 1826), i. 213-14 [1811].

30 See *CN*, i. 1225; *CL*, ii. 1054 and also above footnote 18.
31 *Tieck and Solger: The Complete Correspondence*, ed. P. Matenko (New York, 1933), 429.
32 As, e.g., the irony of Sophocles and Shakespeare. For Tieck on the complex 'high irony' see I. Strohschneider-Kohrs, *Romantische Ironie in Theorie und Gestaltung, Hermaea*, 6 (Tübingen, 1960), 131.
33 *BL*, ii. 182. Raysor's conclusion, *Sh C*, i.xxiii, is misleading.
34 *Tieck's Nachgelassene Schriften*, ed. Köpke (Leipzig, 1855), ii. 173-74, 217.
35 *Ludwig Tieck und die Brüder Schlegel*, ed. Ludeke (Frankfurt, 1930), 99.
36 Köpke, *op. cit.*, ii. 132.
37 *Sh C*, i. 197-98.
38 *CL*, iv. 745-46.
39 Köpke, *op. cit.*, i. 375-76.
40 *CRD*, ii. 62-3.
41 E.H. Zeydel, *Ludwig Tieck in England* (Princeton, 1931), 96.
42 While never completing his Shakespearean plan, Tieck did succeed in publishing *Das Altenglische Theater, Supplemente zum Shakespere* (1811), *Shakesperes Vorschule* (Pt I in 1823, Pt II in 1829, but Pt III unpublished), *Vier Schauspielen von Shakespere* (1836).
43 Griggs, 265.
44 *CRD*, i. 352.
45 *ibid.*, i. 387.
46 Griggs, 267.
47 *ibid.*
48 *CL*, v. 190-91.
49 O. Walzel, 'Methode? Ironie bei F. Schlegel und bei Solger', *Helicon*, i. (1938), 35. See also Köpke, *op. cit.*, ii. 238.
50 Matenko, *op. cit.*, 531.
51 Griggs, 267.
52 See Rosemary Ashton's *The German Idea: Four English Writers and the Reception of German Thought 1800-1860* (1980), ch.I. See also *CRD*, ii. 59-60, 446-47 on Tieck's Catholicism and on *Faust*.
53 *CL*, iv. 742.
54 *ibid.*, iv. 737-38. See Coleridge's marginalia on Solger in the British Library.
55 Matenko, *op. cit.*, 523.
56 *CL*, iv. 750-51, 911; on Wackenröder see *CL*, iv. 743.
57 See J.L. Lowes, *The Road to Xanadu* (1930), 231-32, on animal magnetism.
58 See J. Beer, *Coleridge's Poetic Intelligence* (1977), 220-23.
59 See *Fr.*, i. 154-56nn.
60 *ibid.*, ii. 51; cf. i. 59n[1].
61 See *CL*, iv. 730-31 and 750-51 on animal magnetism and light and sound. See also pp.157-58 of this volume.
62 *CL*, iv. 745.
63 *ibid.*, iv. 749-52, and *Inquiring Spirit*, ed. K. Coburn (1951), 45-50.
64 See Beer, *op. cit.*, 278-80 and 249.
65 *CL*, iv. 793.

66 Marginal note on *The Old Man of the Mountain, The Lovecharm,* and *Pietro of Albano. Tales from the German of Tieck,* trans. Julius Ch. Hare (1831). A MS transcript of the lost note is in Cornell University Library.
67 *CL,* iv. 739.
68 *ibid.,* iv. 744.
69 *ibid.,* iv. 754. He refers to the years of sharp criticism, especially by the *Edinburgh Review.* By 1815 the criticism was beginning to turn into more favourable reviews, as Lockhart's praise of Wordsworth in *Blackwood's Magazine* (1817) suggests.
70 Zeydel, *op. cit.,* 96.
71 *CRD,* iii. 44-5.

7

Coleridge and American Romanticism: the Transcendentalists and Poe

by ALEXANDER KERN

As Samuel Taylor Coleridge (1772-1834) solved his own religious, philosophical, and critical problems, so he was able a generation later to answer American needs. A group of New England Unitarians who were also dissatisfied with the cold rationalism and mechanical psychology of the Enlightenment were able to use his version of German philosophy to create American Transcendentalism. And Edgar Allan Poe, though Southern in background and interested in aesthetics rather than morals, also revolted from rationalism to Coleridgean idealism in *Eureka*.

Yet because of cultural differences between Britain and the new nation, different developments occurred. Let me anticipate my findings. Puritanism remained dominant in New England after 1660, and revival religion was important. Jonathan Edwards, the theologian, as a rational mystic, accepted the passive nature of man in a mechanical world and also emphasized the enthusiasm of conversions. Though his *Freedom of the Will*, as we shall see, gave Coleridge the impression of cold determinism, Edwards anticipated Coleridge's view that the regenerate man was free. The American Unitarians grew out of the Enlightenment and those who read Coleridge became Transcendentalists. Yet because they shared Edwards' Puritan tradition, they became Romantics with a difference. They

113

combined Coleridge's type of idealism with a belief in a divinely ordained, pre-apocalyptic millennialism which would begin in America. Emerson, the central figure in American literature in this union of individual and national destiny, influenced Thoreau and Whitman in a distinctively American way. So Coleridge produced unanticipated results because of the different American environment.

As the discovery of the western world was part of Renaissance expansion so also was the development of New England a late phase of the Reformation. Motivated by Calvinist ideals of separatism, the Puritans saw themselves as chosen people like the Israelites, who were going to a promised land. Divided by the broad Atlantic from a corrupted Europe, they looked forward to an errand into the wilderness[1] and to the establishment of a city on a hill, with the aid of a covenant with God. If they broke the covenant they would be punished like the children of Israel. Thus, as religious zeal declined, prosperity grew, and disasters struck, the clergy preached Jeremiad sermons of doom—as Perry Miller's great history makes emphatically clear.[2] But this European sermon form had itself developed out of prophecy, and the Hebrew prophets were not pessimists. Rather they called on the people to repent so that they could be rewarded by God. Accordingly Cotton Mather in his *Magnalia Christi Americana* in 1702, described John Winthrop, the leader in 1630 of the Massachusetts Bay Colony, as *Nehemias Americanus*, the rebuilder of the New Jerusalem. So Emerson, even after his adoption of Coleridgean ideas, was able to maintain the Puritan typological tradition by combining the individual with the national destiny in a form of soteriology.[3] In contrast, Coleridge was less a prophet than a teacher in his prose patterns.

For all their self-concerned provincialism, the young colonies, as part of the empire, were affected by the changing intellecual climate of Europe, though with a cultural time-lag of a generation or more. After Descartes fathered modern philosophy with his subject-object division, and Spinoza developed his pantheism, the philosophical center of gravity moved to Britain. Not just the presence of major thinkers, but the establishment of paradigm patterns which regulated the approved types of questions and answers caused the shift.[4]

Newton's laws seemed to create an ordered cosmos in which God's interfering Providence had less place. John Locke's mechanical universe was made and wound up by God and then allowed to run without interference. Locke also declared that the human mind with its faculties was passive, its *tabula rasa* receiving impressions which were assembled according to laws of association. Berkeley went farther in the direction of saying that all reality was in the mind of the beholder. However, it was Hume who carried skepticism to the extreme point of denying that the external world was real and that causality could be established. This undercut science on the one hand and religion and morality on the other. No wonder Hume himself gave up philosophy and turned to other fields like history and government. A theological switch had developed. Views of human nature as bound by law became widespread among intellectuals and the mechanical philosophy of Locke took hold. Scientific rationalism and a mechanical religion cut the rigors of the Reformation, and an invisible hand seemed to guide man and society into a course of progress. David Hartley, a Cambridge graduate and physician, also an associationist, influenced both Wordsworth and Coleridge for a time before they found his answers unsatisfactory.

In the colonies thought was also affected. While Jonathan Edwards, who was influenced by both Newton and Locke, developed an idealism similar to, but independent of, that of Berkeley, religion was his first concern. Defending God's sovereignty, he skillfully attacked freedom of the will,[5] arguing against Arminians on their own ground. His concern for individual salvation led him into the Great Awakening, a religious revival movement in which he was aided by George Whitefield, a Methodist enthusiast from England. Edwards in his work on *The Religious Affections,* an impressively subtle psychological analysis applied to conversions, claimed that the regenerate man was free from the causal chain of motivation.[6] Though Coleridge seems not to have known *The Religious Affections,* his argument in *Aids to Reflection* was, as we shall with some irony see, in this respect like that of Edwards.

But despite Edwards' attempts to preserve Calvinism, Locke became America's dominant philosopher. Libertarian religion prevailed among intellectuals like Franklin, while Jefferson and

John Adams were self-professed Unitarians. The optimism which accompanied belief in the natural law of a benevolent deity became a prevailing tone. Locke's natural rights arguments were used to justify the American Revolution—the success and relative moderation of which produced a happiness unlike that following the French Revolution in Europe, where the Terror and Napoleonic nationalism disillusioned previous hopefuls like Coleridge.

In American religion, Edwards' revival movement did not sweep all of New England. Urban churches dominated by elite members of the upper class resisted the emotionalism of revival religion. Charles Chauncy, the pastor of such a church in Boston, attacked the Awakening and engaged in controversy with Edwards.[7] An Arminian, who believed in universal salvation and at the same time advocated the natural rights which led to the colonial break with England, Chauncy was a predecessor of the American Unitarians. This group accepted a mechanical philosophy which did not fit logically with their belief in religious miracles.

While the name Unitarian was kept hidden until 1819, Harvard College was dominated by liberal doctrines. William Ellery Channing, the ablest and most influential of the group in the early part of the century, an intelligent, subtle, and almost saintly man, tended towards Transcendentalism without ever completely accepting its doctrines.[8] Progressive though cautious, he was a precursor. Through his brother-in-law, Washington Allston, he had met Coleridge,[9] but it was not Channing who spread the new views into the circles where they had the most effect.

This was done by the Rev. James Marsh (1794-1842), a Congregationalist minister, a graduate of Dartmouth, but trained at Andover Theological Seminary, and president of the small University of Vermont. By 1826 he had published a translation of Herder's *Spirit of Hebrew Poetry* and in 1829 produced his *magnum opus*, an edition of Coleridge's *Aids to Reflection*. This contained a Preliminary Essay which pointed out key passages where Coleridge put forward the new German philosophical views. In 1831 Marsh also published *The Friend*.[10]

What Marsh tried to do was to revitalize Congregationalism. For him the central issue was freedom of the will, which, as we

116

have said, had been denied by Edwards, who argued successfully that sinful man was incapable of following anything but the strongest motive. Edwards claimed that man deserved punishment for sin because he was free to do, and did, what he willed, though he could not will what he willed. That depended upon God alone. Only when God in His grace granted regeneration to a soul, giving it an extra sense, as it were, to appreciate and enjoy the beauty of God and His creation, was disinterested love possible. Convinced as he was that regeneration depended upon God, Edwards still sought to produce a favorable environment for conversion by preaching powerful sermons depicting the terrors of hell. 'Sinners in the Hands of an Angry God',[11] with its pounding, nail-driving rhythms, produces an effect much like that of the retreat sermon in Joyce's *Portrait of the Artist as a Young Man*.

Coleridge, shrewdly attributing the supposed 'Justice' of Edwards'damnation of sinners to God's right of Property in man,[12] chose freedom. He broke the necessitarian pattern by adapting to his own purposes a German distinction between free Reason, and necessitarian Understanding which was bound by causal law. Coleridge, following Kant, distinguished between the *speculative* Reason which formulates abstract truth and the *practical* Reason which formulates moral truth. This practical reason, very unlike that of Kant, is not a misunderstanding of Kant but a formulation needed by Coleridge to solve his own religious problems.[13] So he states in *Aids to Reflection* that:

> Whenever by self-subjection to this universal Light, the Will of the Individual, the *particular* Will, has become a Will of Reason, the man is regenerate: and Reason is then the *Spirit* of the regenerated man, whereby the Person is capable of quickening inter-communion with the Divine Spirit. And herein consists the mystery of Redemption, that this has been rendered possible to us . . . Reason is preeminently spiritual, and a Spirit, even *our* Spirit, through an effluence of the same Grace by which we are privileged to say Our Father![14]

The relationship between the conceptions of Edwards and Coleridge is interesting. For Edwards true knowledge of the Deity is available to the regenerate man through an added sense, as it were, of the grandeur and beauty of God. Though this is not unlike Coleridge's not quite mystical sense of the practical Reason, the origins were fairly different for the two men. In the Calvinist system of Edwards where the emphasis is upon the sovereignty of God, it is His grace which is the agent, while the recipient cannot freely choose between good and evil. Coleridge, vague on the mechanism, makes the freedom an article of belief.

The ability to come into contact with his God, the Over-Soul, is for Emerson open to all men, not only to the regenerate or elect. In this, he is, by no accident, more democratic, for in the United States the theoretical equality of all men was assumed. If at times Emerson sounds relatively unhappy about the mob, still he recognized the potential of all men without regard to education or wealth to attain a direct relation with God through an intuitive process of Self-Reliance.[15] Emerson and Thoreau, using some of the language of prophecy, imply that any hearer can act, and so exhort or challenge their audiences to lift themselves.

While Marsh did not succeed in reinvigorating conservative Congregationalism, he produced a small but significant group of followers, the Vermont Transcendentalists, and retained his importance as an editor of Coleridge. An edition of *Aids to Reflection* with an introduction by the Episcopalian clergyman John McVickar, failed to displace Marsh, whose Preliminary Essay remained in the British editions. In 1840 Henry Nelson Coleridge wrote Marsh, 'I trust that you are to be the editor of the new edition of the other works', but Marsh died in 1842, and his student W. G. T. Shedd became the editor of the 1853 edition of *The Complete Works of Samuel Taylor Coleridge* in seven volumes, which was long standard. Moreover, John Dewey, the American Pragmatist, as a student at the University of Vermont, was influenced by Marsh's ideas.[16]

The greatest effect of Coleridge was on Emerson (1803-82) who was facing a similar crisis. He was dissatisfied with Locke's mechanical philosophy, and found in the Scottish realists no adequate answer to Hume's devastating skepticism.[17] Moreover, unlike Channing, he got no help from the idealism of Richard Price,[18] and was bothered by German higher criticism of the Bible when he first read *Aids to Reflection* in 1829. The death of his wife and his resignation from the pulpit on religious grounds produced a crisis during which he met Marsh and looked up Coleridge in England. Though Carlyle became a fortunately distant friend, it was Coleridge's writing which showed the greater effect on Emerson's idealism. His interest was reenforced on his return to Massachusetts by the review article on Coleridge of Frederic Henry Hedge who ably presented Coleridge's views, in addition to those of the new German philosophy, as ideas which were worthwhile. Though Hedge criticized Coleridge's diffuseness and lack of coherence, Emerson was impressed by this 'living, leaping logos'.[19]

Primary for him was the distinction between Reason and Understanding which Marsh had pointed out. While Understanding, the logical faculty of the Enlightenment, dealt effectively with nature, Reason dealt with the spirit. As Emerson wrote to his brother, 'Reason is the highest faculty of the soul—what we mean by the soul itself; it never *reasons*, never proves, it simply perceives; it is vision'.[20] What Emerson got from Coleridge was markedly unlike Kant's claim that the *Ding-an-sich*, the noumenon behind the phenomenon, was ultimately unknowable. Emerson, like Coleridge, insisted that the Reason could come into contact with the Over-Soul, one of his names for the Deity, because it was of the same kind. So for the Americans, Transcendental knowledge of what for Kant was roughly transcendent became possible.[21]

Coleridge found through *The Critique of Pure Reason* a solution of the conflict between the empirical and the rationalist schools of philosophy. While Kant criticized both schools and maintained that all knowledge of nature came from experience, experience itself was governed by the *a priori* functions of the mind.[22] Coleridge, while following Fichte's positing of the ego as the free reason, found him inadequate on Nature. On that issue he followed the lead of Schelling, who, however, developed a pantheism, in which the 'It is' became basic.[23] While Schelling moved the static conception of the lawful universe of Spinoza into a dynamic and vital one, Coleridge became, when he was in Malta, too Trinitarian[24] a Christian to accept permanently Schelling's position. McFarland's profound book on *Coleridge and the Pantheist Tradition* is convincing in its conclusion that Coleridge was capable of developing independent positions and even using the verbal counters of other systems to think in a mosaic pattern.[25] So Coleridge wrote, 'Reason is the Power of universal and necessary Convictions, the Source and Substance of Truths above Sense, and having their evidence in themselves. Its presence is always marked by the necessity of the position affirmed . . .' To reuse a previous quotation, Coleridge continues, 'Whenever by self-subjection to this universal Light, the Will of the Individual, the *particular* Will, has become a Will of Reason, the man is regenerate: and the Reason is then the Spirit of the regenerated man, whereby, the Person is capable of a quickening intercommunion with the Divine spirit.' So the saved individual's Reason can communicate directly with God, and the 'I am' is superior to Nature.[26]

Emerson and Alcott and Thoreau, coming out of a Puritan and not an Anglican Church, were less bothered by the fear of panthesim and all accepted it at times, though not, I think, ultimately. *Nature* (1836) represents the high-water mark of Emerson's pantheism. Its first motto he took from Plotinus, one of the fountainheads of the doctrine, to imply that Nature was an emanation from God. 'Nature is but an image or imitation of wisdom, the last thing of the soul, nature being a thing that can only do, but not know.' But the second edition of 1849 had as its epigraph his own verses which imply a rising evolution rather than a descending emanation.

> A subtle chain of countless rings
> The next unto the farthest brings;
> The eye reads omens where it goes,
> And speaks all languages the rose;
> And, striving to be man, the worm
> Mounts through all the spires of form.

One of Emerson's friends, the Transcendentalist preacher, Cyrus A. Bartol, later wrote, 'Pantheism is said to sink man and nature in God, Materialism to sink God and man in nature, and Transcendentalism to sink God and nature in man.'[27] Though the pattern is too neat, the last statement aptly applies to Emerson and his group.

Coleridge, more metaphysical, emphasized the Kantian distinction between pure and practical reason, and argued that the pure Reason would be able to group facts under laws. This interested Emerson, who also had a strong, lifelong interest in science. Yet Emerson and Thoreau made something different of the two levels of dualism. When Thoreau in his early essay 'The Natural History of Massachusetts' talked about a fact flowering into a truth,[28] he meant not finding the natural law; he meant something mystical.

But I must turn to Emerson's *Nature*, his completest if not his most characteristic statement. Recently Barry Wood has demonstrated that the entire work was based on a Coleridgean dialectic available in *Aids to Reflection*. Emerson (who claimed he was no logician) in this carefully worked out essay was much more systematic than usual. In *Nature* itself, the constant use of Reason and Understanding showed Coleridge as his source.[29] But more than that. As readers know, Emerson, the former preacher, habitually moved from the plane of nature to the plane of spirit in his lectures and essays. In *Nature* he used Coleridge's elaborate dialectical scheme as the basis for the unfolding of his entire structured work. Here Emerson brilliantly used Coleridge's 'Noetic Pentad' to move from one section to another and even to solder or weld together the difficult transitions that finally brought him up to his lofty conclusion.[30]

Though he mentioned 'Boehmen' and Schelling, Emerson used Coleridge's dialectic in detail,[31] including both his linguistic and organic metaphors—the former offering material for the 'Language' chapter of *Nature* and the latter the figure for the growth of the soul. First Coleridge applied the pentad to grammatical forms beginning with: 1. The Prothesis *sum* or I am, the verb substantive. Then come: 2. Thesis = Substantive (*res*); 3. Antithesis = Verb (*ago*); 4. Mesothesis = Infinitive (*agere*); 5. Synthesis = Participle (*agens*). While the verbs change, Coleridge significantly begins with the 'I am' which is central to his religion and to his theory of the imagination. Emerson understood and employed this difficult material. In his second illustration, Coleridge suggested that the germinal power of every seed might be generalized under the relation of identity (prothesis). There is a seed in position (thesis), a nourishing environment in opposition (antithesis), an equilibrium (mesothesis), and the composition (synthesis) of a new plant out of the dialectic. In *Nature* Emerson used this structure in each section so that the synthesis became the prothesis of the next section which developed an antithesis on the material side of Nature, and then made a new synthesis.[32] So Emerson started with Soul (me) versus Nature (not me) and produced a harmony of both in a 'perfect exhilaration' of spirit.[33] And in 'Prospects', Emerson, having begun with the eye of Reason, returned to symbols of light, and transformed Coleridge's dynamic to a characteristically American view of the future which added a note of prophecy.

Emerson employed an ascending order, beginning with physical nature which he, unlike Hawthorne, saw as good, with always a slight balance toward the desirable.[34] But Emerson was not satisfied simply with pragmatic conduct. Despite claims that he too strongly emphasized prudential morality,[35] this was not the principal point of *Nature,* which stressed the power to apprehend the spirit behind nature. So he solved his old problem by spiritualizing everything.

In a fine new analysis of the movement as a philosophy, Murray Murphey states, 'Transcendentalism was an attempt to rescue man from nature and reestablish his spiritual character. That is why Emerson's great manifesto was entitled *Nature.*[36] The first sentence seems entirely accurate, yet the way this was done was to elevate Nature by making it symbolize the Spirit. Emerson spiritualized Nature rather than simply separating it from man. For his Reason permitted a direct communion with the Ultimate through Nature as symbol. In a famous passage he wrote, 'Crossing a bare common, in snow puddles, at twilight, under a clouded sky, without having in my thoughts any occurrence of special good fortune, I have enjoyed a perfect exhilaration. Almost I fear to think how glad I am.' Certainly religious sublimity is evident in the word *fear* and in the declaration which followed. 'Standing on the bare ground—my head bathed in the blithe air, and uplifted into infinite space,—all mean egotism vanishes. I am become a transparent eye-ball. I am nothing. I see all. The currents of the universal being circulate through me; I am part or particle of God.'[37] In this religious experience the Eye of Reason was the vehicle of Unity. Emerson's angle of vision had to be correct or the eye-ball became 'opake'.[38] Clearly, this emotional experience was less intellectual than those which Coleridge usually implied, though he was in some sense its source. In any case, the spirit had to be right for the proper effect to occur. Emerson knew well, since *Nature* followed the deaths of his beloved first wife and of his two dear brothers, that the power to produce this delight did not reside in nature, but in man, or in a harmony of both.[39]

'Experience',[40] written after the death of his first-born son, employed the same elaborate dialectical plan as *Nature*, with a series of ascending triads.[41] Perhaps because neither work was designed and delivered as a lecture, he could use a more complex series of Coleridgean pentads in which each synthesis became the prothesis of the next. It appears that Emerson's usually simpler lecture patterns were the result of a recognition of the limitations of his auditors as well as of his own mind. But despite Wellek's mainly accurate statement that Emerson did not follow a German metaphysic,[42] he was sufficiently influenced by Coleridge to have done so in *Nature* and 'Experience'.

Of course, Emerson did not get all his ideas from Coleridge. Compensation he had developed early, and Correspondence he derived from Swedenborg. And he read many idealists and pantheists including: Plato, the Neo-Platonists, Thomas à Kempis, the Cambridge Platonists, Cudworth and More, and a series of mystics including the Hindus, Swedenborg, Boehme, and Oegger.[43] Interestingly, Coleridge read most of these same mystical writers, before he turned from pantheism to Christian orthodoxy.

Before moving on to Coleridge's doctrines of the Imagination and Aesthetics, I turn to the Transcendentalists Alcott and Thoreau. Alcott (1799-1888), a self-educated farm boy, was influenced by Burgh's *Dignity of Human Nature*, which was Lockean and Arminian, in claiming that education can save people. Locke and *A Philosophical Treatise on the Passions and Affections* by Thomas Cogan convinced Alcott that, 'By attending to the education of children, then, we prevent the necessity of regeneration. We prevent them from being depraved.' He was on his way to a correspondence theory when he read *Aids to Reflection* in 1832. This convinced him of the spiritual component of the mind, which Lockean psychology had so effectively obscured. Coleridge's Reason, being identical with the divine spirit, was a source of universal and necessary truth *a priori*—an avenue of direct communication between God and man, and he soon concluded that what was within the mind was God. So, when Alcott talked to Emerson in the summer of 1836, he uttered as the 'Orphic poet' of 'Prospects' words which were like Emerson's own ideas, because both came from Coleridge.[44]

Henry David Thoreau (1817-62)[45] who slowly, like Melville, rose in literary esteem, was profoundly influenced by Coleridge. But since this influence or effect came largely through Emerson, there were also important differences. Thoreau had no such wide-ranging, original mind as either Coleridge or Emerson, but he tested his principles by living them, and he developed a brilliant style. In *Walden* he showed more ability to create a large-scale prose structure than Coleridge or Emerson, and produced an impressive result. But that was not all; his essay 'Civil Disobedience' has had world-wide effect. For clarity I will first discuss the aspects of Thoreau which develop from Coleridge and then those which seem attributable to the American environment.

While Thoreau was not born a Transcendentalist, his crises were psychological rather than theological. By the time he began publication, his philosophy was well formed. The distinctions between Reason and Understanding, between Freedom and Necessity, between the Expedient and the Moral were already internalized and needed only to be expressed. His transition into Transcendentalism was early and easy.

Having absorbed Coleridge's new patterns, he began to think in terms of the dichotomy of Reason and Understanding. Aware of the differences between fact and truth, necessity and freedom, he was constantly trying to bridge the gap. More mystical than either Emerson or Coleridge, he sought to gain and then to express in figurative language, contacts with the level of spirit. Some of his finest writing depends upon his attempts to convey these almost ineffable experiences in symbolic language. While these ecstasies decreased in frequency, they never did cease,[46] and produced great passages in the later *Journals* and essays.

'Resistance to Civil Government', the first and less negative title of 'Civil Disobedience' (1849), is built upon the Coleridge distinction between lower and higher levels of insight and conduct. Thoreau is completely aware of the difference between free and mechanical levels when he decides whether people are acting as 'men or machines'. And like Coleridge in *Aids to Reflection*, Thoreau also attacks the ethics of Paley's *Principles of Moral and Political Philosophy*. Both Coleridge and Thoreau object to the fact that Paley bases his moral calculus on expediency, rather than on the higher level of moral insight. Differences in vocabulary, however, make it seem that Coleridge reminded Thoreau of Paley's work which he had studied as a text at Harvard a decade before.[47]

The philosophical attempt to unite man and nature, empiricism and idealism, was one that Thoreau learned from Coleridge. This complex line, strong in American Pragmatism, is one which has baffled many scholars. Joel Porte, who finds it difficult to understand the nature of the synthesis, argued that Thoreau was not an idealist at all and that he dealt only with the material of the senses.[48] This seems to oversimplify his position. But if it is correct, it is so only in the sense that Edwards meant—namely, that the redeemed soul received an added sense to apprehend the manifestations of God. And this seems like the pattern of Coleridge when he wrote, 'Reason is indeed far nearer to SENSE than to Understanding: for Reason (says our great HOOKER) is a direct Aspect of Truth, an inward Beholding, having a similar relation to the Intelligible or Spiritual, as SENSE has to the Material or Phenomenal'. But 'they differ *in kind*'.[49] And this counters Porte's argument. If Thoreau is not an idealist, neither are Edwards, Coleridge, and Emerson, who all share related positions.

There is a final relationship to Coleridge that is for Thoreau of major importance. As Beer says of Coleridge that his requirement was to be at a remove from himself to attain a double vision,[50] so Miller and Cavell find this in Thoreau. In an early journal of 1839, Thoreau wrote of the poet,

> Nature will not speak through him but along with him . . . He then poetizes when he takes a fact out of nature into spirit. He speaks without referring to time or place. His thought is one world, hers another. He is another Nature,—Nature's brother . . . . Each publishes the other's truth.[51]

Miller commends this 'doubleness' of *Walden* which can be

placed beside *The Prelude*. It is 'the growth of a poet's mind', and despite all its wealth of concrete imagery it is centered not upon nature, but upon nature's brother, the intelligence of the artist.[52] Cavell, himself a philosopher, states this in philosophical terms, saying that while Emerson in an un-Kantian way holds that the senses are the scene of illusions, Thoreau's *Walden*, in effect, provides a transcendent deduction for the concepts of the thing-in-itself and for determination—something Kant ought so to speak, to have done'. Cavell continues, 'When I said that Kant ought to have provided a deduction of the thing-in-itself, I meant that he had left unarticulated an essential [category] of objectivity itself, viz., that of *a world apart from me in which* objects are met. The externality of the world is articulated by Thoreau by its nextness to me.'[53] Cavell's philosophically sophisticated and literarily sensitive analysis clearly demonstrates the relationship of Emerson and Thoreau to the Kantian thought which Coleridge transmitted. Emerson, according to Cavell, saw the effluence of God as streaming through him, at least in his period of early greatness. Thoreau by use of his intuition came up with something closer to an aspect of Coleridge in being conscious as artist of his consciousness and so furnishing a deeper, more knowable, grounding of the thing-in-itself, as Kant should have done.[54]

However much Coleridge influenced Thoreau, his transatlantic background made for differences in results. The half-settled continent and American frontier produced a different response to nature than that of Coleridge. The virgin land mothered a different myth and symbol,[55] and Thoreau's fine essay 'Walking', if double in structure, caught the mood of westering as of going to the holy land. Yet, though attracted to the wild, Thoreau was profoundly shocked by the inhuman power of brute nature at the top of Mt. Ktaadn. He sought a middle landscape, as at Walden Pond, between the machine and the garden,[56] where instead of blowing his oaten stop, he hoed beans. While closer to Wordsworth than to Coleridge in attitudes toward Nature, still, the Americans saw their nature as national destiny.[57]

This also involved the post-Puritan prophetic tradition in the United States. New England religion contained a strong emphasis upon the Old Testament and on Prophecy. While Emerson displayed a prophetic tone in 'The American Scholar', Thoreau built the entire structure of *Walden* upon the scheme of prophecy, as Cavell has clearly emphasized.[58] Like Ezekiel and Jeremiah whom he cites, Thoreau alternated denunciation of ignorant materialists, promises of hope for those who reform, and contemporary fact. If in the nineteenth century few could utter 'Thus saith the Lord', Thoreau wrote as one who knew the truth that if men would only perceive it, they could put foundations under their castles in the air and thus change their lives.[59]

Sacvan Bercovitch, recognizing the prophetic element, emphasizes the optimism in the Jeremiads of Emerson and Thoreau, who while denouncing materialism, perpetuate the myth of America's future in a kind of religion of the republic.[60] Unlike Fourier, Marx, or Engels, they are not social reformers. Yet Thoreau got close enough to reform on the issue of slavery to advocate not only passive resistance, but even violence and death in war.[61] Consequently Thoreau's prickly personality has been strongly attacked by conservatives. Leon Edel, thinking of the anti-war hippies and campus resistants of 1970, even charged him with using nature as a drug.[62] Still Bercovitch is mainly right. Coleridge's emphasis on a 'clerisy' showed his concern for the cultured but also culture-bound appendage of the leisure class, which Thorstein Veblen claimed was emphasizing the economically useless accomplishments of sports, manners, classical learning, and proper prose.

To turn now from the epistemological to the literary portion of Coleridge's influence on American romanticism, we can see that Coleridge produced important effects, immediate as well as long-run, through the impact of his critical theory and of his practical criticism. The *Biographia Literaria* was well known in America, so the German distinctions between Imagination and Fancy, and Genius and Talent rather quickly became known to the Transcendentalists. Of them Emerson and Jones Very were the best poets, and Thoreau, while he gave up the art partly because of Emerson's discouragement, showed considerable talent. William Ellery Channing (nephew of Dr. Channing and first biographer of Thoreau) especially showed what was defective in the New England acceptance of

127

Coleridge's literary theories.

In order to see how Coleridge's ideas operated, we must once more quote the entire complex set of definitions as set out in Chapter XIII of the *Biographia Literaria* in order to examine the nature of the ideas themselves before endeavouring to show how and why they were applied or not applied.

> The IMAGINATION then, I consider either as primary, or secondary. The primary IMAGINATION I hold to be the living Power and prime Agent of all human Perception, and as a repetition in the finite mind of the eternal act of creation in the infinite I AM. The secondary Imagination I consider as an echo of the former, co-existing with the conscious will, yet still as identical with the primary in the *kind* of its agency, and differing only in *degree,* and in the *mode* of its operation. It dissolves, diffuses, dissipates, in order to recreate; or where the process is rendered impossible, yet still at all events it struggles to idealize and to unify. It is essentially *vital,* even as all objects (*as* objects) are essentially fixed and dead.
>
> FANCY, on the contrary, has no other counters to play with, but fixities and definites. The FANCY is indeed no other than a mode of Memory emancipated from the order of time and space; while it is blended with, and modified by that empirical phenomenon of the will, which we express by the word CHOICE. But equally with the ordinary memory the Fancy must receive all its materials ready made from the law of association.[63]

McFarland has demonstrated in depth that the general source for all three faculties was the *Philosophische Versuche*[64] of Tetens, whose name Kathleen Coburn rescued when she discovered it had been omitted from a previously published selection of notebook entries[65] called *Anima Poetae* (1895). Tetens' psychological theories solved Coleridge's problems so that, having overcome his pantheism, he could freely turn to aesthetic theory.

Clearly Coleridge combined abstract religious ideas with a searching introspection in defining the Primary Imagination. Triumphantly, he linked the I AM of German philosophy with the God of Moses. For Exodus, 3:14 states: 'And God said unto Moses, I AM THAT I AM; and he said, Thus shall thou say unto the children of Israel, I AM hath sent me unto you.' I AM, transliterated into Jehovah (i.e. Lord) as the creator God, is the concept which placed the Reason above the 'It is' of Nature. Having settled his religious problem, Coleridge rarely wrote again about the Primary Imagination.

The new idea here, developed from Tetens' *Dichtkraft*,[66] is the Secondary Imagination, the free, shaping, creative power of the poet. This is the Imagination Coleridge subsequently described and employed. The Fancy he had already used, the inferior mode of memory derived from Hobbes and discussed by Wallace Stevens in the twentieth century. Yet Imagination was not rigorously separated from Fancy, and Coleridge advocated the use of both to produce superior art.

Among the American Transcendentalists the Secondary Imagination and the Fancy were disregarded. Inspiration or intuitive insight was the important element, and the shaping faculties were not given a theoretical place by the New England Transcendentalists. Flashes of Reason were vital, but because they could not create the detailed action of a novel or drama, the central group was unable to compose successfully plotted works, not even narrative poems.[67] Fiction was characterized as a set of lies. Post-Puritans could see made-up stories as nontrue, in the way logical positivists could see literature as nonsense. Thus Hawthorne's brother-in-law, Horace Mann, preferred uplifting biographies to Hawthorne's fiction for school libraries, and Emerson could call *The Scarlet Letter* 'ghastly'.[68]

Though Emerson and Thoreau revised what they wrote, neither one saw much use for the secondary imagination. They thought in terms of unitary symbols rather than of the complex symbol that is the entire work of art. For *Walden* Thoreau found an excellent organizing principle, but despite more material than he could ever use, he never produced another effective book plan. While Emerson and Thoreau worked with care (*Walden* had at least six revisions),[69] Ellery Channing was too satisfied with his own inspirations to do proper revising, so Thoreau characterized his work as 'sublimo-slipshod', and Poe attacked it.

Coleridge's emphasis upon the symbol-making power of the imagination had a profound effect upon Emerson and Thoreau, and produced a unified sensibility which has continued, despite

129

T. S. Eliot's pronouncement.[70] Emerson, accepting Coleridge's religious connotations, insisted that there is 'no fact in nature which does not carry the whole sense of nature'; so that the base, even the obscene can become illustrious. Small and mean things are also symbols. 'Bare lists of words are found suggestive to an imaginative and excited mind',[71] like that of Whitman. Though Emerson, more cautious in verse form than in thought, did not often achieve this freedom, he did succeed in the beginning of 'Hamatraya', where he combined in lists of names and products a sequence of symbols with an irregular metre:

> Bulkeley, Hunt, Willard, Hosmer, Meriam, Flint
> Possessed the land which rendered to their toil
> Hay, corn, roots, hemp, flax, apples, wool and wood.

Interestingly, Emerson's preference for traditional techniques prevented him from appreciating Wordsworth until he learned from Coleridge what was contained in the symbols. Thus he wrote of Wordsworth's allegedly feeble poetic talents, 'More than any poet his success has been not his own but that of the Idea or principle which possessed him and which he has rarely succeeded in adequately expressing.'[72]

While Coleridge's concept of unity will appear again with Poe, his emphasis on the organic was echoed often in America. This old idea, a central concept in the Romantic complex, took several forms in America. Emerson's 'metre-making argument' implied that inspired material had and would find its own form. Both Emerson and Thoreau held that art was organic in the further sense of 'the impossibility of any man's being a good Poet without first being a good man'.[73] This Coleridge quotation from Ben Jonson fitted well in New England where attacks on Goethe were common. Conversely Thoreau held that 'Steady labour with the hands which engrosses the attention also, is the best method of removing palaver out of one's style both of talking and writing'.[74] Certainly Thoreau's own style with its brilliantly gnarled details of woodchucks, pumpkins, and wild apple trees represents such a disciplined activity. As for Coleridge's weakness of character, Emerson showed disappointment without discounting the value of the ideas, when he read De Quincey's account:

Coleridge loses by De Quincey but more by his own concealing uncandid acknowledgement of debt to Schelling. Why could not he have said generously like Goethe I owe all? As soon as one gets so far above pride as to say all truth that might come from him . . . [is] not his truth . . . then he may be indebted without shame at all.[75]

Edgar Allan Poe (1809-49), with a different sense of unity and of beauty, found in Coleridge a different set of emphases which he was able to use in his own poetry, fiction, and criticism. Like the Transcendentalists, whom he often attacked, Poe was subject to the same influences of rationalism and the romantic reaction, and was affected by both. Though born in Boston, he was raised in Virginia on the margin of gentility and had to earn his own living. Since neither poetry nor fiction could gain him an adequate income, he turned to journalism, editing, and reviewing.

Poe's aesthetic doctrines included the main categories of Imagination, Pleasure, Beauty, and Effect.[76] Poe accepted Coleridge on the Imagination, but while interested in novelty as a popular writer, he held that only God and not man could create anything completely new.[77] Like Coleridge, Poe also claimed that the immediate aim of poetry is pleasure not truth, that the highest pleasure comes from the contemplation of beauty, and that poetry is itself the rhythmical creation of beauty.[78] Yet parts of Poe's formulation were directly based upon A. W. Schlegel's *A Course of Lectures on Dramatic Art and Literature*, translated by John Black (London, 1815). Poe's review for the *Southern Literary Messenger*, September, 1835 (reprinted in *Works*, viii. 43-7) is an almost Coleridge-like pastiche from Schlegel. In addition, Poe got the supernal quality of beauty from Schlegel's analysis of the northern, Christian world view as opposed to the classical temper, and the longing for beauty as a cause for the proper melancholy of poetry.[79] There are, of course, Coleridgean elements of Imagination in Poe's conception of Ideality, and the emphasis on indefiniteness came from both Coleridge and Schlegel. While Coleridge stressed the organic form of the work, Poe's emphasis on the effect of the technique proved closer to Schlegel.[80]

Poe's brilliant handling of unity of effect in 'The Philosophy of Composition' and in his impressive review of Hawthorne's *Twice Told Tales* has a complex origin. That a poem or story had to be short, as was necessary for magazine journalism, found precedence in the *Biographia Literaria*. The subordination of all parts to the whole follows Coleridge's artist who could produce a 'tone and spirit of unity, that blends, and (as it were) *fuses*, each into each, by that synthetic and magical power to which we have exclusively appropriated the name of imagination'.[81] Poe at times did include local satire in his major works—as when Ligeia represented German Transcendentalism and Rowena Anglo-Saxon common sense.[82] Yet the unity is not damaged, even when the covert aim is recognized.

Coleridge's own poetic practice also had significant though less easily demonstrable influence on Poe, whose rhythmical and highly rhymed stanza patterns are related to Coleridge's tradition. By an irony of incorrectness a review by 'Outis', probably C. C. Felton, one of the Transcendentalist poets, said that the quaint repetition of 'The Raven' was a palpable imitation of the *Ancient Mariner*.[83] To this Poe effectively replied. Yet the metre and devices of 'The Raven' do imitate Elizabeth Barrett Browning's 'Lady Geraldine's Courtship' and Thomas Holley Chivers' *Isadore*.[84]

Poe's late work *Eureka* (1848), called his masterpiece by Hoffman,[85] also shows Coleridgean influence, since its universe is based upon the very dialectic in a passage from the Marsh *Aids to Reflection*: in *Eureka* 'TWO POLAR FORCES OF ONE AND THE SAME POWER' show 'A TENDENCY TO REUNION'[86] to nothingness. But, Poe concluded by saying that the alternation of nothingness and creation might repeat with 'every throb of the Heart Divine'.[87] I am convinced that this is Coleridgean idealism, symbolizing Poe's terror of annihilation while demonstrating that Truth and Beauty are one. But in any case he was able to use Coleridge's theories, and some gained from Schlegel, to construct an aesthetic which influenced the French symbolists and much modern criticism.

In conclusion, it is clear that Coleridge, more than Wordsworth, Carlyle, or any German writer, precipitated American Transcendentalism. His identification of Reason with Spirit became the catalyst which broke the Lockean and Associationist bond of mechanical necessity. The emphasis on insight, intuition, and imagination permitted a contact with nature which has dominated subsequent American literature and thought. And through the influence of Emerson this insight served to fix and prolong the myth of the promised land, at least down to Jay Gatsby's time. In the area of aesthetic and critical theory, the Transcendentalists accepted Coleridge's emphasis on the primary imagination and assumed that inspired insight would find its organic form. They did not gain from Coleridge a theory for the construction of plotted wholes. While Hawthorne could enter into his notebook a one-sentence statement of the idea for a novel and then develop it, Emerson and Thoreau could not. It took Poe's emphasis on other aspects of Coleridge's complex doctrine to work out a theory of effects—one which justified close reading as the necessary basis for judgment. Finally, the magnificent burst of recent Coleridge scholarship has both elevated his own reputation and contributed to the current romantic revival in Britain and the United States.

NOTES AND REFERENCES

1 P. Miller, *Errand into the Wilderness* (Cambridge, Mass., 1958).
2 P. Miller, *The New England Mind: The Seventeenth Century* (New York, 1939); *The New England Mind: Colony to Province* (Cambridge, Mass., 1953).
3 S. Bercovitch, *The Puritan Origins of the American Self* (New Haven, 1975), 1.
4 T. S. Kuhn, *The Structure of Scientific Revolutions* (Middletown, Conn., 1966).
5 J. Edwards, *Freedom of the Will*, ed. P. Ramsay (New Haven, 1957), *passim*.
6 J. Edwards, *Religious Affections*, ed. J.E. Smith (New Haven, 1959), 206.
7 P. Miller, *Jonathan Edwards* (New York, 1949), 167-77.
8 A. Kern, 'The Rise of Transcendentalism' in *Transitions in American Literary History*, ed. H.H. Clark (Durham, N.C., 1954), 258-59.
9 *CN*, ii. 2794.
10 J. Duffy (ed.), *Coleridge's American Disciples: The Selected Correspondence of James Marsh* (Amherst, Mass., 1973), xiv, 124n.
11 J. Edwards, *Religious Affections*, 205; J. Edwards, 'Sinners in the Hands of an Angry God', in *Jonathan Edwards: Representative Selections*, ed. C.E. Faust and T.H. Johnson (New York, 1935), 155-72.
12 S.T. Coleridge, *Aids to Reflection: Together with a Preliminary Essay, and Additional Notes* by J. Marsh (Burlington, Vt., 1829), 91, 105-6. This has been reprinted in *Selected Works of James Marsh*, ed. P.C. Carafiol (New York, 1976), i.

13 R. Wellek, 'Emerson and German Philosophy', *Confrontations* (Princeton, 1966), 194, stubbornly speaks of Kant as misunderstood by Emerson—or rather by Coleridge—without seeing that they were solving their own problems. T. McFarland, *Coleridge and the Pantheist Tradition* (1969), Chs. I-IV, proves that Coleridge knew what he was doing as a creative thinker.

14 Coleridge, *Aids to Reflection*, 137-38.

15 R.W. Emerson, *The Complete Works of Ralph Waldo Emerson*, centenary edition, ed. E.W. Emerson (Boston, 1903-4), ii. 64, 66.

16 Duffy, *op. cit.*, 30.

17 Kern, *op. cit.*, 265-66.

18 *ibid.*, 254; E. Flower and M. Murphey, *A History of Philosophy in America* (New York, 1977), i. 400-10.

19 F.H. Hedge, 'Coleridge's Literary Character', *Christian Examiner*, xiv (1833), 108-29.

20 R.W. Emerson, *The Letters of Ralph Waldo Emerson*, ed. R.L. Rusk (New York, 1939), i. 412-13.

21 Wellek, *op. cit.*, 193.

22 G.N.G. Orsini, *Coleridge and German Idealism* (Carbondale, Ill., 1969), 58.

23 T. McFarland, 'The Origin and Significance of Coleridge's Theory of the Secondary Imagination', in *New Perspectives on Coleridge and Wordsworth*, ed. G.H. Hartman (New York, 1972), 199. Cf. McFarland, *Coleridge and the Pantheist Tradition*, 149-52.

24 D. Sultana, *S.T. Coleridge in Malta and Italy (1969), 287-88*.

25 McFarland, *Coleridge and the Pantheist Tradition*, 32.

26 *Aids to Reflection*, 137.

27 C.A. Bartol, *Radical Problems* (Boston, 1877), 283.

28 H.D. Thoreau, 'The Natural History of Massachusetts', in *Thoreau: The Major Essays*, ed. J.L. Duncan (New York, 1972), 22.

29 C. Strauch, 'The Year of Emerson's Poetic Maturity—1834', *Philological Quarterly*, xxxiv (1955), 360.

30 B. Wood, 'The Growth of the Soul: Coleridge's Dialectical Method and the Strategy of Emerson's *Nature*' in *Emerson's Nature: Origin, Growth, Meaning*, ed. M.M. Sealts, Jr., and A.E. Ferguson, 2nd ed., enlarged (Carbondale, Ill., 1979), 198. This valuable volume includes an excellent new essay by Sealts, 'The Composition of *Nature*', 175-93.

31 R.W. Emerson, *The Journals and Miscellaneous Notebooks of Ralph Waldo Emerson*, ed. M.M. Sealts, Jr. (Cambridge, Mass., 1965), v.30.

32 The entire passage is based on Wood, 'The Growth of the Soul', 201-8.

33 *Emerson's Nature*, 8.

34 Emerson, *Complete Works*, i. 372.

35 J. Porte, *Emerson and Thoreau: Transcendentalists in Conflict* (Middletown, Conn., 1966), 15, 79.

36 Flower and Murphey, *op. cit.*, i. 402. This chapter is by Murphey.

37 *Emerson's Nature*, 8.

38 S. Paul, *Emerson's Angle of Vision* (Cambridge, Mass., 1952), 80-102. Cf. *Emerson's Nature*, 34.

39 *Emerson's Nature*, 8.
40 Emerson, *Complete Works*, iii. 43-86.
41 Wood, *op. cit.*, 208n.
42 Wellek, *op. cit.*, 210-11.
43 K.W. Cameron, *Emerson the Essayist* (Raleigh, N.C., 1945), i, quotes Emerson's sources in such writers. There is a strong Platonic stream in both Emerson and Coleridge, of course.
44 Flower and Murphey, *op. cit.*, i. 400-15. For more detail see O. Shepard, *Pedlar's Progress: The Life of Bronson Alcott* (Boston, 1937), *passim;* R.L. Herrnstadt (ed.), *The Letters of Bronson Alcott* (Ames, Ia., 1969), 22, 643; H.A. Pochmann, *German Culture in America: 1600-1900* (Madison, Wis., 1957), 224-34, 292-304.
45 W. Harding, *The Days of Henry David Thoreau* (New York, 1966), is the best biography.
46 A. Kern, 'Church, Scripture, Nature, and Ethics in Henry Thoreau's Religious Thought' in *Literature and Ideas in America*, ed. R.K. Falk (Athens, Ohio, 1975), 91-2. S. Paul, *The Shores of America: Thoreau's Inward Exploration* (Urbana, Ill., 1958), is the most complete study of Thoreau's mind.
47 H.D. Thoreau, 'Resistance to Civil Government', in *Reform Papers*, ed. W. Glick (Princeton, 1973), 67-8, 86-8; Coleridge, *Aids to Reflection*, 263.
48 Porte, *op. cit.*, 135, 155.
49 Coleridge, *Aids to Reflection*, 263.
50 J. Beer, *Coleridge the Visionary* (1959), 18.
51 Thoreau, *The Journals of H.D. Thoreau*, ed. B. Torrey and F.H. Allen (Boston, 1906), i. 75-6.
52 P. Miller, *Nature's Nation* (Cambridge, Mass., 1967), 181.
53 S. Cavell, *The Senses of Walden* (New York, 1972), 94.
54 *ibid.*, 93, 95-6.
55 H.N. Smith, *Virgin Land, The American West as Myth and Symbol* (Cambridge, Mass., 1950).
56 L. Marx, *The Machine and the Garden* (New York, 1967), 242-65.
57 Bercovitch, *op. cit.*, 186.
58 Cavell, *op. cit.*, *14, 17*.
59 H.D. Thoreau, *Walden* (Princeton, 1973), 324.
60 S. Bercovitch, *The American Jeremiad* (Madison, Wis., 1978), 189-90.
61 Thoreau, *Reform Papers*, 75, 142.
62 L. Edel in *Six Classic American Writers*, ed. S. Paul (Minneapolis, 1970), 190-94.
63 *BL*, i. 202.
64 McFarland, 'Theory of the Secondary Imagination', 206, names J.N. Tetens, *Philosophische Versuche über die menschliche Natur und ihre Entwickelung* (Leipzig, 1777).
65 *CN*, ii. 2375.
66 McFarland, 'Theory of the Secondary Imagination', 211.
67 C. Feidelson, *Symbolism and American Literature* (Chicago, 1953), 120-22, 136, but cf. L. Buell, *Literary Transcendentalism* (Ithaca, 1973), 157-59.

68 A. Kern, 'A Note on Hawthorne's Juveniles', *Philological Quarterly*, xxxix (1960), 242.

69 L. Shanley, *The Making of Walden* (Chicago, 1957), 32.

70 J.R. Barth, *The Symbolic Imagination: Coleridge and the Romantic Tradition* (Princeton, 1977), develops the religious aspect of Coleridge's symbolic theory. Emerson is different in his emphasis on the word as microcosm.

71 Emerson, 'The Poet', in *Complete Works*, iii. 17-18.

72 Miller, *op. cit.*, 176.

73 McFarland, *Coleridge and the Pantheist Tradition*, 196.

74 Thoreau, 'Sir Walter Raleigh', in *Early Essays and Miscellanies*, ed. J.J. Moldenhauer, E. Moser, A. Kern (Princeton, 1975), 212.

75 Emerson, *Journals and Miscellaneous Notebooks*, v. 59.

76 Particularly good on Poe's aesthetics are: N. Foerster, *American Criticism* (Boston, 1928); E.H. Davidson, *Poe: A Critical Study* (Cambridge, Mass., 1957); and F. Stovall, *Edgar Poe the Poet* (Charlottesville, Va., 1969).

77 G. Kelly, 'The Aesthetic Theories of Edgar Allan Poe' (Univ. of Iowa Ph.D. thesis, 1953), 86. Kelly emphasizes Schlegel's impact on Poe.

78 Stovall, *op. cit.*, 137, 142. Cf. G. Kelly, 'Edgar Allan Poe's Theory of Beauty', *American Literature*, xxvii (1956), 321-36. E.A. Poe, *The Complete Works of Edgar Allan Poe*, ed. J.A. Harrison (New York, 1902), xiv. 275.

79 Kelly, *op. cit.*, 98.

80 Stovall, *op. cit.*, 144; Kelly, *op. cit.*, 106.

81 *BL*, ii. 12.

82 C. Griffith, 'Poe's "Ligeia" and the English Romantics', *University of Toronto Quarterly*, xxiv (1954), 16-25.

83 E.W. Parks, *Edgar Allan Poe as Literary Critic* (Athens, Ga., 1964), 100n.

84 H.H. Clark, *Major American Poets* (New York, 1936), 843n.

85 D. Hoffman, *Poe Poe Poe Poe Poe Poe Poe* (New York, 1973), 273.

86 Marsh, *Aids to Reflection*, 287.

87 Poe, *Works*, xvi. 307.

8

The Influence of Cowper's *The Task* on Coleridge's Conversation Poems

by ANN MATHESON

Between August 1795 and April 1798, Coleridge composed the group of poems popularly known as the 'Conversation Poems', following them, later that same year, with the publication of *Lyrical Ballads* in association with Wordsworth. Among the most significant of the Conversation Poems are 'The Eolian Harp', 'This Lime-Tree Bower my Prison', 'Frost at Midnight', 'Fears in Solitude', 'The Nightingale' and 'Dejection'. These poems display a distinctive style which makes it possible to examine them as a group with the purpose of isolating the principal influences which contributed to producing their particular character.

The accepted version of the genesis of these poems is that the best of them were the fruits of the coalescence of minds that occurred when Wordsworth moved to Alfoxden near Coleridge in Nether Stowey in July 1797, and which culminated in the appearance of *Lyrical Ballads* the following year. When George Whalley queried this assumption in his article in *Essays and Studies* in 1958, he drew attention to the existence of an earlier divergence of style in Coleridge's poems, which he argued, manifested itself from the beginning of 1795.[1] It is certain that by the end of 1794, Coleridge was himself dissatisfied with the ornate rhetorical style of earlier poems like 'Lines on an Autumnal Evening'. He gave expression to this unease when he

137

confessed to Southey in December 1794 that 'my *Poetry* is crowded and sweats beneath a heavy burthen of Ideas and Imagery!'[2] And in 1797, Coleridge openly admitted in the preface to the second edition of his *Poems* that the criticisms of turgidity and over-elaborateness directed at his verse had been justified, but he asserted confidently that he 'had pruned the double epithets with no sparing hand; and used my best efforts to tame the swell and glitter both of thought and diction'.[3] Thus, by 1797, Coleridge seemed to feel that he had created a new style in the poems written after the end of 1794: the tangible evidence of this change of mood can be seen in the gentle and contemplative tones of the Conversation Poems. From where then did these new influences emerge? Coleridge's Conversation Poems or 'meditations in blank verse' have been described by Basil Willey as indicating Coleridge's move from Miltonising to Cowperising,[4] that is to say, they represent Coleridge following in the footsteps of William Cowper in search of naturalness and simplicity in verse. This article attempts to examine some of the influences of Cowper's *The Task* on Coleridge's Conversation Poems.

Coleridge's most renowned remark on the poetry of Cowper comes in his letter to John Thelwall, dated 17 December 1796, when he refers to his own ability to absorb the best qualities of all contemporary poets, including the 'divine Chit chat of Cowper'.[5] This comment tends to suggest, however, that Coleridge took the view that Cowper's poetry, however worthy, did not deal with the deep intellectual matters of the mind and, therefore, lacked the high seriousness of true poetry. This view is offset by Coleridge's remark to Hazlitt at Nether Stowey in 1798 that Cowper was the 'best modern poet'[6] and by his reference to *The Task* in *Biographia Literaria* as 'that excellent poem'.[7] For a poet who wished to improve the style of his poetic diction in the direction of simplicity, Cowper was the best model of the period to follow. But first of all, we must ask why and how Coleridge was guided along the route to simplicity of diction. As we have seen, he does later express his own dissatisfaction with the bombastic style of his earlier poems, and it is here that the influence of Charles Lamb on Coleridge's style must be considered.

Lamb, two and a half years Coleridge's junior, corresponded

extensively with Coleridge during the period 1796 to 1797, before Coleridge became preoccupied with the Wordsworths' move to Alfoxden and, as a result, the correspondence between Coleridge and Lamb lapsed for a time. The first letter in the main canon of their correspondence is dated 27 May 1796, and for the next nine months the two poets wrote to each other (unfortunately, Coleridge's side of the correspondence appears not to have survived), often as many as three letters a week winging their way back and forth in the early part of their correspondence. Lamb wrote to Coleridge about literary and critical matters and his correspondence is significant for what it reveals about Lamb's own views on the correct style for poetry, and the influences that his forthright and honest criticism brought to bear on the fashioning of Coleridge's poems.

Lamb's attempts to wean Coleridge away from the sentimentalities of William Lisle Bowles towards a simple and spontaneous style are best seen in his plea in a letter of 8 November 1796:

> Cultivate simplicity, Coleridge, or rather, I should say, banish elaborateness; for simplicity springs spontaneous from the heart, and carries into the daylight its own modest buds and genuine, sweet, and clear flowers of expression.[8]

Lamb presents Coleridge with detailed criticisms of his poems, pointing out here that a simile used is 'far-fetch'd' and there taking issue with ornate phraseology and bombastic terms. The crux of Lamb's critical advice to Coleridge is to cultivate simplicity, but in the same way as he chides Coleridge for failing to attain a true simplicity of style, he is unstinting in his praise when Coleridge achieves success. In a letter of 5 December 1796, Lamb refers approvingly to Coleridge's poem 'Reflections on having left a Place of Retirement' as 'the sweetest thing you ever wrote',[9] and in an earlier letter of 2 December 1796, he commends Coleridge on the style of 'The Eolian Harp', asserting that if he continued to write poems in this vein, 'I shall never quarrel with you about simplicity'.[10] The stress on simplicity is a constant theme throughout the poets' correspondence of 1796 to 1797, and as late as 5 February 1797, Lamb was yet again taking issue with Coleridge for 'sad deviations from that simplicity which was your aim',[11] instancing as examples the use of the phrases 'frost-mangled wretch' and 'green putridity'.

Lamb's preoccupation with simplicity was a reflection of his own admiration for the poems of Cowper, who is referred to time and time again in Lamb's correspondence as the most acceptable poetical model for simplicity and feeling in poetry.[12] In a letter of 10 June 1796, Lamb queries Southey's disparaging remarks on Cowper's *Homer* and asks, 'What makes him so reluctant to give Cowper his fame?' Three days later, Lamb comments (in a rather dry criticism of Coleridge) that Southey's poems were excelled in simplicity and tenderness only by those of Beaumont and Fletcher in *The Maid's Tragedy* and perhaps by Cowper's 'Crazy Kate'.[13] On 7 July 1796, in a poem 'To the Poet Cowper', Lamb applauded Cowper's return to health by calling him 'Of England's Bards, the wisest and the best'.[14] Later that year, in a letter of 5 December 1796, Lamb tells Coleridge of his renewed delight in re-reading *The Task* and he responds to what was obviously a favourable comment by Coleridge when he says in the same letter, 'I am glad you love Cowper . . . I would not call that man my friend, who should be offended with the "divine chit-chat of Cowper"'.[15] He calls him 'my old favourite' in his letter to Coleridge dated 10 December 1796, in which he draws comparisons between Coleridge's affection for Bowles with his own love for the poetry of Burns and Cowper. He confirms Coleridge's regard for Cowper, when he remarks that Coleridge 'conciliate[s] matters when you talk of the "divine chit-chat" of the latter: by the expression I see you thoroughly relish him'.[16] Thus, before their correspondence had lapsed in 1797, Lamb had left Coleridge in no doubt about the direction in which his poetry should develop, and he had provided him with the contemporary model for blank verse poetry to assist him in fashioning his own poems.

Cowper's *The Task* was written during the period July 1783 to September 1784 and it was published in the following year. It was written originally in response to a request by Lady Austen, Cowper's close friend and confidant, for a poem in blank verse on the subject of a sofa, but from these modest beginnings the poem grew and was finally completed in six books, embodying a mixture of autobiography, social comment and descriptive poetry. Cowper employed blank verse as his poetic medium, its flexible rhythms and free-ranging structure being eminently suitable for describing the pursuits of everyday life and conveying these events to his readers in pleasant conversational tones. So what are the ideas held in common by Cowper and Coleridge and what are the influences of Cowper's poetry that can be seen in Coleridge's Conversation Poems?

The Task, as has been explained, is a blend of autobiographical reminiscence and descriptive poetry, in which Cowper refers to his own life and the particular events and situations in it from which he derived pleasure. In Book I of the poem, he describes his love of rural walks:

> For I have lov'd the rural walk through lanes
> Of grassy swarth, close cropt by nibbling sheep.[17]

He reiterates time and time again the superiority of country life over town life, quoting from Varro's lines 'God made the country but man made the town',[18] in support of his view that a life of rural seclusion and simplicity represented a more natural habitat for man than an urban environment with its false and ephemeral values. To convince his readers, Cowper relied on the rhetorical devices of contrast and comparison. In the poem, he contrasts the peace and calm of the country with the empty hubbub of urban life, using the attractions of the former to highlight the falsities of the latter. He illuminates the disadvantages of London by referring to it as 'this queen of cities, that so fair may yet be foul; so witty, yet not wise'.[19] In *The Task*, the poet's ardent love of Nature is given free expression and ranges through the entire poem. To Cowper, Nature was superior to Art because while Art could satisfy the visual senses, Nature was capable of satisfying all the human senses:

> Lovely indeed the mimic works of art;
> But Nature's works far lovelier.[20]

This was a belief which Coleridge restated in 1796 in a notebook entry which reads, 'The limited sphere of mental activity in artist'.[21] Again, Coleridge, in his poem 'This Lime-Tree Bower my Prison', not only showed that he shared Cowper's love of trees but he echoed Cowper in his description of the bower when he referred to the 'shadow of the leaf and stem dappling its sunshine'.[22] Cowper had used the image of light and shade in *The Task* when he described the tree trunks shining 'within in the twilight of their distant shade',[23] and again when he referred to the sun shining through the trees 'Shadow and sunshine intermingling quick'.[24]

Well before the composition of 'Lime-Tree Bower', Coleridge had become disillusioned with Pantisocracy, and his dreams of a common united ideal were being replaced by a deepening religious feeling and a desire for rural simplicity and calm. In a letter of 13 November 1796, Coleridge tells his friend John Thelwall that he is 'daily more and more a religionist'.[25] The Conversation Poems reveal Coleridge's new ardour for country life and for the beauties of Nature. He, too, reiterates Varro's sentiments and he misquotes Varro's phrase as 'God made the city and man made the town'.[26] But Coleridge's view of nature differs from that of Cowper in its final aim. For Cowper, the contemplation of Nature was a vantage point from which to consider the tragic position of fallen man in the world and to reiterate that man's only hope of salvation lay in the grace of God. In *The Task* Cowper felt at one with God through the contemplation of Nature, and he believed that man must have a knowledge of God in order to appreciate his works:

> In that blest moment Nature, throwing wide
> Her veil opaque, discloses with a smile
> The author of her beauties, who, retir'd
> Behind his own creation, works unseen
> By the impure, and hears his power denied.[27]

Coleridge takes Cowper's love of Nature further in his Conversation Poems, and he treats it in a deeper and more significant manner. Through his contemplation of Nature, he desires to achieve a unity with Nature which is almost visionary in mood. In 'This Lime-Tree Bower', the poet describes watching the sunset 'silent with swimming sense till everything seemed less gross than bodily'.[28] Both poets describe the hush of Nature[29] but Coleridge's view of Nature is that in its ideal form, the human spirit is attuned to Nature in a harmonious and joyful union, while Cowper, by contrast, ultimately viewed Nature as a means of directing guilty mankind to God. For this reason, Cowper's descriptions of Nature, when compared with

Coleridge's, seem muted in tone and without the passionate intensity of Coleridge's vision of the union between Man and Nature. The fact that Cowper (according to John Newton and Samuel Greathead) lost confidence in his own salvation after 1773 imposed a further restriction on his view of Nature, which he could inevitably only see as an avenue to divine redemption, thereby accounting for Coleridge's later recognition of 'the sombre hue of its [*The Task's*] religious opinions'.[30]

Cowper's view of Nature as a route to God was also linked to a strong sense of divine retribution, which manifests itself in a similar way in Coleridge's 'Fears in Solitude'. In *The Task*, Cowper sees natural catastrophes as the manifestation of divine retribution for man's evils, and he proffers a stern warning that guilty man may find himself being judged by God, and that society may have to stand judgement for its shortcomings. Coleridge in 'Fears in Solitude' sees the ills of society with foreboding and he warns of the consequences of divine retribution against man:

> Therefore, evil days
> Are coming on us, O my countrymen!
> And what if all-avenging Providence,
> Strong and retributive, should make us know
> The meaning of our words, force us to feel
> The desolation and the agony
> Of our fierce doings?[31]

Of all Coleridge's Conversation Poems, 'Frost at Midnight' is the poem which manifests Cowper's influence most extensively and most directly, even to the extent of echoing some of the same ideas and phrases. In Book IV of *The Task*, Cowper describes the quiet pleasures of a winter's evening by the fireside and the calm of the 'parlour twilight' while he gazed into the fire and imagined 'a waking dream of houses . . . in the red cinders', and, significantly, he continues, 'myself creating what I saw'.[32] He describes watching the sooty film fluttering in the grate,[33] later referred to by Coleridge in 'Frost at Midnight',[34] both poets drawing on the folk tradition in which the presence of a film on the grate was thought to portend the arrival of absent friends. The references in both poems to the calm and secret ministry of the frost[35] and to the hush of Nature

143

in the 'parlour twilight',[36] make it likely that Coleridge had *The Task* in mind when he composed 'Frost at Midnight', particularly since shortly after completing it he quoted some lines from Book V of *The Task* in a letter to his brother George.[37]

It is not known when exactly Coleridge first became familiar with Cowper's poem. In *Biographia Literaria*, he commented that although *The Task* was published in 1785, he was 'not familiar with it till many years afterwards',[38] but by 1796, two years before the publication of 'Frost at Midnight', Coleridge was writing to John Thelwall about the 'divine Chit chat of Cowper' and on 5 December 1796, Lamb wrote to him to say that he was glad that Coleridge loved Cowper. In 1797, Coleridge was planning to write 'The Brook', a poem which was to be in the manner of *The Task*,[39] and in 1799 he refers to Cowper's *Poems* as a present for his German friend Blumenbach.[40] In 'Frost at Midnight', Coleridge, like Cowper, conveys his impressions of the absolute beneficence of Nature and of the superiority of rural life:

> For I was reared
> In the great city . . .
> And saw nought lovely but the sky and stars.[41]

It is interesting to note that later on in *Biographia Literaria* [ii.32] in his critique of Wordsworth's theory of poetic diction, Coleridge revised his former position, expressing scepticism about the alleged superiority of rural to urban life. But whereas, in the case of Cowper, the contemplative mood engendered by the parlour twilight and hush of Nature is an end in itself, in Coleridge's poem the mood induced by the meditative calm of the twilight hour invokes the poet's childhood memories and, from there, he moves on to contemplate his infant son Hartley, and to contrast his own childhood with that of Hartley, until the poem reaches its climax in a statement about the all-pervading influence of God 'Himself in all, and all things in himself'.[42] Again, here, Coleridge, by the greater intensity of his own vision and his expressed joy in the benefits of Nature, goes further than Cowper in bringing his readers within the scope of his poem and enabling them to share in the feelings it expresses as it moves from the particular to the infinite. Coleridge's reader is thus able to share the varied states of mind embedded in the poem through the poet's fusion of description and contemplation.

In *The Task*, Cowper gives free vent to his condemnation of the slave trade, a subject upon which Coleridge, too, held strong and similar views. Cowper's poem was published four years before the subject of slavery was introduced into Parliament by William Wilberforce in 1789, largely as a consequence of strong Evangelical and Quaker pressure for its abolition. It was not until 1807, however, that the General Abolition Bill was enacted by the Fox-Grenville ministry so that, throughout the 1790s, the treatment of slaves and the iniquities of the slave trade continued to be vigorously debated. As an Evangelical, Cowper abhorred the slave trade and the human indignity that he felt it both represented and actively fostered. In Book II of *The Task,* he includes a rousing condemnation of slavery and its toleration by England:

> I would not have a slave to till my ground. . .
> I had much rather be myself the slave, —. . .
> We have no slaves at home—Then why abroad?[43]

He deplored the presumption of one man to chain another and 'exact his sweat', and he asks, 'What man, seeing this, and having human feelings, does not blush?'[44] Coleridge was also opposed to the slave trade. In 1795 he had delivered a lecture on the slave trade in the Assembly Coffee-House on the Bristol Quay, which was later published as an essay 'On the Slave Trade', in the fourth issue of *The Watchman* in 1796.[45] He returned to this theme (still unresolved) in 'Fears in Solitude' when he condemned the slavery and servitude imposed by England upon other races. Drawing upon the image of 'a cloud that travels on, steamed up from Cairo's swamps of pestilence', he alleged that his fellow countrymen had —

> gone forth
> And borne to distant tribes slavery and pangs . . .
> Yet bartering freedom and the poor man's life
> For gold, as at a market![46]

To both Coleridge and Cowper, the concept of the freedom of man was of primary importance; slavery, which represented the denial of individual freedom, was a violation of man's true nature:

'Tis liberty alone that gives the flow'r
Of fleeting life its lustre and perfume.[47]

Ultimately, for Cowper, the true freedom for man was to be achieved through his redemption by the grace of God. This alone enabled man to attain his true stature or, as Cowper puts it, 'Grace makes the slave a freeman'.[48] Cowper's love of freedom was matched, not surprisingly, by his hatred of despotism and injustice. Convinced that man's nature was endowed by God, Cowper was opposed to any manifestation of tyranny or unjust rule as a contravention of the behaviour he expected of men so endowed. Strong views on the injustices that led to the French Revolution are evident in Cowper's poem. He attacks the French monarchy for opposing freedom, the achievement of which he regards as 'the cause of man'.[49] In 'Fears in Solitude', Coleridge, too, condemns both the tyranny of England in supporting the slave trade and the despotism of post-Revolutionary France, which he denounced at the same time in 'France: An Ode'.[50]

There is another parallel between the attitudes of both poets towards their native land. While condemning injustice to man, both Cowper and Coleridge show strong patriotic feelings. In the case of Cowper, patriotism is outweighed only by martyrdom, those who die in the cause of religion being even more worthy than those who die for their native land, because of the greater sacrifice and greater permanence of their action. In *The Task*, Cowper expressed the view that love of mankind was the route to love of society, and hence to patriotism.[51] This quotation was noted by Coleridge in one of his letters[52] and he wrote in the same vein when he produced his introductory address to *Conciones ad Populum*, where he stated that 'the intensity of a private attachment encourages, not prevents, universal benevolence'.[53] The poets do differ, however, to some extent, in their approach to slavery. While Cowper almost uncharacteristically makes a plea for Britain to exercise her civilized nature so that where her 'pow'r is felt, mankind may feel her mercy too',[54] Coleridge's reaction is more bitter and sustained. He also requires a more radical solution. In 'Fears in Solitude', while referring to Britain as the source of all his intellectual and sensuous pleasures as well as the limit of 'all bonds of natural love',[55] his condemnation of slavery and of the way in which Britain's vices were affecting societies abroad through her empire seems to become more strident in proportion to the intensity of his patriotism.

Both poets are united in their dislike of war and the machinery of war. In *The Task*, Cowper criticizes the unfortunate end result of militarism when young men who go to join the militia no longer love or can adapt themselves to the circumstances of rural life on their return, and he condemns the military might of imperialism. He reveals himself as an Evangelical pacifist when he refers to 'universal soldiership' which stabs 'the heart of merit in the meaner class'.[56] Coleridge, too, condemns war and the warmongering of contemporary society in 'Fears in Solitude'.[57] Again, though, Coleridge takes the matter further than Cowper, in that he sees an element of collective responsibility in these actions: because Coleridge belongs to society, he is therefore responsible both for society's actions and for its wrong decisions.

In *Biographia Literaria,* Coleridge makes a significant remark when he comments, in a discussion of his early style, that of contemporary poets, Bowles and Cowper were 'the first who combined natural thoughts with natural diction; the first who reconciled the heart with the head',[58] and he confesses that he himself had once 'adopted a laborious and florid diction' which he had later discarded in his shorter blank verse poems. His style, in fact, had suffered from some of the same defects as those of James Thomson in *The Seasons* (1730) which Coleridge, also in *Biographia Literaria,*[59] pronounces to fall far below *The Task* in 'chastity of diction'. On the other hand, in fairness to Thomson, he had preceded both Cowper and Coleridge not only in fostering a love of Nature but in exploiting, under the far-reaching impact of Newton's *Optics,* the same close studies of light and shade as those of Coleridge in 'This Lime-Tree Bower' and other Conversation Poems.

Cowper and Coleridge, besides sharing some of the same attitudes towards patriotism, militarism, nature and rural life, were above all at one in the view that it was the function of the poet to be concerned for his fellow man. They were also at one in exploring 'the poet's mind' with particular reference to the eighteenth-century principle of the transmutation of pain into pleasure as an integral part of the process of composition. Cowper's fullest expression of this is in Book II of *The Task:*

> There is a pleasure in poetic pains
> Which only poets know. The shifts and turns,
> Th' expedients and inventions, multiform,
> To which the mind resorts, in chase of terms
> Though apt, yet coy, and difficult to win—
> T'arrest the fleeting images that fill
> The mirror of the mind, and hold them fast,
> And force them sit till he has pencil'd off
> A faithful likeness of the forms he views;
> Then to dispose his copies with such art,
> That each may find its most propitous light,
> And shine by situation, hardly less
> Than by the labour and the skill it cost;
> Are occupations of the poet's mind
> So pleasing, and that steal away the thought
> With such address from themes of sad import,
> That, lost in his own musings, happy man!
> He feels th' anxieties of life, denied
> Their wonted entertainment, all retire.
> Such joys has he that sings.[60]

Coleridge's earliest explanation of the same psychological process is in the Preface to the first edition of his poems (1796). It occurs in self-defence against a possible charge of 'querulous egotism' in his poems. 'The communicativeness of our Nature', he observes, 'leads us to describe our own sorrows; in the endeavour to describe them, intellectual activity is exerted; and from intellectual activity there results a pleasure, which is gradually associated, and mingles as a corrective, with the painful subject of the description.'[61] Coleridge here echoes not only Cowper but David Hartley, to whose principle of association he was as much attached in 1796 as to the conversational fluency of Cowper's blank verse in *The Task*. His own later tribute to Cowper's blank verse as 'excellent' includes a distinction between its 'colloquial' nature and the more 'philosophic' blank verse of Wordsworth, which Coleridge called 'Orphic'.[62] While one gets an impression of a certain limited sense of purpose about Cowper's poetry, one is struck by the emotional intensity and the interplay of thought and feeling in Coleridge's Conversation Poems, and by the way in which the material world and the spiritual world become one. Nevertheless, William Hayley's comment in his *Life of Cowper* (1803) was historically accurate:

> Southey, Wordsworth, and Coleridge, in their blank verse, trod directly in the steps of Cowper, and, in the early productions at least, were each, in a measure, what he made them.[62]

NOTES AND REFERENCES

1 G. Whalley, 'Coleridge's debt to Charles Lamb', *Essays and Studies,* xi (1958), 68-85.
2 *CL,* i.137.
3 *PW,* ii.1145.
4 H. House, *The Clark Lectures 1951-52 (1967),* 71.
5 *CL,* i.279.
6 House, *op. cit.,* 71.
7 *BL,* i.16n.
8 **LAMB,** i.55-6.
9 *ibid.,* i.66.
10 *ibid.,* i.59.
11 *ibid.,* i.93.
12 *ibid.,* i.15.
13 'Crazy Kate' was, of course, not a poem but a figure of pathos in *The Task,* i.534ff.
14 **LAMB,** i.36.
15 *ibid.,* i.66.
16 *ibid.,* i.73.
17 *Task,* i.109-10. (All *The Task* references are from the edition of *The Poetical Works of William Cowper* by H.S. Milford, 1934.)
18 *ibid.,* i.749.
19 *ibid.,* i.727-28.
20 *ibid.,* i.420-21.
21 *CN,* i.77.
22 *PW,* i.180, ll.50-1.
23 *Task,* i.303-4.
24 *ibid.,* i.347.
25 *CL,* i.253.
26 *CN,* i.815. In Wordsworth's copy of Varro's *Scriptores de re rustica* (Paris, 1543), Coleridge marked this passage with an 'X' and wrote in manuscript below: 'God made the country and man made the town. Cowper'.
27 *Task,* v.891-95.
28 *PW,* i.180, l.39.

29 *ibid.*, i.240, l.17 and *Task*, iv.308-10.
30 *BL*, i.16n.
31 *PW*, i.260, ll.123-29.
32 *Task*, iv.287-90.
33 *ibid.*, iv.292.
34 *PW*, i.240, l.15.
35 *Task*, iv.308-11 and *PW*, i.240, ll.1-2.
36 *Task*, iv. 308-10 and *PW*, i.240, l.17.
37 *CL*, i.396.
38 *BL*, i.16n.
39 *BL*, i.129. A later (1802) variant of this abortive topographical poem was 'The Soother of Absence', also abortive (cf. *CN*, i.1225, f.26ᵛ).
40 *CN*, i.452.
41 *PW*, i.242, ll.51-3. This passage was twice echoed by Wordsworth in *The Prelude* (iii. 467-68; vi.275-84).
42 *PW*, i.242, l.62.
43 *Task*, ii.29-37.
44 *ibid.*, ii.26-7.
45 S.T. Coleridge, *Collected Works* (Princeton, 1969 -), i.232.
46 *PW*, i.258, ll.47-50 and 62-3.
47 *Task*, v.446-47.
48 *ibid.*, v.688.
49 *ibid.*, v.396.
50 *PW*, i.243.
51 *Task*, v.503-8.
52 *CL*, i.396.
53 This view was also expressed by Burke in his *Reflections on the Revolution in France* (1790): 'To love the little platoon we belong to in society, is the principle . . . in the series by which we proceed towards a love of our country and mankind'. E. Burke, *Reflections on the Revolution in France* (1790), pp.68-9.
54 *Task*, ii.46-7.
55 *PW*, i.262, l.180.
56 *Task*, iv.617-18.
57 *PW*, i.259, ll.88-123.
58 *BL*, i.16.
59 *ibid.*, i.16n.
60 *Task*, ii.285-304.
61 *PW*, ii.1144.
62 *Coleridge's Miscellaneous Criticism*, ed. T.M. Raysor (1936), 251. For another and better-known application of 'Orphic' by Coleridge to Wordsworth's blank verse with specific reference to *The Prelude*, see 'To William Wordsworth', *PW*, i.406, l.45.
63 W. Hayley, *Life of Cowper* (1803), i.xxxii.

9

Scenery and Ecstasy: Three of Coleridge's Blank Verse Poems

by JOHN GUTTERIDGE

In the summers of 1795, 1796 and 1797 Coleridge began three blank verse loco-descriptive poems that tried to encapsulate his spiritual experience of the divine presence in nature. The first two, 'The Eolian Harp' and 'Reflections on Having Left a Place of Retirement', were set in Clevedon where he lived for a short time after his marriage in October 1795; the third, 'This Lime-Tree Bower My Prison', is about the countryside around Nether Stowey where Coleridge settled in early 1797. Although the three poems are now most commonly seen as the foundation of the genre of the 'Conversation Poems',[1] when he wrote them Coleridge seems not to have been trying deliberately to invent a new species of poem. Each deals with a particular incident in his life, and with the ecstatic feelings he derived from contemplating natural scenes. Each poem also transmutes major literary and philosophical sources into a distinctively Coleridgean style: blank verse enlivened by spiritual excitement and strengthened by metaphysical metaphor.

In the spring of 1795 Coleridge was living in Bristol and courting Sara Fricker, whose sister Edith was to marry Robert Southey. Coleridge and Southey were working together on a revision of Southey's epic *Joan of Arc* which was to present many political and religious arguments current in the 1790s in historical guise. They had also been engaged in a series of joint

151

lectures about politics, religion and history, and had been quarrying for material in many out-of-the-way authors. Coleridge's head was full of abstract notions, and most of the poetry he was writing had a political or religious theme. Amongst his minor verse, however, there were some poems, such as 'Brockley Coomb', which were records of walks and visits in the countryside around Bristol.

Coleridge had lived in London for most of his life, and his vacation visits to Ottery St Mary, such as the one in the summer of 1793, had prompted him to write verse which owed a great deal to loco-descriptive traditions. The countryside around Cambridge had not inspired such work, though his walk to North Wales with Joseph Hucks in the summer of 1794 had brought him back to descriptive writing in both letters and poems. His life in Bristol and his affection for Sara Fricker gave him fresh stimuli both to write descriptive verse and to return to writing the complimentary love poems he had written for Mary Evans, Fanny Nesbitt, and other girls while he was at school and at Cambridge.

It was in this frame of mind that he visited Clevedon, a small town on the Bristol Channel some twelve miles from the city, in mid-August 1795 to find the cottage in which he and Sara would begin their married life. While there he began to draft what was to become the first poem of his maturity—'The Eolian Harp'. It was a 17-line poem ending with the image of the harp lodged in the window frame and was dated 'Cleveden, August 20th 1795'.[2] This first version is similar to Coleridge's earlier love poems ('To the Evening Star' and 'The Kiss') and it describes his mood at Clevedon on the evening of 20 August as he sits with Sara listening to the sea outside their new-found cottage. The harp is simply an image of the poet's coy lady; it is used to represent Sara's teasing in very similar vein to the images of cupids in 'The Rose' and 'Cupid turned Chemist'. There is no evidence in the manuscript that Coleridge considered this 17-line draft as anything but a complete poem—a little compliment to Sara commemorating their visit. The manuscript entitles the poem 'Effusion XXXV', and it was to be published as such in Coleridge's first printed collection, *Poems on Various Subjects*.[3]

At the end of July 1795 Joseph Cottle had agreed to publish a volume of Coleridge's poems, and it appears from a letter Coleridge wrote in October that the first six sheets of the volume had been prepared and printed by September when Coleridge visited Thomas Poole in Nether Stowey.[4] The first six sheets to be printed were B-G in *Poems on Various Subjects* (the letters of early 1796 show that sheet A was printed much later)[5] and the interruption of printing that followed had important consequences for 'The Eolian Harp'. Sheet G ends at line 8 of 'Effusion XXXV' which must therefore have been left only half printed in September 1795. The material for sheet H was sent to Cottle by Coleridge when he was living in Clevedon after his marriage and included the printer's copy for the remainder of 'The Eolian Harp'.[6] The version in the printer's copy is based on two drafts: one also in the Rugby Manuscript and one among the Cottle papers at Cornell University. None of these manuscripts is dated, but as the poem was sent from Clevedon, and as it is concerned with Coleridge's love for Sara, the traditional view that the main part of the poem was written shortly after Coleridge's marriage on 4 October is probably correct. The drafts of the poem show that Coleridge laboured over it, taking particular care with the metaphysical passage about the harp. Two months after writing the shorter version of 20 August Coleridge took the opportunity afforded by the accident of the poem being only partly printed on sheet G of *Poems 1796* to expand a lightweight occasional poem into a much more serious treatment of his current preoccupations.

Between Coleridge's visit to Clevedon in August and his residence there in October 1795 his relationship with Southey had turned sour, and he had begun to question many of the political and metaphysical ideas he had espoused earlier in the year. At the same time his intimacy with Sara increased, and this, together with his isolation in the pleasant scenery of Clevedon, seems to have put him in a more relaxed frame of mind. Reviewing his relationship with Southey in an important letter he admitted to a degree of indolence.[7] When he began to expand the harp image of 'Effusion XXXV' he drew on Thomson's *Castle of Indolence* for his descriptions of both the harp, and the philosopher in repose:

153

I.xvi

What, what is Virtue, but Repose of Mind?
A pure ethereal Calm! that knows no Storm;
Above the Reach of wild Ambition's Wind,
Above those Passions that this World deform,
And torture Man, a proud malignant Worm!
But here, instead, soft Gales of Passion play,
And gently stir the Heart, thereby to form
A quicker Sense of Joy; as Breezes stray
Across th'enliven'd Skies, and make them still more gay.

I.xl

A certain Musick, never known before,
Here lull'd the pensive melancholy Mind;
Full easily obtain'd. Behoves no more,
But sidelong, to the gently-waving Wind,
To lay the well-tun'd Instrument reclin'd;
From which, with airy flying Fingers light,
Beyond each mortal Touch the most refin'd,
The God of Winds drew sounds of deep Delight:
Whence, with just Cause, *The Harp of Aeolus* it hight.[8]

In Canto I of *The Castle of Indolence,* and now in 'Effusion XXXV' the aeolian harp is used as an image of pleasant retirement; Thomson's philosopher sinks through philosophic reverie into indolent apathy, but Coleridge, whose letter to Southey of 13 November 1795 shows he was aware of his tendency to indolence,[9] is aroused into active harmony with the forces of the universe:

Full many a thought uncall'd and undetain'd,
And many idle flitting phantasies,
Traverse my indolent and passive brain
As wild and various, as the random gales
That swell or flutter on this subject Lute![10]

Coleridge then went further, however, and pressed the harp into dual service as an image not only of his state of mind but also of his current metaphysical thinking.

Ealier in the year he had consulted Ralph Cudworth's *True Intellectual System of the Universe*[11] for material for his lectures on Revealed Religion; the learned and quaint style of the Commonwealth Platonist seems to have attracted Coleridge and to have left with him a number of phrases and speculative ideas. When he expanded the 17-line version of the poem

154

Coleridge enriched its imagery not only with the atmosphere of Thomson's world of indolent reverie, but also with the language of Cudworth's metaphysical speculations:

> If the oecodomical art, which is in the mind of the architect, were supposed to be transfused into the stones, bricks and mortar, there acting upon them in such a manner as to make them come together of themselves and range themselves into the form of a complete edifice, as *Amphion* was said, by his harp, to have made the stones move, and place themselves orderly of their own accord, and so to have built the walls of *Thebes*; or if the musical art were conceived to be immediately in the instruments and strings, animating them as a living soul, and making them to move exactly, according to the laws of harmony without any external impulse: these, and such like instances, in *Aristotle's* judgement, would be fit iconisms or representations of the *plastick nature*, that *being art itself acting immediately upon the matter as an inward principle in it.*[12]

The many changes in the drafts of 'The Eolian Harp' in the Rugby and Cornell manuscripts show that Coleridge laboured over the section describing the 'universal harp', and that the introduction of the term 'plastic nature' helped resolve many of his difficulties. It was not, however, a purely metaphysical term. In a group of Sermons appended to the edition of the *True Intellectual System* which Coleridge borrowed from Bristol Library the same idea was used for the moral life, again in musical imagery:

> they, that are acted by the *new law of the Gospel*, by the *law of the spirit*, they have an inward principle of life in them, that from the centre itself puts forth itself freely and constantly into all obedience to the will of Christ. The *new law of the Gospel* is a kind of musical soul, informing the dead organ of our hearts, that makes them of their own accord delight to act harmoniously according to the rule of God's word.[13]

It is these ideas that lie behind the mysterious core of 'The Eolian Harp':

> And what if all of animated nature
> Be but organic Harps diversly fram'd,
> That tremble into thought, as o'er them sweeps,
> Plastic and vast, one intellectual Breeze,
> At once the Soul of each, and God of all?[14]

The breeze in the evening scene is an image of the universal mind of God which arouses the souls of all living things, including the human soul, to sing in tune with each other. But this 'plastic' breeze, mediating between spirit and matter, causes more than a purely aesthetic pleasure; it is also the agent of God's will and brings all creatures into moral and spiritual harmony.

Shortly after this passage Coleridge has Sara rebuke him for entertaining speculations which are likely to lead him into evil ways:

> But thy more serious eye a mild reproof
> Darts, O beloved Woman! nor such thoughts
> Dim and unhallow'd dost thou not reject,
> And biddest me walk humbly with my God.[15]

Coleridge was afraid that by enquiring too deeply into the metaphysics behind the pleasant evening scene he would again become 'thought bewildered' as he had been in 1793-4. He found stability in 1794 with Southey and their plans for Pantisocracy, but this relationship had then foundered and he saw his marriage to Sara as both spiritual salvation and a re-birth of human feeling.

In the same Sermons Cudworth had written movingly of the error of seeking truth by reason alone:

> Cold theorems and maxims, dry and jejeune disputes, lean syllogistical reasonings, could never yet of themselves beget the least glimpse of true heavenly light, the least sap of saving knowledge in any heart. All this is but the groping of the poor dark spirit of man after truth, to find it out with his own endeavours, and feel it with his own cold and benumbed hands.[16]

In both the Sermons (p. 50) and the *True Intellectual System* Cudworth presented the rational brain as a vain bubble, an image Coleridge now borrowed:

> The rational soul is itself an active and bubbling fountain of thoughts; that perpetual and restless desire, which is as natural and essential to us, as our very life, continually raising up and protruding new and new ones in us;

> Meek Daughter in the Family of Christ,
> Well hast thou said and holily disprais'd
> These shapings of the unregenerate mind,
> Bubbles that glitter as they rise and break
> On vain Philosophy's aye-babbling spring.[17]

In extending 'The Eolian Harp' on his honeymoon Coleridge remembered a number of images from his reading of Cudworth a few months earlier, and moulded these into a fresh account of both the new life he had found and of the new beliefs that came with his marriage.

The 1796 version of 'The Eolian Harp' progressed from the gales of fancy through the description of tranquil noontime reverie to the metaphor of the Harp of the Universe. These three parts were linked by the themes of philosophic indolence and natural harmony, and while the thoughts they contain may not be completely intelligible the movement of the verse was smooth and the imagery homogeneous. When the poem was reprinted in 1803, however, Coleridge replaced the lines about the birds of Paradise with a simpler statement of the idea of natural harmony:

> Methinks, it should have been impossible
> Not to love all things in a World like this,
> Where e'en the Breezes of the simple Air
> Possess the power and Spirit of Melody![18]

This use of 'should' is ambiguous, referring either to the failure of the Clevedon period of Coleridge's life to reconcile him to all things in love, or perhaps to an Eden with all the characteristics of Clevedon. Coleridge remained dissatisfied with the passage, however, and in the *Errata* page of *Sibylline Leaves* he added the famous lines about the 'One Life' which, although powerful, are nevertheless obscure; their abstract diction is wholly at odds with the continuous sensual descriptions and metaphors of the rest of the poem:

> O! the one Life, within us and abroad,
> Which meets all Motion, and becomes its soul,
> A Light in Sound, a sound-like power in Light,
> Rhythm in all Thought, and Joyance everywhere—[19]

The addition of these lines only in the *Errata* page suggests they were written after the main text of the poem (which had also been revised elsewhere) had been printed. Although dated 20 August 1795 most of 'The Eolian Harp' was written in the autumn of 1795, and it was considerably revised for the editions of both 1803 and 1817. These revisions changed its metaphysical content, but it remained an occasional poem commemorating a particular day, scene and mood.

Reflections on having left a place of Retirement

E.H. Coleridge thought that 'Reflections on having left a place of Retirement', alternatively called 'Reflections on Entering into Active Life', was written in late 1795, but if it had been it would surely have been published in *Poems on Various Subjects*, which was issued in April 1796 rather than in the *Monthly Magazine* number of October 1796, where it first appeared. The descriptions of scenery in the poem suggest the life of spring and summer rathe than the late autumn (the myrtle 'blossoms' whereas in 'The Eolian Harp' the myrtles are 'broad-leaved'), and there is no external evidence of its existence before the autumn of 1796. It is much more likely that the poem was written in summer 1796 long after Coleridge had left Clevedon, and that it was from the first intended for the newly founded *Monthly Magazine* which had carried several poems by Coleridge's friends.[20] The blank verse of the poem is much more even than that of 'The Eolian Harp', suggesting that it was written in a more concentrated way as a retrospective poem looking back to the occasion of Coleridge's leaving Clevedon.

The title and main theme of the poem are concerned with the traditional debate on the relative advantages of active and retired life. The opening movement describes the advantages of retirement in Clevedon, and once again music symbolises the spiritual influence of nature on the human soul. In 'Reflections', however, Coleridge presents forcibly the other side of the argument: that refined feelings can cause slothfulness and self-centred callousness. Coleridge's political commitment was not only to the abstract goals of democracy and freedom, but also to active benevolence, and he claims that it was this cause that called him forth from retirement:

158

> I therefore go—and join head, heart, and hand,
> Active and firm, to fight the bloodless fight
> Of Science, Freedom, and the Truth in Christ.[21]

This was not biographically true as he had already left
Clevedon at the end of 1795 to participate in the Bristol
agitation against the Treasonable Practices and Seditious
Meetings Bills, and then to run *The Watchman*, but it was a
message that would be well received by the liberal readership of
the *Monthly Magazine*.

The debate between activity and retirement had been a
traditional poetic theme since Horace. Coleridge was conscious
of this, and he changed the original motto of the poem, 'A poem
which affects not to be poetry', to a Horatian misquotation,
'Sermoni propriora' when he reprinted it in his volume of 1797.
This tag was often used to identify semi-prosaic poems about
public issues,[22] and places 'Reflections' towards the end of the
Horatian tradition that has been traced by Maren-Sofie
Rostvig.[23] Coleridge added to the traditional debate a visionary
element that enhances the spiritual value of retirement. In the
climb up the 'stony Mount' and the description of the scene
from the top he used first the 'picturesque' device of composing
a picture of an inland scene, and then the 'sublime' convention
of dim vastness. This part of the poem owes much to Crowe's
'Lewesdon Hill'.[24] The artificiality of the passage is pointed up
by the italicised words '*here . . . there*' which mark the transitions
between these descriptive styles. Coleridge then goes further, to
present the harmony with nature he had claimed in 'The Eolian
Harp' in less metaphysical, but still almost mystical, religious
terms. His witness of the scene as God's dwelling place induces
an ecstatic identification with a *spiritus mundi* similar to the
'plastic breeze' of 'The Eolian Harp'. In 'Reflections' this
feeling is not called in question, as it had been in 'The Eolian
Harp', partly because the debate in the poem lies elsewhere,
and partly because the honest emotions Coleridge described are
divorced from speculative metaphysics:

> *Here* the bleak mount,
> The bare bleak mountain speckl'd thin with sheep;
> Grey clouds, that shadowing spot the sunny fields;
> And river, now with bushy rocks o'erbrow'd,

> Now winding bright and full with naked banks;
> And seats, and lawns, the abbey, and the wood,
> And cots and hamlets, and faint city-spire:
> The channel *there*, the islands, and white sails,
> Dim coast, and cloudlike hills, and shoreless ocean!
> It seem'd like Omnipresence! God, methought,
> Had built him there a temple! The whole world
> Was *imag'd* in its vast circumference.[25]

Although this experience has undoubted value for the poet's moral well-being, Coleridge turns from it to consider the possible effects of retirement on his moral life. It is not enough to be good: the true philosopher must also do good, and the peace of Clevedon may result in a decline to the useless self-indulgence of Thomson's philosopher in the *Castle of Indolence:*

> Ah, quiet dell! dear cot! and mount sublime!
> I was constrain'd to quit you. Was it right,
> While my unnumber'd brethren toil'd and bled,
> That I should dream away the trusted hours
> On rose-leaf beds, pamp'ring the coward heart
> With feelings all too delicate for use?[26]

Coleridge does not debate for long with himself, but quickly makes up his mind in favour of the active political life of Bristol. The tone of the concluding lines is that of his Miltonic poems, and it jars with the subtler language of description and debate:

> I therefore go—and join head, heart, and hand,
> Active and firm, to fight the bloodless fight
> Of Science, Freedom, and the Truth in Christ.[27]

The strongest feature of 'Reflections' is the expression of Coleridge's awareness of the spiritual heart of the universe combined with an ability to question himself about the value and significance of such awareness. The poem again uses a particular occasion, the departure from Clevedon, to debate the relative value of different states of consciousness.

This Lime-Tree Bower My Prison

Like 'The Eolian Harp', 'This Lime-Tree Bower My Prison' began as an occasional poem but was heavily revised before publication. It is the first confident statement of Coleridge's faith in the psychological and spiritual therapy afforded by the contemplation of natural scenes. The dialectic of the poem lies in its progression of moods rather than in abstract argument.

The poem began as a celebration of Charles Lamb's visit to Nether Stowey in July 1797, and first appeared in a letter to Robert Southey written shortly afterwards.[28] The plot is simple: Coleridge sits depressed in the lime-tree bower because his injured foot prevents him from joining his friends on a walk in the Quantocks; he imagines Lamb's joy as he views the scenery, so different from the London streets that have confined him for many years, and his sympathy with Lamb leads him to share in his friends' joy, and to end his own depression. The heart of the poem is again a description of spiritual ecstasy stimulated by the natural scene, and Coleridge combines elements of earlier poetry and philosophy to give a novel and eclectic expression to his latest ideas.

The climax of the poem is expanded from an earlier notebook description:

> The Sun (for now his Orb
> Gan slowly sink) ~~behind the Western Hill,~~
> Shot half his rays aslant the heath, whose flowers
> Purpled the mountain's broad & level top,
> Rich was his bed of Clouds: & wide beneath
> Expecting Ocean smiled with dimpled face.[29]

These lines are rather conventional and in expanding them Coleridge both improved the quality of the blank verse description, under the influence of Cowper, and animated them with a new metaphysical metaphor of the hidden light and fire of the nature spirit, derived from Berkeley. Lamb, as already explained by Ann Matheson in the preceding article,[30] had been recommending Coleridge to read Cowper, and to 'cultivate simplicity' in his poetry while banishing elaborateness. In absorbing Cowper's technique, however, Coleridge also took over certain key ideas and phrases, including the view that the elect, who had tutored their souls in the Biblical knowledge of God, would easily perceive God's handiwork in nature and free themselves from the prison of the senses:

> For he has wings that neither sickness, pain,

> Nor penury, can cripple or confine.
> No nook so narrow but he spreads them there
> With ease, and is at large. Th'oppressor holds
> His body bound, but knows not what a range
> His spirit takes unconscious of a chain,
> And that to bind him is a vain attempt
> Whom God delights in, and in whom he dwells.[31]

Cowper also used more mystical language echoed by Coleridge in his description of the experience of discerning the handiwork of God:

> In that blest moment, nature throwing wide
> Her veil opaque, discloses with a smile
> The author of her beauties, who retired
> Behind his own creation, works unseen
> By the impure, and hears his pow'r denied.
> Thou art the source and centre of all minds,
> Their only point of rest, eternal word![32]

In one passage he described the aching of the soul for its heavenly home in words Coleridge borrowed for Lamb's vision of the spiritual life in nature:

> So I with animated hopes behold
> And many an aching wish, your beamy fires,
> That shew like beacons in the blue abyss
> Ordain'd to guide th'embodied spirit home
> From toilsome life to never-ending rest.
> Love kindles as I gaze.[33]

Coleridge drew on all these ideas and phrases in revising his original notebook description of sunset:

> Live in the yellow Light, ye distant Groves!
> And kindle, thou blue Ocean! So my friend
> Struck with joy's deepest calm, and gazing round
> On the wide view, may gaze till all doth seem
> Less gross than bodily, a living Thing
> That acts upon the mind, and with such hues
> As cloathe the Almighty Spirit, when he makes
> Spirits perceive His presence![34]

Coleridge wrote these lines partly to answer a question recently posed by Wordsworth at the end of a poem greatly admired by

162

Lamb, 'Lines left upon a seat in a Yew-tree'. The subject of
Wordsworth's poem sits despondent in scenes of natural beauty
because he has been disillusioned by the failure of mankind to
live up to his ideals.[35] This, says Wordsworth, is a species of
contempt and pride, and he recommends humility as a cure. In
'This Lime-Tree Bower' Coleridge dealt with the same subject,
but suggested a deeper and more optimistic solution.

Coleridge's solution is religious but stops short of overt
Christianity. Portraying his own salvation from depression in
the story of his sympathy with Lamb, he asserts that the
spiritual life of nature is always ready to inspire and raise up
downcast hearts provided they are alert to it. Wordsworth drew
an abstract moral in his 'Yew Tree Lines':

> Stranger! henceforth be warned; and know that pride,
> Howe'er disguised in its own majesty,
> Is littleness; that he who feels contempt
> For any living thing, hath faculties
> Which he has never used; that thought with him
> Is in its infancy.[36]

In 'This Lime-Tree Bower' Coleridge reached a more positive
conclusion:

> Henceforth I shall know
> That nature ne'er deserts the wise & pure,
> No scene so narrow, but may well employ
> Each faculty of sense, and keep the heart
> Awake to Love & Beauty:[37]

The efficacy of this doctrine depends on spiritual experience
and Coleridge's account of it had a metaphysical basis
detectable in the sources and peculiar language of his
description of the sunset. Coleridge annotated the lines on
Lamb's vision 'You remember I am a Berkeleian'.[38] His first
library borrowing of Berkeley in 1796 had been of the later
works, including *Siris,* not of the earlier and better known
works.[39] This is an important clue to the meaning of the passage
in which Coleridge compounded early Berkeley with late
Berkeley and Cowper.

In the *Three Principles* and *Dialogues* Berkeley had argued that
Locke's theory of perception was inconsistent in saying that

163

man can only 'know' the impressions of his senses but that these impressions originate in a material world beyond them: Locke should logically have gone further to say that man could not know that 'matter' existed at all. Berkeley went this far, asserting that conventional notions of 'matter' were unnecessary, and that things existed only in so far as they were perceived; *esse est percipe*.[40] The shared experience of the same sensations by all creatures was guaranteed by God. In his later work, *Siris*, Berkeley left behind these empiricist arguments and wrote about nature in language drawn from neo-Platonism using an idea of the *anima mundi* similar to Cudworth's notion of Plastic Nature:

> As the Platonists held intellect to be lodged in soul, and the soul in aether; so it passeth for a doctrine of Trismegistus in the Pimander, that mind is clothed by soul, and soul by spirit. Therefore as the animal spirit of man, being subtile and luminous, is the immediate tegument of the soul, or that wherein and whereby she acts; even so the spirit of the world, that active fiery aethereal substance of light, that permeates and animates the whole system, is supposed to clothe the soul, which clothes the mind of the universe.[41]

Berkeley's *anima mundi* is a fiery spirit dwelling beneath the surface of things, and like Cudworth's Plastic Nature it bridges the division between the spiritual world and the world of the senses. The indwelling force enlivens natural objects which are usually most unfiery: 'Fire or light mixeth with all bodies, even with water; witness the flashing lights in the sea, whose waves seem frequently all on fire.'[42] In expanding his notebook description of sunset Coleridge called on Berkeley's fiery spirit of the universe to reveal itself to Lamb through his sensations of the sunset, and so to raise his soul into divine ecstasy:

> Ah slowly sink
> Behind the western ridge; thou glorious Sun!
> Shine in the slant beams of the sinking orb,
> Ye purple Heath-flowers! Richlier burn, ye Clouds!
> Live in the yellow Light, ye distant Groves!
> And kindle, thou blue Ocean! So my friend
> Struck with joy's deepest calm, and gazing round
> On the wide view,* may gaze till all doth seem

Less gross than bodily, a living Thing
That acts upon the mind, and with such hues
As cloathe the Almighty Spirit, when he makes
Spirits perceive His presence!

   *You remember, I am a Berkleian.[43]

The second part of this passage is directly indebted to the image
of nature as the *clothing* of God in *Siris* 178 (the more usual
Platonic term 'veils' was substituted for 'cloathe' in later
versions). The difficult phrase 'Less gross than bodily' is
eclectic Berkeley; Lamb's perception is not of matter, ruled out
by early Berkeley, but of a fiery spirit less substantial than
matter mediating between the divine spirit and man's normal
perceptive faculties. In the elated state of Cowper's elect
Lamb's soul receives direct experience of God's agent in nature:
the mind of God which gives coherence to all sense perceptions
in early Berkeley is blended with the fiery living spirit of the
universe of *Siris* to explain how Lamb's soul is directly touched
by God. The *anima mundi* reveals itself to Lamb arrayed in the
colours and sensations of the sunset.

  The spiritual revelation to Lamb and Coleridge's sympathy
with it are central to the broader theme of friendship in 'This
Lime-Tree Bower'. The poem was first sent to Robert Southey,
from whom Coleridge was still estranged, in a letter which
concluded with a breathless appeal for a rapprochement:

> Wordsworth at whose house I now am for change of air has
> commissioned me to offer you a suit of rooms at this place, which
> is called 'All-foxen'—& so divine and wild is the country that I
> am sure it would increase your stock of images—& three weeks'
> absence from Christ-Church will endear it to you—& Edith
> Southey & Sara may not have another opportunity of seeing each
> other—& Wordsworth is very solicitous to know you—& Miss
> Wordsworth is a most exquisite young woman in her mind, &
> heart.—I pray you, write me immediately, directing Stowey near
> Bridgewater, as before.[44]

Perhaps in an attempt to impress on Southey his readiness for a
renewed friendship Coleridge wove into his poem echoes of two
of Southey's poems. They were printed in the second edition of
Southey's poems, which had just been sold out:

> and thence at eve
> When mildly fading sunk the summer sun,
> Oft have I loved to mark the rook's slow course
> And hear his hollow croak, what time he sought
> The church-yard elm,
>
> Oh there are those who love the pensive song,
> To whom all sounds of Mirth are dissonant!
> There are, who at this hour
> Will love to contemplate!
>
> For hopeless Sorrow hails the lapse of Time,
> Rejoicing when the fading orb of day
> Is sunk again in night,
> That one day more is gone.[45]

The croaking rook becomes the link between all the friends in the poem, and Southey is assured that none thinks its croak is 'dissonant':

> My Sister & my Friends! when the last Rook
> Beat it's straight path along the dusky air
> Homewards, I bless'd it; deeming, it's black wing
> Cross'd, like a speck, the blaze of setting day,
> While ye stood gazing; or when all was still,
> Flew creaking o'er your heads, & had a charm
> For you, my Sister & my Friends! to whom
> No sound is dissonant, which tells of Life![46]

In later revision of the poem Coleridge replaced the phrase 'My Sister & my Friends' with 'My gentle-hearted Charles' (drawing Lamb's wrath in the process). This change hid the importance the 'sister', Dorothy Wordsworth, had for the poem; it was she who helped with the expansion of the letter version in the text first published three years later in the *Annual Anthology* 1800.

There is no clear evidence of the date when Coleridge revised the poem, but parallels with Dorothy's writings provide at least a guide. In the *Annual Anthology* Coleridge expanded the four-line description of the dell to twelve:

> The roaring dell, o'erwooded, narrow, deep,
> And only speckled by the mid-day sun;
> Where its slim trunk the Ash from rock to rock

166

Flings arching like a bridge; that branchless Ash
Unsunn'd and damp, whose few poor yellow leaves
Ne'er tremble in the gale, yet tremble still
Fann'd by the water-fall! And there my friends,
Behold the dark-green file of long lank weeds,
That all at once (a most fantastic sight!)
Still nod and drip beneath the dripping edge
Of the dim clay-stone.[47]

The description of the dripping woods is very close to that of the
'adder's tongue' in Coleridge's juvenile poem 'Melancholy',
published in the *Morning Post* on 12 December 1797:

The fern was press'd beneath her hair,
The dark green Adder's Tongue was there;
And still as pass'd the flagging sea-gale weak,
The long lank leaf bow'd fluttering o'er her cheek.[48]

Dorothy described a similar scene in her Journal on 10
February 1798:

Walked to Woodlands, and to the waterfall. The adder's-tongue
and the ferns green in the low damp dell. These plants now in
perpetual motion from the current of the air; in summer only
moved by the drippings of the rocks.[49]

These extensions made the dell a more dispiriting place: an
image of melancholy. In expanding the poem Coleridge then
divided the dell and hill top scenes into contrasting stanzas,
bridging them with a new passage:

The many-steepled track magnificent
Of hilly fields and meadows, and the sea
With some fair bark perhaps which lightly touches
The slip of smooth clear blue betwixt two isles
Of purple shadow![50]

This is a reversion to the use of sublime and picturesque
conventions in 'Reflections', and is very similar to a scene
observed by Dorothy on the Quantocks in Coleridge's
company:

The sea very uniform, of a pale greyish blue, only one distant
bay, bright and blue as a sky; had there been a vessel sailing up it,
a perfect image of delight.[51]

167

These parallels suggest that Coleridge was probably revising the poem in early 1798 and the topography of the Quantocks and Dorothy's journal throw other light on the revisions.

It has generally been assumed that the dell and waterfall of the poem are those discovered by the Wordsworths near Alfoxden. Dorothy mentioned them twice in her letters:

> William and I, in a wander by ourselves, found out a sequestered waterfall in a dell formed by steep hills covered with full-grown timber trees.

> In a glen at the bottom of the wood is the waterfall of which I spoke, a quarter of a mile from the house.[52]

If this is the dell in the letter version of the poem, Dorothy's claim to have found it is at odds with Coleridge's later claim that he sent his friends 'To that still roaring dell, of which I told'. Moreover, the 'full-grown timber trees' would scarcely give the same decaying atmosphere as Coleridge's rift, deprived of sun, and full of twisted ash trees. The valley of the letter version is surely not Holford Glen, but one of the long coombs that stretch back into the hills a couple of miles behind Stowey. Walking up these the friends would indeed have looked down on a 'narrow rifted dell', and at its upper end Quantock Coomb is deep, steep, and criss-crossed by any number of fallen trees. Whether there would have been a waterfall in 1798 is impossible to say now, but the place is certainly dank and gloomy. Half a mile further the path comes to the head of the valley, and emerges on a rounded hill top, covered with gorse and furze, and commanding a fine view over the Bristol Channel, the coastal plain, and the farms around Stowey. On that walk, but not so easily from Alfoxden, the friends would have passed quickly from the scene of a valley in the woods, to an open prospect. The letter version of the poem is about a walk up this long coomb, a walk directed by the absent Coleridge, while the published version was revised to include details from Dorothy's observations of the Alfoxden dell. Coleridge provided the large structures of the descriptions, the walk and the sunset vision, while Dorothy helped fill in the details, so that the *Annual Anthology* description conflates two places.

The other revisions to the poem gave it greater harmony and

balance than the first two conversation poems. Coleridge emphasised the presence of a hidden light in the third stanza to link this description of the bower with that on the hill top. He also rounded out the movement of the poem from alienation, through friendly sympathy and religious joy, to stable benevolence and spiritual well being. In the *Annual Anthology* it is the plot, rather than the argument, of the poem that supports the assertion

> That Nature ne'er deserts the wise and pure,
> No scene so narrow but may well employ
> Each faculty of sense, and keep the heart
> Awake to love and beauty![53]

This confident statement of faith in the power of nature to ameliorate human feeling was repeated and extended by both Coleridge and Wordsworth in the *annus mirabilis* which began in the summer of 1797. It was also the culmination of Coleridge's attempts in the three poems to describe, in blank verse, nature, his ecstatic response to it, and the metaphysical basis of that response. The three poems were a prelude not only to the remainder of the conversation poems but also to the great verse of Coleridge's maturity.

NOTES AND REFERENCES

1 See in particular G.M. Harper, 'Coleridge's Conversation Poems', *Quarterly Review*, ccxliv (1925) and A. Gerard, 'The Systolic Rhythm: The structure of Coleridge's Conversation Poems', *Essays in Criticism*, x (1960).
2 This manuscript and two other drafts of the poem form part of the 'Rugby Manuscript' now held by the University of Texas at Austin. A microfilm of the whole manuscript may be found in the British Library (RP 179 A). The Rugby MS is reproduced in a partial transcription in *PW*, ii. 1021-3.
3 *Poems on Various Subjects* (1796), 96-100.
4 *CL*, i. 162.
5 *ibid.*, i. 186, 193-94.
6 The covering letters for this material are *CL*, i. 186-87 and vi. 1004. E.L. Griggs dated these February 1796, but their mention of 'coming in' to Bristol indicates that they date from October-November 1795 when Coleridge was living at Clevedon.
7 *CL*, i. 172-73; 13 November 1795.
8 *The Castle of Indolence* (1748), 9 and 21.

9 *CL*, i. 172-73.
10 *Poems on Various Subjects*, 98.
11 Coleridge borrowed *The True Intellectual System of the Universe*, 2nd edition, ed. T. Birch (1743), from Bristol Library 15 May-1 June 1795 and 9 November-13 December 1796 (G. Whalley, 'The Bristol Library Borrowings of Southey and Coleridge 1793-98', *The Library*, ser. 5, iv [1949], 120, 124).
12 *True Intellectual System*, i. 155.
13 *Sermons*, 64. This volume of Sermons is bound up at the end of volume two of the 1743 edition of the *True Intellectual System* but paginated separately.
14 *Poems on Various Subjects*, 98-9.
15 *ibid.*, 99.
16 *Sermons*, 41.
17 *True Intellectual System*, ii. 846; *Poems on Various Subjects*, 99.
18 *Poems*, 3rd ed. (1803), 130.
19 *Sibylline Leaves: A Collection of Poems* (1817), xi, *Errata*.
20 Charles Lamb, John Thelwall, Charles Lloyd and George Dyer all published poems in the *Monthly Magazine* in 1796.
21 *Monthly Magazine*, i. 732.
22 R.T. Martin, 'Coleridge's Use of "sermoni propriora"', *Wordsworth Circle*, iii (1972).
23 Maren-Sofie Rostvig, *The Happy Man* (Oslo, 1962-71).
24 C.G. Martin, 'Coleridge and William Crowe's "Lewesdon Hill"', *MLR*, lxii (1967).
25 *Monthly Magazine*, i. 732.
26 *ibid.*
27 *ibid.*
28 *CL*, i. 334-36; circa 17 July 1797.
29 *CN*, i. 157.
30 pp. 138-40.
31 *The Task*, v. 771-78. (References to *The Task* are from *Poems by William Cowper*, 1782-85.)
32 *ibid.*, v. 891-97.
33 *ibid.*, v. 837-42.
34 *CL*, i. 335.
35 *WPW*, i. 92-4.
36 *ibid.*, i. 94.
37 *CL*, i. 336.
38 *ibid.*, i. 335.
39 G. Whalley, 'Bristol Library Borrowings', 122.
40 References to Berkeley are to *The Works of George Berkeley* (1784), i. 24; *Principles* sec. iii.
41 *Works of Berkeley*, ii. 544; *Siris*, 178.
42 *Works of Berkeley*, ii. 551; *Siris*, 195.
43 *CL*, i. 335.
44 *ibid.*, i. 336.
45 *Poems by Robert Southey*, 2nd ed. (1797), 93 and 61.

46 *CL*, i. 336.
47 *The Annual Anthology*, vol. ii (1800), 141.
48 *PW*, i. 74. Cf. also *Osorio*, iv. 17-19.
49 *Journals of Dorothy Wordsworth*, ed. Mary Moorman (1974), 6. Cf. also *CN*, i. 2557 f. 77.
50 *Annual Anthology* (1800), 141.
51 *Journals of Dorothy Wordsworth*, 8.
52 *The Letters of William and Dorothy Wordsworth: The Early Years*, ed. E. de Selincourt, rev. C.L. Shaver (1967), 189 (4 July 1797) and 191 (14 August 1797).
53 *Annual Anthology* (1800), 143.

10

Coleridge, Symbolism and the Tower of Babel

by H. W. PIPER

The purpose of this essay is to look at some of the confusion in scholarly argument about Coleridge's use of symbolism in his poetry, to try to identify the sources of that confusion, and then to examine briefly the ideas about symbolism which Coleridge himself held in the first half of his life.

One of the most obvious things about the discussion of Coleridge's symbolism is that there are almost as many theories as there are critics, and that the critics are just not listening to one another. Each speaks his own language and is deaf to all else. Before we proceed to examine these languages, some representative examples, old and new, of symbolist discussions of the poems may help to make this clear. The first modern attempt at a symbolic analysis, Robert Graves' Freudian interpretation of 'Kubla Khan' in 1921, was rejected by J.L. Lowes[1], who was working from an associative theory of imagination. This particular rejection was made in terms of inaccuracy of detail, but Lowes also rejected all such explanations in principle. He believed that he had demonstrated his theory and that the facts which he had disclosed 'counsel caution in the prevalent pursuit of so-called Freudian complexes'.[2] This did not prevent D.W. Harding from presenting a much more fully worked out explanation of *The Ancient Mariner* in terms of depth-psychology in 1963,[3] but

172

meanwhile Maud Bodkin had produced the first Jungian interpretation in *Archetypal Patterns in Poetry*, in the course of which she complained of Lowes' theory as inadequate.[4] She was seconded by George Whalley in *Poetic Process* which asked, 'Is Lowes correct in regarding the memory as chaotic?' and which stated that 'Coleridge and Jung . . . postulate[d] a Collective Unconscious to accommodate [the primordial images which embody archetypal patterns]'.[5] At about the same period E.E. Stoll was denying any possibility of symbolic interpretation for these poems.[6]

Even the more limited attempt to assign values to particular symbols does not produce any agreement. Reviewing recently the symbolic meanings assigned by various critics to the sun and the moon in *The Ancient Mariner*, A. Delson describes the views of G. H. Clarke, Robert Penn Warren, John Beer, and Kenneth Burke as respectively referring the symbols to 'God, the secondary imagination, a neo-Platonic myth, or opium visions', adding his own view that 'if construed as representing nature, their chief cumulative attribute is . . . of an instability so repetitive as to assume treacherous proportions'.[7] Explanations of Kubla's dome include, among many others, poetry of rounded solidity, a breast-like emblem of fulfilment and satisfaction, decadent artistic talent, and a Sacred Tree.[8]

Similarly, though the views of Lowes seem to have been silently scrapped, attempts which begin by ascertaining Coleridge's later views on imagination or symbolism and applying them backwards in time seem no nearer to finality. An interesting case is the triangular disagreement between M.H. Abrams and Earl Wasserman, Paul de Man and Jerome C. Christesen. Paul de Man considers that in philosophy now the symbol 'appears more and more as a special case of figural language in general', and, working onwards in time from the pre-Romantics, offers associative analogy as the proper description of Romantic symbols, rather than the 'more vital form of analogy', involving the domination of mind over the external world, which Wasserman and Abrams believe to be characteristic of Romanticism. He comments:

> Since the assertion of a radical priority of the subject over objective nature is not easily compatible with the poetic praxis of

173

the romantic poets, who all gave a great deal of importance to the presence of nature, a certain degree of confusion reigns.[9]

Jerome C. Christesen in a recent article attempts to resolve this disagreement with the formula that 'Coleridge's allegory is split symbolism'. Calling attention to the phrase in Coleridge's distinction between symbolism and allegory which describes the symbol as 'the translucence of the Eternal in and through the Temporal', he offers an explanation of Coleridge's symbolism in terms of the myth theory of Mircea Eliade, and says that in the symbolism God appears as a sublimity which mocks the earthly things (the symbols) which embody it,[10] a view which, however true Eliade's theory may be, does not seem much related to the other views under discussion. Meanwhile Coleridge's views on the structure of the mind had been brought perhaps as close as they can be to the symbolism of the actual poems by Lorne J. Forstner. Taking an analysis of Coleridge's theory by J.R. de J. Jackson, he adapts it to the geography of *The Ancient Mariner,* producing a diagram in which the Line is the Understanding, the region south of it containing the Imagination and the unconscious, and the region north of it the Reason and the conscious.[11]

In view of these discords, de Man's observation of 'a certain degree of confusion' seems just. This is not to say that one of the various theories may not be true, and certainly not to say that the critical interpretations which embody them are not sensitive and illuminating. Obviously a bald description of the positions held cannot do justice to the complexity and critical power of the interpretations themselves. Nevertheless it does seem that the whole discussion is being conducted in the language of Babel and that the scholarly edifice is not proceeding upwards. It may clarify the situation a little to observe that the arguments are being carried on in at least three different types of language. First there is the language of rhetoric, treating the symbols as figures of speech like, say, the symbols of Yeats. Then there is the language of philosophy (particularly the German philosophy of the period), treating the symbol as relationship between the poet and the world. Finally there is the language of anthropology and psychology, which bases the meaning of the symbols on one of the several theories of myth (among them the Freudian and the Jungian) which are themselves incompatible with each other. It may be worth looking at the uses of these kinds, if only in a classificatory way to discover which of the disputants are mutually unintelligible.

A prior question to that of the meaning of the symbols in the poems is whether there are any symbols in the poems. Much excellent criticism has dealt simply with the human interest in the stories otherwise supernatural or at least romantic and, indeed, interesting more or less literal interpretations (accounting in different ways for those elements) have been offered of 'Kubla Khan' and *The Ancient Mariner*.[12] Moreover, the question raised by J.L. Lowes in *The Road to Xanadu* needs to be faced. Stoll says, of symbolist interpreters generally, 'what should have impressed them is the great critic's re-creation of the poem from its origins . . . . Moreover the critic not only recovers the original materials but, after Coleridge, puts them together again'.[13] In short, if Lowes is accepted, there is not room for symbolism and one is driven to some such view as that of Stoll, that 'it is a matter in short of a convention',[14] or the view held by M.H. Abrams in 1934, that 'the dream quality of *Kubla Khan* cannot be analysed', and that in *The Ancient Mariner* 'a framework of plot was constructed expressly to contain the pre-existent fabric of dream phenomena'.[15] Those who hold symbolist interpretations need to consider whether the sources which Lowes found were the true ones, and whether the chains of looked-up footnotes, each terminating in a phrase or a word which combined to make the images, did in fact take place.[16] But that is matter for another occasion. Certainly the conclusions which seem to emerge from Lowes' demonstration of his theory have been generally ignored by critics who otherwise accept it, and the reason is probably that the non-symbolist interpretations explain much but not enough. They illuminate the human interest but leave the supernatural or at least romantic aspects, which give the poems so much of their fascination, unaccounted for in poetic terms (except convention or opium). They do not present the poem as a unity in all its parts.

Those critics who set out to interpret the symbols of Coleridge's major poetry as simply figures of speech face immediately a serious problem of method. When Yeats interrogated the spirits who provided the material for 'A Vision', they disclaimed any intention of providing a philosophy:

> 'No', was the answer, 'we have come to give you metaphors for poetry.'[17]

Nevertheless they did provide a system which made the metaphors clear. Coleridge provided no such system, while, on the other hand, much of the fascination of his images lies in their very difference from any traditional system of symbols in English poetry. The critic must find some method of validating his interpretation. One way, favoured by Bernard Blackstone in his broadly Jungian book, *The Lost Travellers*, is to examine the currency of the symbols in other Romantic poetry to find Romantic archetypes. This certainly discovers favourite images but whether it discovers common applications is less certain. Thus, to take an instance, Xanadu's caverns and Shelley's cave in *Prometheus Unbound* can both be included under the different parts of the phrase 'tomb-womb', but whether this means that the caverns, with their lifeless ocean, can then be taken as 'symbols of a primeval and unconscious happiness' is another matter.[18] Alternatively, one can examine the individual symbols of the poem, like Elliot B. Gose, who analyses the symbols of *The Ancient Mariner* into their elements of hot and cold, light and dark, and concludes that 'God the Sun [is] the source of life and love and joy' in the poem. How far one is convinced will depend on how far one prefers this to other ways of analysing natural objects. Again, one can begin at the other end and look directly for a scheme which will explain the behaviour of the symbols. Some of the schemes are provided by classical myths which Coleridge might have known; in 'Kubla Khan' the myth of Cybele for Richard Gerber or the myth of Bacchus for Patricia Adair, and in *The Ancient Mariner* the myth of Isis and Osiris for John Beer.[20] Other schemes are provided by ideas which were of importance to Coleridge in his later life, the secondary imagination for Robert Penn Warren or the structure of the mind for Lorne J. Forstner. With so much before us, how to choose? The great value of these schemes is that they provide the critic with a frame for his insights into the poem, but the schemes themselves are all orphans. Not one has been generally adopted and, to vary the figure, the free coinage of explanations has debased the currency.

A different kind of validation is provided by the theories of myth, for these belong in a scientific field and purport to explain the origin and nature of the symbols in myth. G.S. Kirk, in *The Nature of Greek Myths*, treats, under the heading 'Myths as a product of the Psyche', five different such theories, the Freudian, the Jungian, and those of Cassirer, Levi-Strauss and Mircea Eliade.[21] It is worth bearing in mind that he is rather dampening about all of them, but nevertheless his list will make a useful basis for the classification and discussion of the relevant symbolist theories.

Central to Freudian theory is the 'dream-work' of '*condensing* the material of daytime experience, *displacing* its elements, and *representing* it in symbols and images',[22] and thus the theory offers a clear method for symbolic analysts. Nevertheless there has been comparatively little interpretation of Coleridge's poetry along these lines. The reason is, perhaps, implied by D.W. Harding when he distinguishes between 'general psycho-analytic guesswork which may be plausible as a clinical account of Coleridge', and 'handling of the poem itself'.[23] Clearly there is, for criticism, a great difference between a psycho-analysis of the poet using his poem as evidence, and an account of the poem itself which explains its effect on the reader in terms of what Kirk calls 'the manipulation of emotions and experiences at a less than fully conscious level . . . in those myths that plainly bear on social and personal preoccupations'.[24] Moreover the amount of material provided by what we know, from the poems and elsewhere, is as Lowes pointed out,[25] much less than what a clinical psychiatrist would consider satisfactory. Harding dismisses Graves' explanation, which is essentially an analysis of Coleridge's psyche, as, among other things, ham-fisted. He also rejects David Beres' analysis of *The Ancient Mariner* itself as inept, and quotes, without approval, Beres' discovery in the combination of the moon and the snakes of a symbol of the phallic mother. Harding's own tone is moderate and sensible. He finds in the poem 'a private sense of guilt, intese out of all proportion to public rational standards'.[26] (William Empson, on other grounds, also finds neurotic guilt in the poem.[27])

177

Harding considers that 'much of the poem has a symbolical significance that the writer was not aware of', and the main symbol he discusses, the moon, he finds to be in some contexts 'a rather straightforward emblem of maternal assurance', and in others a symbol of 'a less benign aspect of the mother'. But he does not erect any general system of symbols in the poem, and he values the symbolic elements for 'their hint of a direction in which to move rather more than a literal meaning'.[28]

Although Jung's theory is not universally accepted even among psychologists, perhaps particularly among psychologists, the reader of literary criticism will not need a description of it. Indeed the Jungian interpretation of literature has so flourished that it has become almost a separate genre. Jungian analysts do not experience the same difficulties or constraints as the Freudian ones for they do not face any problem in validating their symbols. Though the task of showing how the archetypes work in the poem always remains for each critic to solve, finding them originally is simpler because the stock of symbols is known. Maud Bodkin, George Whalley, Bernard Blackstone and Kathleen Raine may differ in detail but nevertheless they are seeking their archetypes in the same pool. Thus, in 'Kubla Khan', Blackstone finds Beulah, the Sybil, the erotic cave-womb (which is here 'impenetrable'), the father-figure, the insulted god and the Labyrinth.[29] To a selection of these Kathleen Raine would add only the Sacred Tree (represented as both a river and a dome), the Abyss (in Abyssinia) and Apollo's lyre.[30] It makes entrancing reading but it does present problems of communication. Those who believe Jung's theory to be true will be convinced; those who find 'the very idea of archetypes . . . most dubious'[31] will not, and between believers and unbelievers there will always be a bottomless abyss.

Cassirer's theory of mythical consciousness is based on what Kirk calls 'ponderous neo-Kantian epistemology'.[32] It postulates that when the external world 'overcomes a man in sheer immediacy', the subjective becomes objectified and confronts the man as a god or a demon or a symbol. Normally this symbol expresses simply religious awe, though some symbols can have a more complex meaning because of their structure.[33] The most important critic of Coleridge to acknowledge the inspiration of

Cassirer is Albert S. Gerard in *English Romantic Poetry*, in which he sees Cassirer as the fruition of the Romantic theory of the symbol and sets about finding its origin through a careful examination of Coleridge's early poetry. He sees in 'The Eolian Harp' of 1795 'a pantheism which could not but clash with Coleridge's religious belief', that is, with his pious adherence to Christian transcendentalism'.[34] He finds that Coleridge escaped from pantheism by developing a theory of symbolism described in 'Religious Musings', developed in 'The Destiny of Nations', and summarised in the phrase 'counterfeit infinity'. (Gerard's argument suffers a little in cogency from his impression that the 'first draft' of 'The Destiny of Nations' was written after 'Religious Musings', instead of before 'The Eolian Harp'.[35]) In this theory 'the whole of nature and each of its parts are genuine symbols', the corporeal forms themselves have no substance, and the function of the symbols is to refer the beholder to God.

There may be some doubts as to whether this happened, and in quite this way, because, as will appear later, the idea that nature reflects at once both human emotion and God was to be found in Coleridge's poetry and prose some months before he wrote 'The Eolian Harp' (and indeed can be found as far back as Akenside[37]) and because the exact phrase, apostrophising God as Nature's Energy, which made Coleridge later describe 'The Destiny of Nations' (mid 1795) as Unitarian and pantheistic, recurs in 1796 in 'Religious Musings', both times without any qualification.[38] But for our immediate purposes the most important point is that this is a narrowly delimited idea of symbolism and does not seem to provide Gerard with any way into Coleridge's three major poems, on which his only relevant remark is that in *The Ancient Mariner* the images of evil are allegorical.[39] The word images cannot be accidental. If all symbols refer us to God, then evil must be content with mere images and one could have in the same poem symbols of good and images of evil.

Mircea Eliade believes that the purpose of all myths is to evoke the creative era of God or the gods, since 'any tale that restores for a time the mythical past is . . . helping humans to share in the power of the divine actions *in illo tempore*'.[40] Jerome C. Christesen's explanation of Coleridge's symbolism follows

NEW APPROACHES TO COLERIDGE

these lines. He finds that 'Kubla Khan' and *The Ancient Mariner* suggest possible visionary symbols which evoke the Creation either by recreating Paradise or by communicating 'an incredible yet paradigmatic event'. This has been obscured by Coleridge's own suggestions of allegory, as in the glosses to *The Ancient Mariner,* but the true purpose of the symbols is to remind us of 'the Creator *in illo tempore*'. In the symbol Christesen analyses most closely, an ice-scene from a letter of 1799, he finds that 'God appears in the text of the world as he appears in the Book of Job, in order to mock the pretence involved in any symbolical manifestation'.[41] Christesen recognises that the sense in which he uses the word 'symbol' does not apply 'to any literary use of "symbols" in the broad modern sense', but he insists that the sense which he expounds is the only one intended by Coleridge.[42] For those present-day critics who 'unwarily' use the word in a broader sense, confusion is inevitable.

The myth theory of Levi-Strauss does not yet seem to have made any appearance in Coleridge criticism. His method of analysing the variant forms of a myth to bring out its binary structure, and hence its social or personal concern, would not lend itself easily to the analysis of single poems, but an explanation on this basis may yet be found.

This leaves the theories which use the language of the philosophy which Coleridge adopted in his later life. (To apply these to his earlier poetry obviously involves believing that Coleridge anticipated his German contemporaries and only borrowed their words when he needed them for his own ideas.[43]) Coleridge's own later statements about symbolism are not as numerous or concordant as one would wish. As Patricia Ward says, they comprise 'a few brilliant statements which adapt in a meaningful way the symbol as seen by Schelling and Schlegel to the Englishman's own aesthetic theories, but Coleridge the theorist never becomes spokesman for the symbol to the degree with which the Germans were its enthusiasts'.[44]

Some of these statements deal with ordinary senses of the word, as in 'symbols and emblems' or in 'states of inmost being . . . cannot be conveyed save in symbols',[45] but there are two longer passages in which Coleridge develops a special theory. One is 'On Poesy or Art', largely borrowed from Schelling, in

180

which Nature, being already the product of the mind, and therefore sharing our life, speaks to us through symbols, and it is the task of the poet to make Nature still more fully mental. The other is a passage from *The Statesman's Manual* in which Coleridge discusses the symbolism of Scriptural history and describes the symbol as follows:

> A symbol is always characterised by a translucence of the Special in the Individual, or of the General in the Special, or of the Universal in the General; or above all by the translucence of the Eternal in and through the Temporal. It always partakes of the reality which it renders intelligible.[46]

This has produced a variety of elucidations, from the view that it was all a muddle on Coleridge's part, and Coleridge's own unfortunate example of a sail as the symbol for a ship, through the explanation that the symbol must be consubstantial with its conception, to the symbol as an intimate unity between the image and the supersensory totality that the image suggests, and to the symbol as participating in the One Life.[47]

J.V. Baker, in *The Sacred River*, takes the passage in *The Statesman's Manual* to indicate that Coleridge held a symbolist theory of literature, but the symbols he quotes are those found by Robert Penn Warren and others on quite different grounds and they do not seem to have much to do with the theory.[48] Earl R. Wasserman, on the other hand, avoids applying it to literary symbolism. Taking up a position based on Schelling, he says that 'for Coleridge the goal of art is "to make Nature thought and thought Nature"'. This means that what the poet finds in Nature is essentially subjective because 'every object is dead ... it is vital only insofar as the self is viewing itself in the object'. It recognises that this theory cannot be translated into the life of a poem, and that it does not provide a process for the transformation of images into symbols. In his view 'the most important role for Coleridge's epistemology is to provide a dramatic form for a group of poems [for exemplar 'This Lime-Tree Bower My Prison'] in which the self becomes a self by objectifying itself so as to identify finite and infinite'.[49] In other words, it is a theory about the relationship of the poet with

Nature and will be exemplified only in those poems in which the poet sets out to describe that relationship. Now it is true, as J.A. Appleyard and A.S. Gerard point out,[50] that in 1795 Coleridge deemed 'all that meets the bodily sense . . . Symbolical', but his use of the word at that time (and his practice of poetry) does not necessarily have the sense that he was to give to the word twenty years later, after his reading of Schelling and with all Schelling's implications of subjectivity. The sense at this date must be judged from the text of the poems themselves and it is notable that in them Nature employs the human faculties and not vice-versa.[51]

This has been a review of types of theory and many individual critics could not be accommodated, but one theorist who remains is Coleridge himself. The rest of this essay will discuss the views which he held in the first half of his life, as the present writer sees them, but two preliminary points need to be made. The first concerns the distinction which has emerged between the symbol as a relationship between the poet and Nature, which may be called natural symbolism, and the symbol as a figure in a poem, which can be called literary symbolism. Coleridge had views about both kinds. Natural symbolism is described in poems in which the poet records an encounter in which he finds religious meanings in the forms of Nature. It can only become literary symbolism in narrative or other fictional poems when these meanings in the forms of Nature are transferred with them. Literary symbolism on the other hand need not derive its images from Nature, and when it does they can be images which the poet could not possibly have encountered.

The second point concerns Coleridge's religion, about which some curious remarks have been made. Statements that he did not write as a Christian before 1817 or that his poetry of the seventeen-nineties contained 'cheerful godlessness' are as far from the truth as statements that in 1795 he was an orthodox Christian or interested in the defence of the established church.[52] In fact, he was a Unitarian preacher (though not a paid one) until he left for Germany in 1798. He was thus always a Christian, however heretical, and his religion in the seventeen-nineties was strongly biblical as well as strongly philosophical. Of the two pantheisms distinguished by Hegel, he never believed that 'Alles ist Gott' (the a-moral pantheism?) but he did believe the Spinozist or oriental pantheism, that 'das Gottliche nur sei . . . das Wesen der Dinge' (the essence of things).[53] In Coleridge's concept of Nature God played three parts, as the substance behind the shadow, the all-conscious Presence, and the ever-acting Energy in 'The Destiny of Nations', and Nature's essence, mind and energy in 'Religious Musings'. The 'Ode to the Departing Year' shows that his adoption of Berkeley did not essentially alter his belief in God's providential activity in Nature.[54] It is this belief, Christian yet with a powerful stress on Immanence (call it pantheism with Hegel or panentheism with Inge, as you wish) and, as Coleridge said in *Biographia Literaria*,[55] regarding material Nature as essentially spirit, that forms the setting for Coleridge's theory of natural symbolism.

Coleridge's interests in the two kinds of symbolism began at about the same time in mid-1795 but it will be convenient to deal first with natural symbolism. In the *Lectures on Revealed Religion*, delivered in June 1795, Coleridge has several references to this idea.

> The Omnipotent has unfolded to us the Volume of the World, that there we may read the Transcript of himself. In Earth or Air, the meadow's purple stores, the Moon's mild radiance, or the Virgin's form Blooming with rosy smiles, we see portrayed the bright Impressions of the eternal Mind . . . To the philanthropic Physiognomist a Face is beautiful because its Features are the symbols and visible signs of the inward Benevolence or Wisdom—to the pious man all Nature is thus beautiful because its every feature is the Symbol and all its parts the written Language of infinite Goodness and powerful Intelligence.[56]

These are clearly related to the passage he wrote about the same time for 'Joan of Arc':

> For all that meets the bodily sense I deem
> Symbolical, one mighty alphabet
> For infant minds.[57]

There is nothing wholly new in this: the idea that Nature provides both divinely ordained similitudes for human feeling and also converse with God is to be found in Akenside; the idea that it provides an alphabet to be read is in Young; and the application of the word 'symbol' to any special manifestation of God in Nature (though Coleridge generalises it) is in Priestley.[58] As Thomas MacFarland has shown,[59] Coleridge as a thinker worked by agglomerating ideas and he here produced a clear enough theory of the discovery of God in Nature, but there is nothing neo-Kantian about it and it is not new enough to account for the change which Coleridge and Wordsworth brought to English nature poetry. W.K. Wimsatt[60] has suggested that the chief mark of this change is a greater attention to the detail of the landscape together with a greater depth of response on the part of the poet. A probable source of this change would seem to be Hartley's theory (hinted at in the 'Joan of Arc' passage) that all sense impressions were meant to produce eventually theopathy, to train up to God. This combined with his Unitarian belief that God as Nature's Energy was providentially active in Nature in a much more immediate way than the Newtonian watchmaker, would mean that contact with Nature was more than the reading of a volume which had been left open: it would be an encounter with a living spirit intent in teaching himself in every sense impression and one could expect an even greater intensity in the recording of the scene and in the meanings learned. In 1797-98 this sense of contact with a living spirit became even more intense.

Coleridge's acquaintance with what we would now call literary symbolism came with his reading in 1795 of Sir Isaac Newton's *Prophecies of Holy Writ*,[61] and particularly of its second chapter 'Of the Prophetic Language', which detailed a large number of biblical symbols with their allegorical significances, these being usually political or historical. Coleridge jotted one of these symbols in his notebook—a ruler is signified by his riding on a beast—and proceeded to use a number of the others in his poetry between 1795 and the end of 1796, again normally with a political significance. Thus the fogs around the rising sun stand for the attempts to oppress the French Revolution, the fall of stars for the fall of the aristocracy, earthquakes for the ruin of England, whoredom with the Daemon Power for the apostasy of the established church, and the pangs of childbirth for the bringing forth of a new kingdom (in this case Nature brings forth twins, Equality and Peace). Newton's statement that riding in clouds is put for reigning over much people and the movements of clouds for wars produced the images of an English cloud ridden by Oppression and a French ridden by Envy, pursuing each other over the battlefields of Europe.[62] Another of Newton's significances, rain and dew for the graces and doctrines of the Spirit, and defect of rain for spiritual barrenness, may have played a part in *The Ancient Mariner,* if Newton's help was needed with so ancient a symbol.

More significant than these symbols themselves was the scheme they brought with them. The importance of the Apocalypse to Romantic thought has been pointed out more than once.[63] In this case the Apocalyptic prophecies not only linked these symbols but also provided new ones. Coleridge had, for poetical purposes at least, something like a literal belief, as well as a political-allegorical one, in the coming Millennium and this fuelled his interest in Burnet's *The Sacred Theory of the Earth,* which provided a natural explanation for the Apocalypse, and also an interest in those passages of Darwin's poetry which seemed to supplement it. Thus Burnet's rotting ocean of the Last Days was reinforced by Darwin's putrifying and phosphorescent sea to issue as the slimy ocean of *The Ancient Mariner.* Burnet's caverns of the fallen earth found their way into the post-lapsarian Xanadu, while the breezes which Darwin thought might bring the Millenium became the paradisal breezes of Coleridge's poetry.

These last examples bring up the point that in the poetry of 1797-8 the use of these images was no longer as political allegory. They had become charged with deeper, more emotional, and perhaps more personal meaning. The process by which this happened can perhaps be glimpsed in a notebook entry of late 1796,[64] possibly written under the influence of opium. This describes the Second Coming, the central event of the Apocalypse story, with the colours, a hint of the images, and certainly the terror that invest part of *The Ancient Mariner.* The symbolism had ceased to be allegory and had become entwined with Coleridge's own neurotic guilts.

There was one form of symbolism which played its part in the poems of 1797-8 and that is the Gothic mode which formed an emotional symbolism, though not a very intellectual one, for Romantic poetry. Coleridge's main comment on the Gothic romance was that the powers given to evil in it made moral seriousness impossible,[65] but apparently the Gothic of Percy's *Reliques,* particularly 'Sir Cauline', was more acceptable. One of the attractions of the Gothic must have been that, like the vision and the reverie, it freed the poems from the immediate demands of experience and common sense, and allowed the symbols to shape themselves around the inner emotions. Certainly, with the reverie and vision, it marks the difference between the three major poems and the conversation poems and its use by Coleridge was the most important step in its naturalization into English Romantic poetry.

There are limits to what any explication of symbols can do in the criticism of a poem. The great poems of 1797-98 are not puzzle pieces to be rearranged by a new idea: they have been enjoyed for nearly two hundred years, the cental effect of each is in no doubt, and any explication which denies it must be wrong. It is impossible to miss in 'Kubla Khan' the theme of Paradise and the prophet, bard or seer who through the power of joy rebuilds it (even Perdita Robinson, writing to Coleridge in 1800, knew that the poem described 'the New Paradise' and that the dome in this context was 'thy Temple'[66]), or in *The Ancient Mariner* the alternation of agony and joy in a world whose strangeness reflects each, or in *Christabel* Part I (the part written in 1798) the confrontation between innocence and the sinister, and the strangely mixed vision or dream that comes when they touch. For that matter some of the central symbols, Paradise itself, thirst and water, darkness and midnight, are so ancient that they too cannot be missed. Nor can an explication of symbols provide the sort of narrowly-defined meaning that allegory does, for symbols have a generality in their action: Yeats calls them 'shadows thrown upon the intellect'.[67] What an explication of the symbols can do is to make clearer how the poems work, and what is central, even if as an area rather than a line, in their meaning.

What follows is not intended as full analyses of the major poems (these have been given elsewhere[68]) but merely as an indication of the function and importance of these forms of symbolism in the poems. 'Kubla Khan' then is a reverie and a vision on the theme of Paradise, which has always meant, from the very word Eden, pleasure or joy. This much is obvious enough, but Paradise is a complex symbol the parts of which are themselves symbols. There are, in the first place, three states of Paradise, the primal Paradise of *Paradise Lost* Book IV, the fallen Jerusalem haunted by demons of Book I, and the restored Millennial Paradise of *Revelation* with the Temple in the heavens. The fully articulated symbol itself includes the mountain, the fountain, the ravine, the river, the trees and the Dead Sea, (to which can be added Burnet's caverns as a sign of the post-lapsarian state). In the first part of the poem, when Kubla builds his pleasure-dome in a fallen world, it is the interplay of these elements which makes the structure of the poem, while the second half moves from the song of the first Paradise, Mount Abora, to the vision of the restored Paradise. The symbolic meaning to be drawn from this cannot be tied down too exactly, and any reading which stresses the power of joy to create the vision of new Paradise cannot be wholly wrong, but the symbolism suggests that for Coleridge the poet was prophet as well as bard.

In *The Ancient Mariner*, probably written very soon after 'Kubla Khan', all three kinds of symbolism can be found. It begins in the Gothic mode, which provides an everyday world strange enough to harmonise with the story and a medieval voyage in which the marvels can occur and the new knowledge be learned. The marvels themselves are produced by the forces of Nature, and the world of the voyage, though poetically transformed, is the world of natural forces as Coleridge and his contemporaries understood them. Much comes from travel books and from Darwin and even the action of the winds is modelled on contemporary understanding. Nevertheless this is the world of divine Nature, of the divine energy giving its ministrations (severe as they may be) and pouring its influences on the Mariner until he is 'healed and harmonized' by 'love and beauty'[69] in the great paean to the beauty of the world in the fifth part of the poem. But there is another level to the poem and another symbolism, the Apocalyptic. The poem is a mimesis of the Apocalypse, with the burning heat and rotting ocean of the Last Days, the Millennial wind, the rising of the dead, and the singing in heaven. The poem stops this action between the Millennium and the Last Judgement, with the Last Trump and the sea giving up its dead, and so the Mariner is left to relive his experience and ponder his knowledge again and again. The effect of this symbolism is to bring, into what might otherwise have been a poem of pure healing, all Coleridge's neurotic guilt as well as his sense of release into joy, and to give the poem sombre depth as well as ecstasy.

In *Christabel* Part I, the Gothic structure is provided by the two figures from 'Sir Cauline', Christabel, the daylight heroine of that poem, and the eldrich lady who appears by moonlight. Their relationship in *Christabel* is expressed by the metaphors of false mother and child, and of midnight anti-marriage, but the symbolism which surrounds them is symbolism of Nature, and it is Nature with a difference. The delayed spring, the rejoicing owls, the green parasites, the mastiff who howls at midnight and a shroud, belong to sinister aspects of the world and they attach themselves to Geraldine. They raise profound questions about the goodness of nature, and it is a pity that when Christabel had dreamed that strange dream that promised to reconcile all, she awoke in 1800 to a very ordinary Gothic romance in the second part.

There is a postscript to this. In 1802, in making a distinction between Imagination and Fancy, Coleridge decided that though the Greek religion did not progress beyond Fancy, the Hebrew poets were poets of Imagination,[70] whose work participated in the One Life. In Wordsworth's hands this idea became, in *The Excursion*, the idea that all ancient religions (even, at times, the Greek) were intuitions of the religion of Nature. From there it passed to the younger poets to provide in mythology a means of expressing their sense of the world and of man as a play of forces and influences, and there is a direct line to be traced between Coleridge's letter of 1802, and such poems as *Manfred, Prometheus Unbound* and *Hyperion*. Thus Coleridge played a seminal part in the development of four modes of Romantic symbolism - the symbolism of Nature, apocalyptic, Gothic and mythological symbolism. This is an achievement which should not be obscured either by his own later mystifications on the subject, or those of his latter-day critics.

NOTES AND REFERENCES

1 J.L. Lowes, *The Road to Xanadu* (Boston, 1927), 545-48.
2 *ibid.*, 366.
3 D.W. Harding, *Experience into Words* (1963).
4 Maud Bodkin, *Archetypal Patterns in Poetry* (1934), 40.
5 G. Whalley, *Poetic Process* (1953), 65, 169.
6 E.E. Stoll, 'Symbolism in Coleridge', *PMLA* (1948).
7 A. Delson, 'The Symbolism of the Sun and the Moon in The Rhyme of the Ancient Mariner', *Texas Studies in Language and Literature* (1974), 709.
8 G. Wilson Knight, 'Coleridge's Divine Comedy', in *English Romantic Poets*, ed. M.H. Abrams (1960), 164; H. House, *Coleridge*, 1953, 118; G. Yarlott, *Coleridge and the Abyssinian Maid* (1967), 141; Kathleen Raine, 'Traditional Symbolism in *Kubla Khan*', *Sewanee Review* (1964), 637.
9 P. de Man, 'The Rhetoric of Temporality', in *Interpretation*, ed. C.S. Singleton, (Baltimore, 1969), 176, 179, 180.
10 J.C. Christesen, 'The Symbol's Errant Allegory: Coleridge and his Critics', *English Literary History* (1976), 651.
11 L.J. Forstner, 'Coleridge's "Ancient Mariner" and the Case for Justifiable Mythocide: An Argument on Psychological, Epistemological and Formal Grounds', *Criticism* (1976), 225.
12 Elizabeth Schneider, *Coleridge, Opium and Kubla Khan* (New York, 1966), 241 ff.; W. Empson and D. Pirie, *Coleridge's Verse* (1972), 35 ff.
13 Stoll, *op. cit.*, 224.
14 *ibid.*, 225.
15 M.H. Abrams, *The Milk of Paradise* (Cambridge, Mass., 1934), 46, 36.
16 For one doubter see N. Fruman, *Coleridge the Damaged Archangel* (1972), 119.
17 W.B. Yeats, *Selected Prose*, ed. A.N. Jeffares (1964), 235.
18 B. Blackstone, *The Lost Travellers* (1962), 207.
19 E.B. Gose, Jr., 'Coleridge and the Luminous Gloom', *PMLA* (1960), 240.
20 R. Gerber, 'Keys to *Kubla Khan*', *English Studies* (1963); Patricia M. Adair, *The Waking Dream* (1967), 122 ff.; J. Beer, *Coleridge the Visionary* (1959), 115 ff.
21 G.S. Kirk, *The Nature of Greek Myths* (1974), 69-94.
22 *ibid.*, 72.
23 Harding, *op. cit.*, 67.
24 Kirk, *op. cit.*, 72-3.
25 Lowes, *op. cit.*, 366.
26 Harding, *op. cit.*, 65, 59.
27 Empson, *op. cit.*, 39.
28 Harding, *op. cit.*, 71, 87, 89.
29 Blackstone, *op. cit.*, 64, 46, 179, 207, 180, 232.
30 Raine, *op. cit.*, 636-37, 638, 639.
31 Kirk, *op. cit.*, 77.
32 *ibid.*, 266.

33 *ibid.*, 80.
34 A.S. Gerard, *English Romantic Poetry* (Berkeley, 1968), 13, 47, 42.
35 *ibid.*, 45.
36 *ibid.*, 61.
37 See note 58 below.
38 'The Destiny of Nations', l.461, 'Religious Musings', l.49. Cf. Gerard, *op. cit.*, 49, where he discusses the pantheistic implications of identifying the forms of nature with spiritual energy.
39 Gerard, *op. cit.*, 35.
40 Kirk, *op. cit.*, 63-4.
41 Christesen, *op. cit.*, 644, 645, 650.
42 *ibid.*, 642. Christesen is generalising a remark by M.H. Abrams which Abrams presumably restricted to *The Statesman's Manual*, rightly in view of Coleridge's many other remarks on symbolism.
43 R.L. Brett, 'Coleridge's Theory of the Imagination', *Essays and Studies* (1949), 88; Gerard, *op. cit.*, 13.
44 Patricia Ward, 'Coleridge's Critical Theory of the Symbol', *Texas Studies in Language and Literature* (1966), 32.
45 S.T. Coleridge, *Miscellanea, Aesthetic and Literary* (1885), 249; *BL*, ii. 120.
46 S.T. Coleridge, *Collected Works* (Princeton, 1969 -), vi. 30.
47 Fruman, *op. cit.*, 204-5; R. Wellek, *A History of Modern Criticism* (1955), ii. 174; W.J. Bate, *Coleridge* (New York, 1968), 163; de Man, *op. cit.*, 174, 176; Gerard, *op. cit.*, 89.
48 J.V. Baker, *The Sacred River* (Louisiana State U.P., 1957), 104-11.
49 E.R. Wasserman, 'The English Romantics: The Grounds of Knowledge', *Studies in Romanticism* (1964), 29, 30, 31.
50 J.A. Appleyard, *Coleridge's Philosophy of Literature* (Cambridge, Mass., 1965), 49; Gerard, *op. cit.*, 61.
51 'This Lime-Tree Bower my Prison', ll.61-4.
52 S. Potter, *Coleridge and STC* (1935), 232; D.G. James, *The Romantic Comedy* (1948), 197; Gerard, *op. cit.*, 42; Brett, *op. cit.*, 78.
53 D.W. Hegel, *Samtliche Werke* (Stuttgart, 1959), xv. 110. Coleridge once made a similar distinction himself in *BL*, ii. 112-3.
54 'The Destiny of Nations', ll.23, 460, 461; 'Religious Musings', l.49; 'Ode to the Departing Year', l.94 app. crit.
55 i. 91.
56 S.T. Coleridge, *Collected Works*, i. 94, 158.
57 'The Destiny of Nations', ll.18-20. In 'Religious Musings', ll. 9-14, Coleridge describes Jesus of Nazareth as a symbol of God, connecting this to natural symbolism by the Unitarian explanation of such texts as John xiv. 9, 'He that hath seen me hath seen the Father'. Cf. J. Priestley, *Theological and Miscellaneous Works*, ed. J.T. Rutt (1817), ii. 465, 451.
58 *The Pleasures of Imagination* (1744), I. 99-108, III. 279-86, 629-33; *Night Thoughts*, Night Nine l. 167; J. Priestley, *Matter and Spirit* (1782), 148.
59 T. McFarland, *Coleridge and the Pantheist Tradition* (1969), 29 ff.
60 W.K. Wimsatt, *The Verbal Icon* (New York, 1958), 108-9.

61 Sir Isaac Newton, *Opera*, ed. S. Horsley (1779), vol. v.
62 'The Destiny of Nations', ll.448-50, 'Religious Musings', ll.309-14, 320-22, 329-34, Ode to the Departing Year', ll.33-7 app. crit., 'The Destiny of Nations', ll.421-37 and app. crit.
63 M.H. Abrams, *Natural Supernaturalism* (New York, 1971); H.W. Piper, *Nature and the Supernatural in "The Ancient Mariner"* (Armidale, 1956); *The Active Universe* (1962).
64 *CN*, i. 273.
65 *Coleridge's Miscellaneous Criticism*, ed. T.M. Raysor (1936), 371.
66 M. Robinson, *Poems* (1804), i. 226-28.
67 W.B. Yeats, *Selected Criticism*, ed. A.N. Jeffares (1964), 50.
68 H.W. Piper, 'The Two Paradises of *Kubla Khan*', *Review of English Studies* (1976); '*The Ancient Mariner:* Biblical Allegory, Poetic Symbolism and Religious Crisis', *Southern Review* (Adelaide), 1977; 'The Disunity of *Christabel*', *Essays in Criticism* (1978).
69 'The Dungeon', ll.29-30.
70 *CL*, ii. 865-66.

11

Coleridge and Wordsworth: Influence and Confluence

by JOHN BEER

In recent times the question of 'influence', formerly a concept taken so much for granted as to be virtually unexamined, has been opened up in a new and interesting way. Following Walter Jackson Bate's *The Burden of the Past and the English Poet*, which described the problems experienced by poets in writing when everything seemed already to have been said, Harold Bloom's *The Anxiety of Influence* read the same situation in Oedipal terms, each poet being seen as a son who was afraid of being consumed by his father and who asserted himself by 'misreading' his predecessors, to make a 'strong' text of his own.[1]

Bloom ranged widely in his discussion of the question; he looked both narrowly at Wordsworth's relationship with Milton, as shown in 'Home at Grasmere' and his sonnet to Milton, and broadly at Oscar Wilde, whom he saw as drawing upon the whole of English Romantic literature. His most extended study of a single author, however, took place in an essay published separately and devoted to Coleridge, a prime instance for him of the potentially great poet who becomes disabled through the anxiety of influence.[2] After showing how the early poem 'Religious Musings' was virtually taken over by Milton, he took his reader through Coleridge's address to his child at the end of 'Frost at Midnight' (seen as a misreading of Eve's address to Adam), the element of lust in 'Kubla Khan'

192

and 'Christabel' (a 'counter-sublime' to Milton's), 'Dejection' (a misreading of 'Lycidas') and 'To William Wordsworth' (seen as assimilating Wordsworth's *Prelude* to *Paradise Lost*); he concluded by tracing a negative sublime in 'Limbo' and 'Ne Plus Ultra'. Coleridge's mistake, however, had been not that he allowed himself to be influenced by Milton, but that he did not then wrestle hard enough. Had he done so, he might have produced a very strong text indeed; instead, he had turned aside to become preoccupied with the 'Organic Analogue', a less satisfactory mode of proceeding.

That there is an important truth in this interpretation cannot be doubted. It ought to be examined closely, however, before being accepted without qualification. Coleridge's anxiety, for example, has been documented and discussed by several authors, including David Beres and Thomas McFarland.[3] But anxiety can take many forms, and in Coleridge's case it might be said that he suffered less from an anxiety *of* influence than an anxiety *to be* influenced—that he repeatedly leant towards strong characters in the hope that they would steady his course. In his first year at Cambridge this role was undertaken by his friend Middleton;[4] afterwards, as Anthony Harding has pointed out, it was assigned in succession to Southey and to Thomas Poole. To Southey he wrote reproachfully after their rupture: 'I did not only venerate you for your own Virtues, I prized you as the Sheet Anchor of mine'; and to Poole he wrote a year or two later as 'the man in whom *first* and in whom alone, I had felt an *anchor!*'[5] Towards Wordsworth he felt an even greater respect, agreeing with Poole that he was 'the greatest Man, he ever knew' and describing him as 'the only man, to whom *at all times* & in *all modes of excellence* I feel myself inferior'.[6] 'The Giant Wordsworth' (as he also called him[7]) was to prove for a time his most successful support as a poet.

If there was an 'anxiety' of Bloom's kind in the Wordsworth-Coleridge relationship, it was probably more on Wordsworth's side than on Coleridge's—though it was hardly Oedipal. Wordsworth's poetry benefited immeasurably from the stimulus of Coleridge's speculations, which constantly opened new perspectives in his dealings with the past; yet he was unwilling to acknowledge his debt publicly[8] except in very general terms—and probably did not even notice how much he owed to his friend. If Coleridge had a fault, by contrast, it was — as Poole charged[9] — one of 'prostration' before Wordsworth. This kind of self-subordinating anxiety eventually became inhibiting to him as a poet.

My purpose here, however, is not to discuss such questions in detail, or to argue again the question of Coleridge's unacknowledged borrowings and the kind of anxiety they suggest (though more remains to be said on that subject) but to turn the discussion in a different direction by pointing out that for some periods of his life Coleridge was relatively free from anxiety, and that such periods should be looked at as steadily as those in which anxiety was prominent. One such period began in 1797 and continued for two or three years: its ending was signalled in March 1801, when he wrote of his poetic imagination as being dead and claimed that Wordsworth, by showing him what true poetry was, had made him know that he himself was no poet.[10] The period between, during which most of his major poems were written, was also his least Miltonic.

My own interpretation of the phenomenon, then, would take its point of departure from Bloom's basic premises but develop them rather differently. The influence of Milton which proved detrimental in poems such as 'Religious Musings' was, I would argue, the influence of that Milton who wished to establish a theocracy based upon the traditional Law of God. Coleridge's wrestling with this Milton took place centrally—and almost unconsciously, it seems—in his writing of 'Kubla Khan', where the very language can be seen as coming to affirm the visionary Milton at the expense of the moralizing Milton.[11] Just as Blake thought that the antinomian energies of Milton caused him to be 'of the devil's party without knowing it', so 'Kubla Khan' bends Milton's mythology towards the service of a different God from the orthodox Christian one. After a few years there would be a return to a more conventional Milton, but in the meantime Coleridge had so completely overcome the legalistic power of his predecessor that he did not need to wrestle with that any further. Instead he could draw the visionary Milton into his service when he needed to and for the rest be free to explore new fields.

Were this the whole story, however, Milton would simply have given place to Wordsworth as chief influence. Yet in the years immediately following, and in spite of Coleridge's deep respect, there is surprisingly little evidence of such dominance over Coleridge's writing. Instead, the two poets are to be seen collaborating and working side by side as equal partners. They had found a *modus vivendi* which allowed each to flourish in his own way while they discussed eagerly and intensely the possibility of a new kind of poetry. In addition this temporary mode of cross-influence, not disabling but productive, helped them to discuss the question of influence itself. And at both levels they were evolving a language and imagery which are relevant to the whole question under discussion.

I have maintained elsewhere[12] that one of the most effective means of intellectual exploration for Romantic writers lay in the exploitation of 'unstable images' — images where the relationship between the literal and metaphorical meanings is itself left in question. In the case of 'influence' we have a word where unstable imagery is built into the very word itself. Bloom has made much of the word 'influenza', which means, traditionally, an astral sickness; as long as one is dealing with the anxiety of influence that metaphor holds. But in its original root, of course, the word means no more than an in-flow, and it is that larger, less dramatic concept that evidently appealed most to Coleridge and Wordsworth. At this time, as they contemplated the state of society and pondered how to ameliorate it, the sickness that concerned them lay in human nature, as revealed in political actions, and they looked to 'influence' as a positive means of therapy. The French Revolution had proved inefficacious as a remedy for society's ills; but if one could not heal human nature by violent change, were there not perhaps forces in nature herself that might assist by way of influence? For a time they talked of possible beneficial inflows from the world of inanimate life. Wordsworth's lines,

> One impulse from a vernal wood
> May teach you more of man,
> Of moral evil and of good,
> Than all the sages can . . .[13]

are matched by Coleridge's lines about the possible power of nature to heal the criminal:

> Thou pourest on him thy soft influences

195

Thy sunny hues, fair forms, and breathing sweets,
Thy melodies of woods, and winds, and waters,
Till he relent, and can no more endure
To be a jarring and a dissonant thing
Amid this general dance and minstrelsy . . .[14]

Unless one could wholeheartedly believe in such powers of influx, however, (and it is clear that sentiments such as these were intended as dramatic and exploratory, not as affirmations carrying the poet's personal endorsement) the question of influence must be taken further back, into the depths of human nature itself. As Bloom himself maintains, the anxiety of influence is concerned ultimately with factors such as Goethe's 'the energy, the force, the will'.[15] It is also, and necessarily, concerned with fluency in all its manifestations. And as we begin to examine the last factor we see that that, in particular, holds a central place in the imagery of the two poets.

Some existing studies, particularly of Wordsworth, bear closely on the theme. M.H. Abrams, for example, has discussed the image of the 'correspondent breeze' and Colin Clark has discussed the rhetorical part played by such correspondences in poems such as 'Tintern Abbey'.[16] We may still find room for further exploration, however, as with one particular area of symbolism—which happens to suit our present context aptly.To consider the nature of fluency as a fact of human nature was to invoke almost automatically an imagery of flowing water. I want to suggest that the existence of such a concern did in fact affect the way that these two poets used such images, even when they might seem simply to be writing about the natural world and that it is therefore always worth inspecting any mention of fountains, brooks, streams and rivers for signs of such further significances.

They were not, obviously, the first to make emblematic use of such imagery. The fountain or stream, employed to a moral end, was common enough in previous poetry. But in those earlier usages there was a casual, disengaged quality: there was no sign that the writer had seen his image as more than a hook on which to hang an idea. Thomson's *Castle of Indolence*, published in 1748, contains a typical example:

From virtue's fount the purest joys outwell,

Sweet rills of thought that cheer the conscious soul;
While vice pours forth the troubled streams of hell,
The which, howe'er disguised, at last with dole
Will through the tortured breast their fiery torrent roll.[17]

The basic imagery here seems to derive from classical mythology, with its apparatus of heavenly and hellish streams. There is a not dissimilar use of it in Coleridge's 'Religious Musings'.[18] But when we turn to Coleridge we also find that even an early rhetorical usage could bear the marks of further consideration. Writing his long and indignant letter of reproach to Southey in 1795 after the collapse of the Pantisocratic scheme, he went on to voice his faith that 'however foul your Stream may run here, yet that it will filtrate & become pure in its subterraneous Passage to the Ocean of Universal Redemption'.[19] (One senses the bitter pleasure that Coleridge takes in using this vivid and forceful image — an image of a kind which he had discussed with Southey during their collaboration together.[20])

Already, in that use of the image, there is a side-glance from traditional emblematisation to the world of actual nature and its processes, one reason for which can be traced in the accidents of local upbringing. Both Wordsworth and Coleridge had the fortune to be brought up in landscapes which were honeycombed by springs and streams. One could not grow up in the Lake District without being aware of water flowing and pouring on all sides — often from seemingly inexhaustible sources. In Somerset and Devonshire, similarly, springs, streams and underground rivers were everywhere present. In Coleridge's own birthplace at Ottery St Mary there were two such springs, one of which (students of 'Kubla Khan' may be interested to know) rose near a house with the name of 'Paradise'. When he later came to live in Nether Stowey, a stream, the 'dear Gutter of Stowey' as he once called it,[21] flowed down the street past his house.

Such local phenomena were the subject of scientific investigation. In 1797, the very year in which 'Kubla Khan' was most probably composed,[22] Richard Polwhele published his large *History of Devonshire,* which included a long section on the Devonshire streams and the havoc which they sometimes wrought when they overflowed. And Polwhele's discussion reveals (as we may also learn from other contemporary writers) that the working of springs was at that time still a matter of considerable mystery:

> It was supposed by Dr Halley that springs are produced by vapour: and this hath long been the popular notion. Yet many of our modern philosophers are of opinion, that perpetual springs are derived from the sea, by ducts and cavities running thence through the bowels of the earth, like veins and arteries in the human body; and that the sea itself acts like a hydraulic machine to force and protrude its waters through those cavities, to a considerable inland distance.[23]

Polwhele was a member of the Society of Gentlemen at Exeter, for which Coleridge helped prepare a paper during one of his university vacations;[24] Archdeacon Hole, another member of the Society, was also interested in springs and their workings. There were various further reasons why Wordsworth and Coleridge should have been attracted to the question, most of them having to do with contemporary interest in the topic of the 'active universe'. The suggestion which I want to pursue here, however, is that they also found in this mysterious process of rivers and springs an unusually apt model for their study of fluency in human nature. That model offered the sense of dual process: on the one hand the simple linear progression of the stream flowing into the river, the river augmenting itself into a stately flood and finally being swallowed up in the sea, on the other the complementary awareness that this was not the whole of the process—that one must also take into account the mysterious and ebullient forces which were always making that simple progression possible by a cyclical and renewing process that followed a different pattern altogether. This model, applied to the processes of human nature, might transform the time-dominated consciousness of eighteenth-century man into something altogether more complex.

The imagery of springs and rivers already available from eighteenth-century poetic tradition, was, as we have noted, a generalized and simple one. It was fairly clearly Coleridge who strengthened that tradition by drawing on the symbolic usages to be found in writers such as Jacob Boehme and the neoplatonists, where nature was viewed as a system of energizing centres, manifested in the illumination of the mind and the reinvigoration of the heart.[25] Rediscovered at the end of a century in which belief and scientific law had become steadily more dominant, it offered an invitation to construct a human philosophy based on the idea not of a mechanical universe, gradually running down into death and darkness, but of a 'universe of life', full of self-renewing resources.

I have discussed elsewhere the relevance of such a paradigm to 'Kubla Khan'; it is one that is half figured in Milton's description of the rivers of Paradise:

> There was a place,
> Now not, though Sin, not Time, first wraught the change,
> Where *Tigris* at the foot of Paradise
> Into a Gulf shot under ground, till part
> Rose up a Fountain by the Tree of Life;
> In with the River sunk, and with it rose
> *Satan* involv'd in rising Mist . . .[26]

Milton's lines invite an allegorical reading, suggesting as they do that Satan's self-involvement with a fountain that sprang up near the Tree of Life was itself a foreshadowing of the process of sin that he was introducing there, and which would destroy that very fountain. A Coleridge who was already alert to the imagery of springs would be likely to spot this allegorical point and develop it still further as he contemplated the fact that it was the sense of life itself that was becoming lost to modern man. On such a reading, Kubla Khan, constructing a pleasure dome near the river that ran through vast caverns to a sunless sea, was embarked on an enterprise that would in the end simply confirm the world of death in which he lived, since the energies of appropriation would, in less propitious circumstances, turn themselves readily into energies of destruction. Such a world-view ignored the fountainous nature of the true creative act where a work of art was not a construction created by the decree of a tyrant but a bonus in the world of life, produced effortlessly by the action of true genius. This mythological element in the poem would further suggest that the current 'Gothic' view of the self, which envisaged the unconscious as a vast and horrific series of caverns surrounding the inevitable flow of the human existence to darkness and death, held sway over the eighteenth-century mind only because that had lost touch with any sense of the self-renewing life impulse which could at any time break into the time-ridden consciousness with revivifying power.

Wordsworth uses an equivalent imagery in his poetry as when he says, speaking of his youth, 'Caverns there were within my mind which sun/Could never penetrate'.[27] In his work, however, such images are haunted by the Coleridgean significance without quite embodying it. The springs and streams which appear everywhere resonate in his mind with possible symbolic implications but are either constituted so firmly in the natural world that the reader might miss those implications altogether or absorbed into a parallel metaphor (as when, in the 1799 *Prelude,* he speaks of the 'spots of time' as possessing a 'fructifying virtue' by which our minds are 'nourished, and invisibly repaired'[28]). It is to Coleridge that we turn for more explicit statements—though it may also be remarked that in giving them he can sometimes offer descriptions of the natural world which match anything that Wordsworth has to offer. So one finds him in 1799 observing the movement of an eddy in a stream and delighted by the fact that it takes the form of a flower:

> The white Eddy-rose that blossom'd up against the stream in the scollop, by fits & starts, obstinate in resurrection—It *is the life* that we live.[29]

This sight of a movement of energy which yet flowers into form has become for him an emblem of the life-process itself. Again, one finds him observing the gentle action of a spring in a bed of sand:

> The spring with the little tiny cone of loose sand ever rising & sinking at the bottom, but it's surface without a wrinkle . . .[30]

He goes on to append the initials of William and Dorothy Wordsworth, Mary and Sara Hutchinson: by now the image of life has also become suggestive of the working of a peaceful common life between friends.

This brings us to one of the most intricate parts of the investigation, for there are times when the imagery of spring and stream on the one hand and of heart and blood-stream are so intimately inter-related as to suggest that Wordsworth and Coleridge were seeking for a total rapprochement which might also throw light on the workings of the subconscious—as if, indeed, they thought that an important element of the work of the subconscious might actually take place in the bloodstream itself, rather in the way that D.H. Lawrence was to suggest a century later. It was nothing new to speak of sensations being felt in the heart in that age of sensibility; but Wordsworth, in 'Tintern Abbey', speaks of 'Sensations sweet,/Felt in the blood, and felt along the heart': a striking usage, which suggests that he is identifying the whole process of a sensation, its first springing impulse and then its after-existence in time with the process of blood springing in the heart and then passing into the bloodstream. Nor should one forget the description of the baby that is still at one with the life of its mother in Book Two of *The Prelude*:

> Along his infant veins are interfused
> The gravitation and the filial bond
> Of Nature that connect him with the world.[31]

So far as this range of ideas formed part of the thinking of the two poets, it belonged to the most adventurous period of their speculations together. But there was a less controversial area of the speculation which they could also pursue. If, as one was almost bound to do in their time, one regarded thinking as a process of association, in the way that Hartley had laid down, the idea of a streamy process was bound to form part of that conception, as providing the medium within which any process of association must necessarily take place; and one could not study that for long without becoming aware of elements in the whole process which seemed devoid of conscious control. Coleridge, it will be remembered, speaks in a later notebook of the '*streamy* Nature of Association, which Thinking = Reason, curbs and rudders'[32] (rather as if he were thinking at one and the same moment of a horse galloping in a current of air and a boat sailing in a stream of water). One would also become aware that this process of streamy association continued during sleep and more especially during dreams, a fact which never ceased to intrigue Coleridge.[33] So one is not far from the concept of two levels of consciousness in the body, the one controlled, exercised by day as we make our way through a time-governed existence, the other rolling on perpetually and behaving more like an underground river or spring, able, among other things, to well up in memories taken from any point in the time-stream of the past. And such a concept does indeed seem relevant to the kind of thinking that we find in *The Prelude*.

A full exploration of the imagery of fountains, streams, rivers and the sea in Wordsworth's autobiographical poem is beyond our present scope: I would simply mention the range of metaphoric and speculative reference which seems to be involved, ranging from the suggestion that the perpetual sound of moving water from the River Derwent flowing past his father's house by night and day might have had a palpable and physical effect upon his growth as a poet to the overt imagery of a brook or river which he applies to the composition of the poem itself at various stages. He can use the imagery in an almost totally conventional moral manner, as when he writes of his former nurse's 'clear but shallow stream of piety'; he can also use it as a *leit-motif*—a scene-setting element for the description of an event in which the subliminal forces of his personality were powerfully brought into play. The diversity of usage might in itself be said to correspond with the versatility of the subconscious powers involved.

It is at the end of *The Prelude,* however, when Wordsworth is writing of the Intellectual Love which he claims as at once his major theme and inspiration that the image of spring and stream finally come into their own:

> This faculty hath been the moving soul
> Of our long labour: we have traced the stream
> From darkness, and the very place of birth
> In its blind cavern, whence is faintly heard
> The sound of waters; followed it to light
> And open day; accompanied its course
> Among the ways of Nature, afterwards
> Lost sight of it bewildered and engulphed:
> Then given it greeting as it rose once more
> With strength, reflecting in its solemn breast
> The works of man and face of human life;
> And lastly, from its progress have we drawn
> The feeling of life endless, the great thought

By which we live, Infinity and God.[34]

Many further occurrences of the imagery can be traced in Wordsworth's writings, sometimes in poems written many years later; the resonances involved seem to have haunted him for the rest of his life. But it is to *The Prelude* that one returns for the most wide-ranging and at the same time most central usages; and it is there equally that the stimulus of Coleridge's speculative mind is most fully acknowledged. That stimulus seems to affect not only the ideas in the poem, but even the very mode of construction. Early in his enquiry Wordsworth writes of the difficulties which it involves:

> Who knows the individual hour in which
> His habits were first sown, even as a seed,
> Who that shall point, as with a wand and say
> 'This portion of the river of my mind
> Came from yon fountain'?[35]

And having asked that question, in the second book, he goes on immediately to address Coleridge as 'one/More deeply read in thy own thoughts'; one to whom 'The unity of all has been reveal'd'.[36]

Talking about the nature of poetic process many years later, Coleridge wrote:

> The common end of all *narrative*, nay, of *all*, Poems is to convert a *series* into a *Whole*: to make those events, which in real or imagined History move on in a *strait* Line, assume to our Understandings a *circular* motion—the snake with it's Tail in it's Mouth.[37]

In a recent essay on *The Prelude*, M.H. Abrams has suggested that when we consider the shape of that poem as a whole, a circularity of form emerges.[38] This is, I believe, true: the onward progress of the poem is accompanied by a subterranean cyclical sense which rounds itself finally in the last book of the poem—Coleridge's snake with its tail in its mouth. And perhaps the total process is more complicated and subtle than that. It may be that in order to grasp the full significance of the poem's shape we ought to pursue all the implications of the stream image that Wordsworth himself used during his poem's progress: not only the constant return to original springs, but eddyings in the current,[39] windings back towards the source, the influx of new currents. Such an approach not only helps to thwart any over-schematic version of the poem's shape and symbolism but directs attention to Wordsworth's interpretation of his own growth as a poet. The straight line always resolving itself into a circle insistently dominates and contains lesser processes; it is also of the nature of his own life as he has here presented it that even while flowing on in straightforward progress through time it has found itself inexorably penetrated at every point by memories which reinforce it, cyclically, with a sense of its original springs. The poem was dedicated and partly addressed to Coleridge, but it was also addressed, at least in apostrophe, to that 'Wisdom and Spirit of the Universe' which he characterized (in a formula every word of which deserves to be attentively weighed) as

> Thou Soul that art the eternity of thought,
> That giv'st to forms and images a breath
> And everlasting motion . . .[40]

Whether or not this way of writing *The Prelude* is to be regarded as successful so far as the reader is concerned, it is clear that it worked for Wordsworth himself as providing a means of approaching questions of power and influence as they had worked, multifariously, in the course of his own growth. It offered a way of contemplating their direct action in earlier years:

> I sought not then
> Knowledge; but craved for power, and power I found
> In all things; nothing had a circumscribed
> And narrow influence; but all objects, being
> Themselves capacious, also found in me
> Capaciousness and amplitude of mind;
> Such is the strength and glory of our youth![41]

It also worked, a good deal more intricately, as he came to contemplate the decline of such direct influence and to consider the processes by which he had been enabled to preserve a consistency with his original self. Sometimes he saw that consistency as maintained through a revisitation of the visionary power: and at such times the presence of streams, real or imagined, is often an important feature. The long vision of apocalyptic power in the Simplon Pass took place against such a landscape:

> The brook and road
> Were fellow-travellers in this gloomy pass,
> And with them did we journey several hours
> At a slow step.[42]

The encounter with the discharged soldier took place in a scene where the road's surface

> glittered in the moon
> And seemed before my eyes another stream
> Creeping with silent lapse to join the brook
> That murmured in the valley.[43]

The imagery of an accompanying stream is also used forcefully and more overtly to describe the influence upon him of Dorothy, who

> now speaking in a voice
> Of sudden admonition — like a brook
> That does but *cross* a lonely road, and now
> Seen, heard and felt, and caught at every turn,
> Companion never lost through many a league—
> Maintained for me a saving intercourse
> With my true self . . .[44]

With this praise of Dorothy for providing an intercourse with his 'true self', the stream image earlier associated with the actual voice of Derwent and other brooks heard in childhood emerges as metaphor for an influence assisting the continuity of a life, the consistency of which has not been that of a road. A striking and similar use of the image is to be found in the Essay on Epitaphs, where he describes the ideal epitaph-writer as one who can persuade the reader that he has mounted 'to the sources of things' and penetrated

> the dark cavern from which the river that murmurs in every one's ear has flowed from generation to generation.[45]

There is also a strong suggestion that that murmur could sometimes be powerfully reinforced. When the climactic vision on Snowdon came, an important element in it was

the roar of waters, torrents, streams
Innumerable, roaring with one voice![46]

Close attention to such passages throws a good deal of light on Wordsworth's use of water imagery throughout his poetry; here we may simply draw attention to the striking (and very characteristic) reversal of this process, by which he later echoes such thinking without quite reiterating it, through making literal what was formerly a metaphor. In the Duddon Sonnets, the image of the companion stream which he had used for Dorothy becomes actualized in the presence of the Duddon, as he traces it from its springs to the sea. There are still metaphorical associations, worked out in the separate sonnets that make up the sequence, but the device of addressing himself to the stream itself allows Wordsworth to explore them without such strong hints of further metaphysical implications as haunted his earlier usages of the imagery.

It is no accident, perhaps, that the Duddon Sonnets are better in quality than much of Wordsworth's later poetry. In those years his verse too often exhibits strength without power, as if he needed some reincursion of former influences before his poetic gift could function resonantly. This falling away, however, he seems hardly to have noticed, except in the Immortality Ode. Coleridge, by contrast, was fond of lamenting that he had 'power without strength'. His sense of weakness, which had informed the repeated attempts to find a 'steadying influence', and often resulted in over-idealization of a current friend, had continued to be exhibited in expressions of overwhelming outflow towards Wordsworth, where the imagery of fluency emerges in impossibly generous terms:

> To W[ordsworth] in the progression of Spirit . . . — O that my Spirit purged by Death of its Weaknesses, which are alas! my *identity* might flow into *thine*, & live and act in thee, & be Thou.[47]

Such a forfeiture of identity, particularly when directed towards a man so mindful of his own selfhood as Wordsworth, was not only inauthentic at the human level (he records elsewhere an 'anguish of involuntary Jealousy' towards Wordsworth in a dream)[48] but self-disabling. Coleridge was later to wager bitterly (and wrongly, as it turned out) that Wordsworth

206

would, if he published *The Prelude*, leave out certain parts which he owed to Coleridge's thought; he would also complain that the Wordsworths had thwarted every effort of his to 'roll onward in a distinct current of [his] own'.[49]

Wordsworth, decidedly separate, used the same imagery, but to circumvent the problem. In a bitter little poem about the change in Coleridge's behaviour after his return from Malta[50] he complained that Coleridge, who had formerly been for him a 'consecrated fount/Of murmuring, sparkling, living love' was now a 'comfortless and hidden well'. The more telling image, however, in terms of their relationship, is to be found in the first stanza, where he described Coleridge as having been 'a fountain at my fond heart's door'. There is a telltale separateness in the image which bespeaks Wordsworth's instinctive decorum. He came closest to breaking it down, perhaps, with the graceful compliment to Coleridge in his preface to the Duddon Sonnets, where he recalls Coleridge's former design of writing a poem called 'The Brook' and continues, 'There is a sympathy in streams, "one calleth to another;" and, I would gladly believe, that "The Brook" will, ere long, murmur in concert with "The Duddon"'. He then proceeds to comment on the common tradition concerning 'the power of waters over the minds of Poets'.[51]

The source of Wordsworth's quotation was the Prayer Book version of Psalm xlii: 'One deep calleth another, because of the noise of the water-pipes', and that image of deep calling to deep would probably best express his own conception of ideal mutual influence between poets. Coleridge, by contrast, preferred an imagery of ebullience and mingling. Both poets, however, by their use of this most unstable of all Romantic images, were bearing witness to the new status of influence in their time: that it would no longer work through socially agreed forms and norms, but must work primarily in the subconscious of artists, by way of processes as mysterious as those of streams and rivers that ran through untraceable caverns and re-emerged as ebullient springs where they would least be looked for. As he became a martyr to such instabilities Coleridge found various further images, including that of a restless sea, to picture his own condition, while linking Wordsworth with images of stability. In his most complex account of Wordsworth's powers, written after hearing the completed 1805 *Prelude*, his imagery veers from tide to current and then to something more like a fountain:

> Of tides obedient to external force,
> And currents self-determined, as might seem,
> Or by some inner Power; of moments awful,
> Now in thy inner life, and now abroad,
> When power streamed from thee, and thy soul received
> The light reflected, as a light bestowed . . .[52]

From this it is a short step to seeing the mature Wordsworth established in 'the dread watch-tower of man's absolute self'. And as he contemplates that achievement he is able to find a correspondingly tranquil image to describe his response:

> My soul lay passive, by thy various strain
> Driven as in surges now beneath the stars,
> With momentary stars of my own birth,
> Fair constellated foam, still darting off
> Into the darkness; now a tranquil sea,
> Outspread and bright, yet swelling to the moon.[53]

Wordsworth's self-image comes to be that of a stable entity existing in association with fluencies: an edifice by a stream, a mountain haunted by shooting stars.[54] Coleridge could look up to him, using his lighthouse image, or seeing him in a kind of super-Adamite splendour ('It is good for him to be alone'[55]). He seems to have applied to him the tribute of Pliny to Pompeius Saturninus: 'Whether I sit down to write anything myself, or to revise what I have already written, or am in a disposition to amuse myself, I constantly take up this same author; and as often as I do so, he is still new.'[56] Where Coleridge could value Wordsworth's writing for its versatile objectivity, Wordsworth, by contrast, appreciated above all the *fluency* of Coleridge's mind: after his death he pictured his conversation as 'a majestic river', that of a man with the power of 'throwing out in profusion grand central truths' or a figure of which every mortal power was now 'frozen at its marvellous source'.[57] Although he had seen little of him for the previous twenty years, he said, his mind had been 'perpetually present' with him.[58] In their relationship with each other the two men had exhibited very importantly, in fact, two opposing types of possible influence.

And, paradoxically, it was when they explored the underlying issues together, evolving a whole imagery of fluency and stasis[59] as they did so, that they achieved the kind of unity in diversity which is the most successful kind of influence, a mutually profitable confluence which poets in our later, anxious culture have found it still more difficult to achieve.

NOTES AND REFERENCES

1 1971 and N. Y., 1973 respectively. For another discussion of these problems as they relate to Romantic poetry, see my essay 'Influence and Independence in Blake' in *Interpreting Blake*, ed. M. Phillips (1979), 196-261.

2 'Coleridge: The Anxiety of Influence' in *New Perspectives on Coleridge and Wordsworth*, ed. G. Hartman (N. Y., 1972), 247-67.

3 See esp. D. Beres, 'A Dream, A Vision and a Poem: A Psycho-Analytical Study of the Origins of the Rime of the Ancient Mariner', *Intnl. Journal of Psycho-Analysis*, xxxii (1951), 97-116, and T. McFarland, 'Coleridge's Anxiety', in *Coleridge's Variety*, ed. Beer (1974), 134-65.

4 *CL*, i. 15-17; v. 192-93.

5 *ibid.*, i. 173, 491. See A. Harding, *Coleridge and the Idea of Love* (1974), 7-8.

6 *CL*, i. 325, 334.

7 *ibid.*, i. 391.

8 The nearest he came to such a public acknowledgement was his statement in 1814, concerning the unpublished *Prelude*, that it was 'addressed to a dear Friend' (unnamed), to whom his intellect was 'deeply indebted'. (Preface to *The Excursion*, *WPW*, v. 2.) Privately he had earlier been more forthcoming: see, e.g., *CL*, i. 538; *Letters of William and Dorothy Wordsworth (1787-1805)*, ed. E. de Selincourt, rev. C.L. Shaver (1967), 464.

9 *CL*, i. 584.

10 *ibid.*, ii. 714.

11 I have argued this in a forthcoming paper entitled 'The Language of "Kubla Khan"'.

12 'Wordsworth and the Face of Things', *The Wordsworth Circle*, x (1979), 17.

13 *WPW*, iv. 57.

14 *PW*, ii. 586-87.

15 Bloom, *op. cit.*, (note 1 above), 52.

16 M.H. Abrams, 'The correspondent breeze: a romantic metaphor', *Kenyon Review*, xix (1957); revd. in *English Romantic Poets*, ed. Abrams (N. Y., 1960); C. Clark, *Romantic Paradox* (1962), esp. pp.44-53.

17 St. xxxvi.

18 'So property began, twy-streaming fount,/Whence Vice and Virtue flow, honey and gall.' (ll.204-5), *PW*, i. 116-7.

19 *CL*, i. 168.

20 *ibid.*, ii. 961.
21 *ibid.*, i. 217. Coleridge's spelling here is 'Stowy'.
22 See, e.g., M.L. Reed, *Wordsworth: The Chronology of the Early Years* (Cambridge, Mass., 1967), 208-9nn.
23 p. 31. For an early discussion of this topic in poetic form, see ll. 743-835 of 'Autumn' in Thomson's *The Seasons* (1726-30).
24 *BL*, i. 12.
25 See my *Coleridge's Poetic Intelligence* (1977), esp. ch.ii.
26 *Paradise Lost*, ix. 69-75. See also my *Coleridge the Visionary* (1959), 235-40, 261, 274 etc.
27 *Pr.*(1805), iii. 246-7.
28 This is not of course to deny that Wordsworth sometimes offers an explicit symbolic interpretation in other contexts (see, e.g., *Pr.*[1805], vi. 553-72; xiii. 40-84).
29 *CN*, i. 495 f.54.
30 *ibid.*, i. 980.
31 *Pr.*(1805), ii. 263-64.
32 *CN*, i. 1770.
33 It could also disturb him when what streamed on were ideas and images which would have been censored by the conscious mind. Even here, however he believed that the images of those whom he 'loved and revered' were safe from desecration. (See, e.g., *CN*, ii. 2543, 2600.) I am grateful to Donald Sultana for drawing my attention to these and one or two other references.
34 *Pr.*(1805), xiii. 171-84.
35 *ibid.*, ii. 211-15.
36 For further tributes see *Pr.*(1805), vi. 305-16; xiii. 246-68.
37 *CL*, iv. 545.
38 M.H. Abrams, '*The Prelude* as a Portrait of the Artist' in *Bicentenary Wordsworth Studies*, ed. J. Wordsworth (Ithaca, N. Y. and London, 1970), esp. pp. 180-87; see also his *Natural Supernaturalism* (1971), 79-80, 287-88.
39 In Coleridge's view, however, the eddying must be coupled with a sense of progress: an 'eddying, instead of progression, of thought' is numbered by him among Wordsworth's defects (*BL*, ii. 109). For further discussion of the image of eddying see my *Coleridge the Visionary* (1959), 239-40 and *Coleridge's Poetic Intelligence* (1977), 214-17.
40 *Pr.*(1805), i. 429-31.
41 *ibid.*, viii. 754-60.
42 *ibid.*, vi. 553-56.
43 *ibid.*, iv. 372-75.
44 *ibid.*, x. 910-16.
45 Wordsworth, *Prose Works*, ed. W.J.B. Owen and J.W. Smyser (1974), ii. 79.
46 *Pr.*(1805), xiii. 58-9.
47 *CN*, ii. 2712.
48 *ibid.*, ii. 3148.
49 *ibid.*, iii. 4243; *CL*, i. 631n[2].
50 'There is a change - and I am poor . . .' *WPW*, ii. 34.

51 *Poems* III, 1820, 38-9. (*WPW*, iii. 504). For Coleridge's 'The Brook' see p. 144 of this volume (Ann Matheson's article).

52 *PW*, i. 404-5.

53 *ibid.*, i. 408.

54 See the 'Kirk of Ulpha' sonnet in the Duddon sequence and 'There is an eminence' in the Naming of Places poems (*WPW*, iii. 259-60; ii. 115). Wordsworth's choice of a burial-place by the Rotha at Grasmere is also relevant for the first, as is the conclusion to the 'Effusion in the Pleasure-ground on the banks of the Bran' (*WPW*, iii. 102-5; and see my *Wordsworth in Time* [1979], 150-2).

55 From Allsop's Recollections: *Table-Talk* (1917), 470. He also found Wordsworth's self-segregation and 'Self-involution' qualities which were 'hurtful' and matters of 'disinterested Apprehension': see *CL*, i. 491; ii. 1013.

56 Quoted by Coleridge, without direct reference to Wordsworth, and in Latin, *CN*, ii. 1944. Quoted in English from *CN*, ii. 1944n by N. Fruman (*Coleridge the Damaged Archangel* [1972], 304), who also notes that when the passage is actually applied to Wordsworth in *The Friend* (*Fr.*, i. 183) this sentence does not appear, and assumes that this is an indication of guilt on Coleridge's part concerning plagiarisms from Wordsworth (though the sentence in question would have been out of place at that point in *The Friend*). Fruman's failure to translate the Latin original for himself enables him to make play at Coleridge's expense with the words 'His works are never out of my hands', for which there is no corresponding Latin in Coleridge's quotations, whether in the *Notebooks* or *The Friend*.

57 Wordsworth, *Prose Works*, ed. A.B. Grosart (1876), 441; *WPW*, iv. 277.

58 *Letters of William and Dorothy Wordsworth: The Later Years*, ed. E. de Selincourt (1939), ii. 710.

59 For further discussion of this imagery and its implications in Wordsworth's poetry, see my *Wordsworth in Time* (1979), *passim*.

12

Coleridge's Political Papers in Malta

by DONALD SULTANA

> I am weary of correcting false assertions.
>> Coleridge on Brougham's *Colonial Policy of the European Powers* (Br. Lib., Egerton 2800 f.106)

Coleridge's first political paper in Malta as under-secretary to Sir Alexander Ball, the Civil Commissioner (in effect, the first British Governor of Malta) during the war with France under Bonaparte, has become the subject of confusion leading to a long chain of errors affecting two other political papers. The confusion is in the latest edition of Coleridge's *Essays on His Own Times* in the *Collected Works of Coleridge*. For the editor, Professor David Erdman, has stated[1] that apparently no copy of Coleridge's first political paper survives, whereas a version of it, dated 7 July 1804, in Ball's hand and with his signature, is in his unpublished correspondence with Nelson in the National Maritime Museum at Greenwich.[2] An earlier version, dated 3 July 1804, which was undoubtedly the basis of Coleridge's paper, survives in the Melville Papers in the Scottish Record Office at Edinburgh.[3] This version, hitherto unknown, is complemented by a letter of 20 June 1804 from Ball to Lord Melville in the same set of papers. Melville (*alias* Henry Dundas) was the First Lord of the Admiralty in the Tory ministry formed by William Pitt in place of one under Henry Addington the day before

Coleridge's arrival at Malta on 18 May 1804 for his health and in the hope of obtaining temporary employment from Ball.

The Melville 'prototype' of Coleridge's political paper, although signed by Ball, is in the hand of the Rev. Francis Laing, Ball's private secretary, whose departure for England in H.M.S. *Agincourt* was the immediate occasion for Coleridge's employment by Ball. For Ball's other secretary, Edmond Chapman, was at Odessa on a corn-buying mission. Coleridge was, therefore, called in on 4 July. He was a former leader-writer for Daniel Stuart's *Morning Post* and *Courier,* for which he still intended to send Stuart political information from Malta and Sicily on a much fuller scale than he had lately done from Gibraltar with a report of naval accidents.[4] He was called in from the house of his host, Dr John Stoddart, an advocate in the Court of Vice-Admiralty lately established as a prize-court completely independent of Ball's civil government, so that Professor Erdman's information[5] representing Ball as if he were at the head of the Vice-Admiralty Court is historically inaccurate.

Ball needed Coleridge's help 'to dilate and dress' a paper that he had sketched out, with Laing's assistance, for the new ministry in the interval between Coleridge's arrival at Malta and his employment by Ball. In that interval Ball had himself referred to Coleridge, although not by name, but as 'a gentleman' entrusted with the paper of 3 July. He had done so in a footnote to a long letter that he had started writing to Granville Penn,[6] an under-secretary at the Colonial Office and Ball's principal channel for communication with the cabinet.

The paper passed to Coleridge by Ball in Laing's hand was entitled 'Sketch of the Political Views of France in the Mediterranean'. It complemented another and much longer paper[7] about the Regency of Algiers (the most powerful of the Barbary Powers) with special reference to a treaty newly signed by Bonaparte and the Dey of Algiers. The treaty gave the French military and commercial facilities near the port of Bona, which was familiar to both Coleridge and Laing from their classical studies at Cambridge and Oxford respectively[8] as the ancient site of Hippo. Ball was fully persuaded that the French intended to colonize North Africa as compensation for Bonaparte's loss of St Domingo and his sale of Louisiana to the

United States. In the event of colonization, France would not only reap commercial and political advantages greater than those that could be drawn from the sugar colonies of the West Indies, but would exclude Britain from the Mediterranean. France might even form an alliance with Russia, who, although neutral for the time being, was never averse to acquiring territory and extending her sphere of influence in the Balkans (which she shared with Austria, the other great power) at the expense of Turkey's declining empire.

Ball considered it essential, therefore, that Egypt, which Bonaparte had seized from Turkey in 1798 in an expedition from Toulon via Malta, which he had also captured from the Order of St John, should be prevented from again falling to France in a fresh invasion from Toulon, which Nelson was blockading with a fleet based at the Maddalena Islands off Sardinia. For this purpose Ball had drawn up a 'Plan for the Defence of Alexandria' in consultation with Major Missett, the British Consul at Alexandria, who had reported that Egypt, which had been restored to Turkey under the Treaty of Amiens in 1802, was in rebellion against the Sultan at Constantinople and again in danger from France. Ball's 'Plan', therefore, was designed to admit a British garrison into Alexandria from Malta to enable the native rulers in rebellion against Turkey— the Mamelukes, as they were called—to resist a French invasion. Alternatively, a British garrison would forestall a French offer of military assistance to the Mamelukes, who had sent an emissary called Selim Effendi to Malta to ask for arms from Britain through Ball.[9]

Whatever Ball's *private* and long-term designs as an imperialist may have been, it was not his intention to press *officially* for British colonization of Egypt. For that would have offended Turkey, Britain's former ally in war before the Peace of Amiens. It would also have alienated Russia, whom Pitt was anxious to bring again into the war in an alliance with Austria and Prussia in the Third Coalition against France. Accordingly Ball's 'Plan' envisaged a limited operation on the model of the so-called 'disposable force' of British troops held in readiness at Malta for the defence of Messina against a possible French invasion of Sicily from the mainland.[10] Professor Erdman's assertion, therefore, that the garrisoning of Alexandria 'never was' Ball's 'goal' or 'immediate interest'[11] is directly contrary to the relevant dispatches on Egypt from Ball and other officials in the Colonial and Foreign Office papes in London.[12] Ball's 'Plan', in fact, was to remain his central aim as late as December 1804, when Coleridge was to sum it up admirably for him in the climax of a paper called 'Observations on Egypt' specifically written for the ministry. 'We must then at our own cost and hazard', Coleridge was to write on Ball's behalf, 'fortify and garrison Alexandra with a force sufficient to exclude all invaders, of all nations, and assist the inhabitants in forming a government adapted to their customs.'[13]

If Ball, therefore, was to stand the slightest chance of a hearing from the ministry for his 'Plan', it was vital for him to avoid such language as 'we must take it [Egypt] ourselves'. Yet that is precisely what Professor Erdman has represented him as writing to the ministry through Coleridge in the draft of an earlier paper on Egypt of July 1804,[14] without recognizing at the same time that, if that paper had been intended for the ministry, it would make nonsense of Professor Erdman's denial[15] that 'as a political journalist Coleridge was now committed to the cause of imperialism'. The passage just cited, therefore, was not 'closest to Ball's dictation', as Professor Erdman has asserted,[16] and his denial that it provided a 'contrast'[17] to the other cited passage from the December paper on Egypt again betrays a lack of knowledge of the relevant documents on the subject. Both papers were not 'primarily Ball's documents, his position papers'.[18]

Ball had made his 'position' perfectly clear, well before Coleridge appeared on the scene in Malta, when he had communicated his 'Plan for the Defence of Alexandria' to the late ministry of Addington through Lord Hobart, the Colonial Secretary, on 1 November 1803.[19] He had never advocated the conquest of Egypt either officially to Hobart or unofficially to Penn, whatever he was afterwards to say *privately* to Coleridge. Even his 'Plan' for garrisoning Alexandria with British troops had been submitted by him in the most cautious language and in an apologetic tone in full recognition that Egypt was 'a subject that does not immediately relate to my official situation' in Malta.[20] His 'Plan' had elicited no active response at all from the late ministry. In consequence he decided to make a fresh approach to the new ministry of Pitt soon after news of the change of government in Britain reached Malta on 13 June before the arrival of the *Agincourt* to take a convoy to England.

Neither Ball, however, on calling in Coleridge on 4 July, nor Coleridge himself indicated how many copies of 'Sketch of the Political Views of France in the Mediterranean' Ball intended to 'send home to the Ministry', as Coleridge was to put it to Daniel Stuart[21] immediately after he had worked on Ball's paper on the eve of the *Agincourt*'s departure. Certainly Ball intended to communicate direct with Melville through Laing. For he considered Melville to be 'the boldest of the present ministers' and to have 'the most comprehensive mind'.[22] His opinion of Melville, therefore, was directly contrary to Coleridge's former detestation of him[23] when Coleridge, as a republican, had vigorously campaigned against the war with France. Irrespective, however, of Coleridge's political views, which had undergone a sharp change since 1796, of which Ball might well have been apprised in the letters of recommendation that Coleridge had brought with him to Malta, Ball was resolved to inform Melville not only of the allegedly explosive situation in Egypt but of the new threat to British interests that had arisen in Barbary from the pro-French policy of the Dey of Algiers. In particular, Ball meant to emphasize, in the context of Bonaparte's alleged imperialist designs in the Mediterranean, that 'much may be inferred' from the military and commercial facilities recently granted to France.

Before Ball called in Coleridge, therefore, on 4 July, he had already begun to write a letter to Melville on 20 June to introduce Laing to him as bearer of the 'Plan for the Defence of Alexandria' and of a 'Precis[*sic*] of the Political State of the Barbary Powers whose importance may soon be the subject of discussion in the cabinets of Europe'. Laing, moreover, was instructed to show Melville a copy of a third paper designed to prove 'the importance of Malta to a British Fleet cruising off Toulon'.[24] For Nelson had been openly decrying Malta as of little value to Britain on account of the island's distance from Toulon. In consequence Ball had circulated a paper to the cabinet through Granville Penn as far back as January 1804.[25] Besides answering Nelson's criticisms, especially the contention that Minorca was a better naval base than Malta,

Ball had recommended a regular system of supply ships for the Mediterranean fleet to offset Malta's distance from Toulon. In addition he had underlined that Malta's value was not merely strategic as 'the key to Egypt', which was the phrase commonly applied to Malta by the British press as a barrier to a French descent from Toulon upon Egypt, which was itself commonly described and valued as 'the key to India',[26] where Britain's richest source of imperial power lay. Ball had also emphasized Malta's *political* importance in sustaining Sicily as part of the fragile Kingdom of Naples, and in exerting British influence upon the Barbary Powers and in the Morea, where French agents were allegedly inciting the Greeks to rebel against Turkey.

Ball had even ventured to send Nelson a copy of this paper in the hand of Alexander Macaulay,[27] the Public Secretary of Malta, whom Coleridge was to succeed in January 1805. For Ball was genuinely devoted to Nelson, under whom he had served in the Battle of the Nile when Nelson had destroyed the fleet of the French expedition to Egypt, and had afterwards ordered Ball to sail for Malta in command of a squadron and blockade the French garrison that Bonaparte had left there under General Vaubois. Nelson, for his part, fully reciprocated Ball's regard, as Coleridge was afterwards to bear witness in *The Friend*.[28] Their friendship was perhaps best attested by the regular correspondence that had been passing between them since the renewal of the war. Nelson recognized the vital part that Ball had played in effecting the surrender of the French in 1800 after a two-year blockade in command not only of his squadron but of the Maltese insurgents, who had risen and besieged the French garrison under Vaubois, exactly contrary to Professor Erdman's information[29] that it was the Maltese who had been 'under French siege'.

Ball, then, on 20 June 1800 wished to show Melville a copy of 'Observations on the Importance of Malta to a British Fleet cruising off Toulon', that he had circulated the previous January when Melville had been out of office. For Melville had stressed Malta's value to Britain in the debate of 23 May 1803[30] on the renewal of the war with Bonaparte mainly on account of Britain's refusal to withdraw from Malta and hand it back to the Order of St John, as stipulated in the Treaty of Amiens.

Ball's principal preoccupation, however, when he had started writing to Melville, had not been the issue of Malta's retention by Britain, but the alleged designs of France on Egypt and Barbary, as was reflected even in the letter of 1 or 2 July that he had started writing to Penn without at first specifying the exact day of the month. By the time, however, that he finished both letters, and dated the letter to Penn '4 July 1804', news had reached Malta from England that Pitt was opening negotiations with Russia for the formation of the Third Coalition against France, and that the newspapers were asserting that 'it would be policy in Great Britain to give up Malta to Russia',[31] who was pledged to return it to the Order of St John. In consequence Ball hastened to add a long postcript to both his letters to Melville and Penn warning them that 'this subject is of such vast importance that it behoves us to consider very maturely before we decide upon it'; and he proceeded to detail Malta's importance to Britain in relation to Egypt and Barbary, besides arguing that Russia already had the use of a naval base at Corfu in the Ionian Isles as 'the key to the Adriatic'. Finally he revived the fear that, without Malta, Britain might be excluded from the Mediterranean.

All these ideas and arguments, hitherto loosely scattered in the two letters to Melville and Penn, were put together in a much more coherent and succinct form in the 'Sketch' of 3 July that was passed to Coleridge when Ball called him in on 4 July to take over from Laing. He was also given a draft of the long paper on Algiers, including statistics of that regency in the hands of Ball and Laing.[32] The *Agincourt* was then expected to sail within twenty-four hours, but, in effect, she did not sail till late on 6 July. Coleridge, therefore, was afterwards able, on completing his work for Ball, to avail himself of the little extra time to write a hurried letter to Stuart[33] in a mood of self-satisfaction and confidence for the future, so that Professor Erdman's information[34] that 'writing these papers did not give him [Coleridge] high spirits', needs to be qualified. For, although Coleridge certainly complained *later* that 'I have no Heart for Politics',[35] and became more and more homesick, especially under the burden of administrative duties on taking over from Alexander Macaulay as Public Secretary in January 1805, *initially* 'writing these papers', precisely on Algiers, Barbary and

Egypt, *did* give him 'high spirits' as a novel and stimulating experience. Accordingly he flattered, or rather deluded, himself into believing, as he put it to Stuart in the letter of 6 July,[36] that 'I hope I shall return in Spirit a regenerated Creature', and that 'if I live, I shall be made a perfect [man of busin]ess'.

He also enclosed for Stuart in 'a scrawl' some rough and loose notes, which he accordingly called 'Sybilline [*sic*] Leaves' in anticipation of the title that he was to give to his collected poetical works of 1817 in allusion to the 'fragmentary and widely scattered state in which they have been long suffered to remain'.[37] The 'Sybilline Leaves' for Stuart contained political information for the *Courier*, which Coleridge claimed 'will give you *my Ideas* [*sic*] on the Importance of the Island',[38] but without explaining how exactly his ideas differed from those of Ball and Laing. At the same time he took care to urge Stuart that, if he found the information of interest to his readers, he should not incorporate it in the *Courier* 'in the same words', as a precaution against a possible charge of a leak of official correspondence to the press. This was a hint, therefore, as well as an important technical point with a bearing on the form and style of a later paper, as to how he proposed to deal with official material of potential press interest to Stuart. Moreover, even if a leak were to be suspected in official circles in London, he protected himself against possible discovery by advising Stuart that, although he already considered himself 'as a sort of diplomatic Understrapper' hidden in Ball's palace, Stuart was to speak of this to no one.[39] Finally he promised Stuart that 'by the next opportunity I trust . . . I shall send you . . . something worth Reading' in comparison with 'the scrawl' of 'Sybilline Leaves' and in return for news that Coleridge hoped to have received from Stuart about the political situation in England following the change of ministry.

Stuart, for his part, had published in the *Courier* of 25 May[40] the report of the naval accidents that Coleridge had sent him from Gibraltar, thereby disproving Professor Erdman's suggestion[41] that nothing had come from Coleridge for the *Courier* from Gibraltar. Moreover, the *Courier* had published on 24 May[42]—again despite information to the contrary from Professor Erdman[43]—a report that a rupture was imminent between Britain and Spain, the late ally of France before the

Peace of Amiens. The British minister to Madrid, John Hookham Frere, Coleridge's future patron, had allegedly asked for his passport.

As for the 'Sketch', to which Coleridge was given access on 4 July, it reflected the sequence of the preoccupations in Ball's mind, as they had already been revealed in the letter to Melville. For the first part was taken up with Egypt and Barbary, whereas the second part was largely a replica of the long postscript to Melville and Penn on the importance of Malta in the context of Britain's reported intention to cede it to Russia in the interests of the Third Coalition. There was very little, therefore, in the way of *original* matter, that Coleridge appears to have had to add to the 'Sketch' other than perhaps to make copies of it and 'dress' its style slightly by tidying up a few phrases and constructions, particularly in the latter paragraphs, on the evidence of the version of 7 July (now at Greenwich) that Ball dispatched to Nelson, the day after the *Agincourt*'s departure, with a covering letter that 'I have compressed it as much as possible without losing the substance'. Its title was also slightly amended to 'A Political Sketch of the Views of the French in the Mediterranean', so that the version of 7 July appears to be the finished copy of Coleridge's first political paper in Malta, although both versions of 3 and 7 July would seem to underline that the paper was really in substance the joint production of Ball and Laing rather than of Coleridge despite his claim of originality for the 'Sybilline Leaves' on Malta's importance that he had scrawled for Stuart.

Stuart himself, on receiving Coleridge's letter of 6 July by Laing in late September after the *Agincourt* had anchored and performed quarantine at Portsmouth, would appear to have echoed in the *Courier* of 4 October Ball's warning that, if Malta were given to Russia for the Third Coalition, Britain would be 'excluded' from the Mediterranean. For Stuart argued in an editorial that 'to abandon Malta without an equivalent in the Mediterranean would be a measure which Mr Pitt, we think, would hardly adopt; and Russia, we have no doubt, will consider the Seven Isles [Ionian Isles] as a much more desirable possession'. In the same editorial Stuart announced that 'we had prepared an article in which we had dealt fully upon the policy of this country with respect to the Mediterranean'. Presumably the article was based on Coleridge's 'Sybilline Leaves', and it is unfortunate that it was deferred 'till tomorrow' owing to unexpected 'hot news' of a naval victory that called for instant publicity. In the event the article was never published.

As for the paper on Algiers that was passed to Coleridge at the same time as the 'Sketch', he appears to have made the same minor stylistic corrections to it on the evidence of a number of revisions in his own hand written into the draft in Ball's and Laing's hands, which is now at Toronto.[44] Coleridge absorbed some of the details in the Algiers paper so thoroughly that he afterwards recalled them in *The Friend*[45] without omitting even the statistics of the Dey's treasury. Naturally he emphasized the treaty between Bonaparte and the Dey giving France military facilities near Bona, which Coleridge, echoing a footnote in both Laing's 'Sketch' of 3 July and Ball's letter to Penn, spelt out as 'the very spot where the ancient Hippo stood'. Coleridge likewise afterwards reproduced very closely in *The Friend*[46] parts of Ball's 'Observations on the Importance of Malta to a British Fleet cruising off Toulon', precisely in the original context of Ball's disagreement with Nelson over Malta's value to Britain. On the other hand, Coleridge appears to have had reservations about the fashionable view of Malta as 'the key to Egypt' on the ground, among other reasons, that 'Malta does not lie in the direct course from Toulon to Alexandria', so that he might conceivably have taken this line in the 'Sybilline Leaves' that he had enclosed for Stuart. If so, it might account for his claim of originality of ideas. In any event, since Ball *did* believe that Malta *was* 'the key to Egypt', it is not likely that he would have permitted Coleridge to include any dissident observations on that subject in the 'Sketch' for the ministry.

As Ball had promised Melville, in his letter of 20 June, a copy of 'Observations on the Importance of Malta to a British Fleet cruising off Toulon', it would appear that Coleridge was not only given access to that paper but might have been asked to make the copy for Melville, if Laing had not already done so himself before handing over to Coleridge. In that paper of 24 January and in the 'Sketch' of 4 July Ball had said all that he had wanted to say—indeed all that he could say—to the ministry on the subject of

Malta's importance, supplemented by his letters to Melville and Penn. The 'Sketch' of 4 July, as it had evolved under pressure of international events, had come to be, in effect, if not in title, a 'Political Sketch, concentrating on the importance of Malta'. Yet Professor Erdman, who does not appear to have read the Ball papers at Greenwich, particularly the 'Sketch' of 7 July,[47] has represented Coleridge as writing for Ball on 13 July, just a week after the composition of this 'Political Sketch, concentrating on the importance of Malta', *another* paper for the ministry, which is described as 'a sequel to Ball's earlier "Political Sketch"'.[48] But this sequel is also described as again 'concentrating on the importance of Malta'. It cannot be, therefore, that Coleridge wrote for Ball to send to the ministry a duplicate of what Ball had just sent them the week before. Professor Erdman, moreover, twice gives[49] as his source for his assertion that this third political paper of Coleridge's was written 'for Ball' to be sent to the ministry a reference to a book, *Samuel Taylor Coleridge in Malta and Italy*,[50] in which the exact opposite is stated, namely, that Coleridge could not possibly have written this paper for the ministry, but that he wrote it for Stuart, as he had promised in the letter of 6 July, for publication in the *Courier* and afterwards as a pamphlet.

It is true, as Professor Erdman explains,[51] that Coleridge afterwards drew on this third paper for the version that he published in *The Friend*. But that version, in so far as it dealt with Malta's importance, was largely a variant of Ball's 'Observations on the Importance of Malta to a British Fleet cruising off Toulon' and of the 'Sketch' of 4 July. Coleridge himself admitted[52] that the second part of *The Friend* version was taken up with Malta's importance, while the first part, which he called a 'disquisition', consisted, again on his own admission,[53] of a long discussion, in *1804*, of the reasons why the ministry had gone to war with France over Malta in *1803*. But this was precisely what the ministry had themselves explained in the official manifesto that they had published on the renewal of the war. It would have been unnecessary, therefore, to say the least, for Ball to send them such a paper. Moreover, the abstruse style of the 'disquisition' in *The Friend* version, interspersed as it is with verse quotations from Coleridge's favourite seventeenth-century poets, would have been utterly unsuitable for a paper for the ministry from Ball. Coleridge himself explained[54] that he wrote the paper in answer to 'the Opposers of the present War', namely, the Whig Opposition in the House of Commons led by Charles James Fox, who had allegedly argued that 'on Malta we rested the peace; for Malta we renewed the War'. On that ground alone, therefore, it would have been an intolerable intervention on Ball's part in home politics if he had sent the ministry Coleridge's paper.

Coleridge admittedly did state, at the opening of *The Friend* version[55], that 'the considerations I am about to submit to the Reader, were written by me during my residence at Malta— were written at the instance of Sir Alexander Ball'. But this does not mean that he wrote this third paper 'for Ball' to be sent to the ministry. Ball certainly may have *encouraged* him to write it in the knowledge that Coleridge as an experienced leader-writer for a national newspaper in Britain was under a pledge to remit political information from Malta to Stuart, whose *Courier* might thus come to support both Ball's 'Plan for the Defence of Alexandria' and his recent plea to the ministry against Britain's reported intention to cede Malta to Russia in the interests of the Third Coalition. Ball, indeed, may well have encouraged Coleridge to contribute not only to the *Courier* but to the *Malta Gazette* that he had recently established to counter the influential French propaganda of *Le Moniteur* throughout Barbary and the Mediterranan, thereby strengthening his case for Malta's *political* importance and providing himself with a fresh argument for Britain's retention of Malta. In fact, he had himself explained to Melville in the letter of 20 June that 'the *Malta Gazettes* and other powerful tracts which I circulate all over the Mediterranean are working a great change in the minds of the people—and have alarmed the Bashaw of Tripoli, who is already enlisted under our protection, and is sensible that his safety and that of all the other states depends on our retention of this important island to check the ambitious views of the French'.

For this purpose Ball had been receiving political pamphlets from Penn[56] for translation into Italian, the official language of Malta and the *lingua franca* of the Mediterranean, thereby explaining Coleridge's forecast to Stuart, in the same letter of 6 July,[57] and in the same mood of 'high spirits' for the future, that

'I shall soon be able to speak & write both F[rench] and Italian'. In fact, he not only read one of the pamphlets received by Ball from Penn; he even referred to it, precisely in his third political paper in Malta, on the evidence of it in *The Friend*.[58] For in the pamphlet in question Lord Minto, a former ambassador at Vienna and a powerful advocate of Britain's retention of Malta, had argued that 'France had an undoubted right to insist on our abandonment of Malta', since the late ministry of Addington had foolishly pledged themselves to it in the Treaty of Amiens. Accordingly Coleridge, who had himself supported both Addington and the Treaty of Amiens in his earlier phase of anti-war journalism, took issue with Minto in his own political paper on Malta, thereby providing further proof against Professor Erdman's assertion that Coleridge's paper was written 'for Ball' to be sent to the ministry. For Minto's argument had formed part of a speech in parliament in the debate of June 1803 on a motion of censure of the late ministry of Addington over the Treaty of Amiens. Pitt's ministry, therefore, several of whom had agreed with Minto and had voted against Addington in the censure debate, would not have taken kindly to a paper from Ball with a stricture on Minto or even a semblance of an apologia for Addington and the Treaty of Amiens.

The best refutation of Professor Erdman's assertion and at the same time the best direct proof that Coleridge wrote this paper for Stuart and afterwards for separate publication as a pamphlet in imitation of the political tracts, including Minto's, that Ball had been receiving from Penn, was provided by Coleridge himself. For, on completing both this paper and another one on Egypt, the draft of which, as already explained, was of July 1804, but which Professor Erdman has also asserted was written 'for Ball' to be sent to the ministry, Coleridge wrote to Stuart about the two papers on 22 October.[59] He did so from Syracuse after he had crossed to Sicily in confident hopes of raising money for his return journey to England with the papers through Stuart. 'I leave the publication of the Pacquet, which is waiting for Convoy at Malta for you,' he told Stuart, 'to your own opinion—If the information appear new or valuable to you, & the letters themselves entertaining, etc publish them/ only do not sell the Copy right of more than the right of two

Editions to the Book-seller . . .'

The papers, therefore, formed part of a series of letters from the Mediterranean, not unlike Coleridge's earlier letters from Germany, also for separate publication,[60] and subsequently incorporated in *The Friend*[61] as 'Satyrane's Letters' in a rehashed form, like the paper on Malta. Both the draft on Egypt and the paper on Malta appear to have been originally intermixed, as was traditional, with travel material in journal form. The evidence for this lies in a letter of 1 August 1804,[62] that Coleridge had written from Malta to Sir George Beaumont, one of his patrons in England, before he had crossed to Sicily. For he had informed Beaumont that he was sending 'a series of Letters to you—containing my few very few adventures, and my topographical and political Information', exactly as he had sent his information about the topography and politics of Germany to an earlier patron, Josiah Wedgwood.[63] In the letter from Syracuse he had also informed Beaumont that he was addressing the political and other letters for him to the care of Stuart at the *Courier* office, but that, before sending them off, he would 'add to my pacquet the Journal of my hasty Tour' of Sicily, about which he also appears to have written a political paper, on the evidence of a draft now extant at Toronto.[64]

His hope of prevailing upon Stuart to sell the packet to a bookseller after making use of it for the *Courier* evidently rested on the 'new information' contained in the papers on Malta and Egypt. For he had attempted to qualify the view on which journalists in Britain, including Stuart, had fed the British public for so long, that Malta was 'the key to Egypt', and Egypt 'the key to India'. He had argued, instead, that the notion of Malta as 'the key to Egypt' was too 'exclusive' in that it did not take sufficient account of Egypt's *potentially* fertile natural resources, which made that country desirable for colonization by France *for its own sake* rather than as a means of subverting Britain's imperial power. As a corollary to this argument, therefore, he had entered into a long discussion of the topical question of the purpose of Bonaparte's expedition to Egypt in 1798, naturally taking the line that its principal purpose had not been 'the subversion of our empire in India'.

The evidence that this was the 'new information' that he had exploited for Stuart and the British public in the two papers, and that they were inseparably related to each other in a sequence that has eluded Professor Erdman's observation, lies in a retrospective allusion to the Malta paper in the opening paragraph of the July draft of 'Observations on Egypt'.[65] For unfortunately the packet for Stuart and Beaumont was burnt *en route* at Gibraltar as 'plague-papers',[66] which drew the lament from Coleridge that with the packet 'there perished my fine travels addressed to Sir George Beaumont', as if in confirmation of the conjecture that the political information had been intermixed with travel material in journal form, so that Professor Erdman's suggestion,[67] that 'in retrospect Coleridge seems to lump together his political letters for Stuart and "my fine travels addressed to Sir George Beaumont"', may perhaps call for qualification.

In the absence of the packet for Stuart and Beaumont, its contents have to be inferred from the version of the Malta paper in *The Friend* and from the July and December versions of 'Observations on Egypt', thereby explaining the crucial importance of the opening paragraph of the July draft as evidence in refutation of Professor Erdman's assertion that the paper on Malta and the draft on Egypt were written 'for Ball' to be sent to the ministry. The paragraph reads as follows:

> From the commencement of the disputes which terminated in the present war, the public have been taught to value Malta for its protection of Egypt, and Egypt as a barrier of India. In this opinion I see nothing objectionable but its exclusiveness. It is a good point of view but ought not to be the only one. *In a former paper I have exhausted this subject in relation to Malta*[68] but the same result and similar reasonings apply to Egypt with a force proportionate to its incomparably greater natural wealth, and commercial capabilities.

By 'a former paper' Coleridge meant, of course, the paper now extant in *The Friend* version, but Professor Erdman, while admitting that this was the paper 'drawn upon for *Friend* No 22',[69] has repeated the error that this 'is the paper prepared for Ball on 13 July 1804', which has been proved to have been non-existent. In the passage just cited Coleridge is obviously writing in his own person, and he continues to do so throughout the paper, using, in the main, the first person singular, although occasionally he interchanges it, as was common practice, with the second person plural, which he also used for his own person in the Malta paper in *The Friend*.[70] His use of this letter form of writing, therefore, was in keeping with his own description of the political papers on Malta and Egypt to Stuart on 22 October from Syracuse. Moreover, it was in marked contrast to the formal, objective style of the December version of 'Observations on Egypt', which Coleridge wrote for Ball and the ministry merely to supersede 'a less correct paper',[71] also on Egypt, but unfortunately lost *en route* to London. The first person singular, therefore, which ran throughout the July draft of 'Observations on Egypt', entirely disappeared from the December version, so that Coleridge, in effect, adopted *two* styles for the two papers.

Again, in the passage cited above from the July draft of 'Observations on Egypt' Coleridge is addressing 'the public' in his own person, and he continues to do so throughout the paper, which has specific references to 'the public', or implications that 'the public' are intended, as in the following two passages. The first is from the concluding paragraph, in which Coleridge returns to the 'key-to-India' view of Egypt:

> Let Egypt then continue to derive an importance in the public opinion from its possible *immediate* relation to our empire in the East.

The second passage,[73] which introduces a characteristic observation to which reference will again be made in another context, reads as follows:

> I am sensible that these reflections will be treated by many as dreamlike speculations on dim and distant contingencies, that lose much even of their plausibility when contrasted with the actual experience and historical detail of what the French did and were able to do during the considerable time, in which they remained masters of Egypt.

Professor Erdman, however, pursuing the logic of his mistaken idea that this draft was written 'for Ball' to be sent to the ministry, in other words, that it was the draft of the lost paper on Egypt, which the December version was designed to

227

supersede, has denied that Coleridge is writing in his own person, and that he is addressing the British public through the *Courier* or a pamphlet. Instead, Professor Erdman has alleged that every single 'I' in the July draft denotes Ball, and that throughout the paper Ball is addressing the ministry.[74] Accordingly Professor Erdman has interpreted the two passages cited above from the opening and concluding paragraphs of the July draft as 'advice from Ball to the politicians who influence editors';[75] and the reference to what 'the public have been taught' to value about Malta and Egypt is, according to Professor Erdman,[76] 'a point ministers must take into consideration'. But Ball, on the evidence of his official communications with the ministers, never lectured them on their relationship with 'the public' in England, let alone on their influence upon editors, even if the ministers were prepared to tolerate such gratuitous advice from a subordinate in Malta. Ball was sensible and responsible enough to know that these were subjects unrelated to his situation in Malta, so much so that all but one of the references to 'the public' in the July draft, including the passages cited above, are not to be found in the December version of 'Observations on Egypt' precisely because it was written for the ministry.

Professor Erdman, in short, has not only interpreted the July draft out of context of Ball's situation, character and official papers but has failed to perceive the *two* styles adopted by Coleridge in the two papers, corresponding to the different audience addressed in them. There was no 'movement', therefore, from the July draft to the December version, contrary to Professor Erdman's assertion.[77] Nor is his denial that the July draft is in letter form[78] valid. For the absence of a superscription or subscription from it, *as part of a series of letters* intermixed with travel material in journal form from an author writing from abroad, was quite common, as can be seen from contemporary political and other travel-books, such as E. Blaquiere's *Letters from the Mediterranean* (1813) and P. Brydone's *Tour through Sicily and Malta* (1774), to which there is a reference in the surviving draft of Coleridge's paper on Sicily.[79] Coleridge had himself already dropped the superscription from the series of letters that he had addressed to Josiah Wedgwood from Germany on 'the history of the Bauers',[80] and he was to drop both the superscription and subscription from the rehashed 'Satyrane's Letters' in *The Friend*.[81] It is the adoption of the first person singular for the July draft and the address to 'the public' that link it with the traditional letter form. Moreover, as its opening paragraph which has already been cited, makes clear, it came *after* the paper on Malta, which might have had the usual initial superscription in the *fair* copy.

Nor should its *timing* pass unconsidered as further evidence against Professor Erdman's interpretation of the meaning of 'I' and 'the public' in it. For when Coleridge dispatched the packet of political papers to Stuart in October 1804, he intended to return to England after wintering in Malta.[82] It would be he, therefore, not Ball, who, on resuming his leader-writing for Stuart, would take issue, by means of the paper on Malta, with 'the opposers of the present war', just as it would be he, not Ball, who would question, by means of 'Observations on Egypt', whether what 'the public have been taught' to believe about Egypt was 'truth or error'.[83] Moreover, Coleridge would be unhampered, unlike Ball, by the official policy of Pitt's ministry towards Turkey and Russia with reference to Egypt as a province of the Sultan, so that he would openly proclaim to 'the public' that 'we must take it [Egypt] ourselves' as a much more *radical* measure than Ball's 'Plan for the Defence of Alexandria'.

As for the last passage cited above, containing the sentence

> I am sensible that these reflections will be treated by many as dreamlike speculations on dim and distant contingencies etc.,

Professor Erdman has offered no editorial comment on it with reference to its 'I' and 'many', but common sense would appear to suggest that they should not be taken as denoting Ball and the ministry respectively. Moreover, a knowledge of Ball's character would again have ruled him out as sanctioning the passage or encouraging Coleridge to write it on his behalf for the ministry. For Ball, as Coleridge was himself to describe him,[84] was interested only in the 'factual', 'practical' and 'active' as opposed to the 'speculative' and 'abstract'. The passage, therefore, could never have 'flowed' from his thinking, which is how Professor Erdman has actually represented the origin of another passage[85] merely because it contains a military reference to a fortress on the Red Sea in the context of

Coleridge's discussion of Bonaparte's route to India, on which account Professor Erdman has denied that the passage could have been intended by Coleridge for 'the public' or readers of the *Courier*. But he has not explained why Coleridge, irrespective of the source of his information, should have thought such readers to be uninterested in such a topical subject. Moreover, Coleridge, who was a voracious reader of books of all kinds, drew on Ball's library, with its volumes of travels, geography and history,[86] precisely for 'Observations on Egypt',[87] so that it may be no more than another assertion on Professor Erdman's part that Coleridge obtained his information about the Red Sea fortress from Ball, or that Ball even dictated it to him. Ball, in fact, had never visited the Red Sea in his naval career, and Coleridge's information may just as well, if not more likely, have come from Selim Effendi, who, in Coleridge's own words to Stuart,[88] was 'the Mamaluke Minister at Malta, with whom I was very intimate', and who, again according to Coleridge, supplied him with facts, precisely for the paper on Egypt, *as an eye-witness*, unlike Ball in respect of the Red Sea fortress.

Far from thinking that 'the public' would be uninterested in a discussion of the purpose and implications of Bonaparte's route to India, Coleridge appears to have exploited it not only for its own sake and in relation to his own general thesis but as another technical device to differentiate the July draft on Egypt as a paper for Stuart. For he wrote up the draft to a length that Stuart would consider perfectly suitable for a pamphlet or as part of a series of political letters from the Mediterranean. On the other hand, its length would have been utterly unsuitable for a paper to the ministry from Ball, even without considering that Ball repeatedly stressed in his official correspondence that he had taken pains to make his communications 'compact'.[89] The length of the July draft, therefore, at once rules it out for the purpose asserted for it by Professor Erdman, who appears to have discounted too lightly the perfectly plausible possibility that the draft might have *grown out* of the lost official paper on Egypt but not *condensed into* it, as he appears to have thrice suggested.[90] The draft, in other words, might have *followed*, not *preceded*, the lost paper for Ball in a sequence exactly contrary to that suggested by Professor Erdman, but perfectly in keeping with the earlier parallel of the 'Sybilline Leaves' about Malta's importance, that Coleridge had passed to Stuart for the *Courier* on 6 July immediately *after* he had completed a paper on the same subject for Ball.

The parallel of the 'Sybilline Leaves', therefore, which has eluded Professor Erdman, serves to throw light not only on the sequence of the July draft of 'Observations on Egypt' but on its *genesis* in relation to Coleridge's *technique* and method of publication, which Professor Erdman has also entirely overlooked in his general disregard of the paper's historical context. The technique and the method of publication flowed, in effect, from 'the mystery' inseparable — as Disraeli was to put it—[91]from 'the craft of publishing' in the early nineteenth century, of which Coleridge had long made himself a master. For he had not only published extensively both verse and prose under different pen-names or anonymously but had rehashed used or borrowed material from a multitude of sources for his political, literary and philosophical writings. Accordingly he had not scrupled, in passing to Stuart the 'Sybilline Leaves' on Malta's importance, to include even apparently *facsimile* official material on the strict understanding that, if it were published, it should not be 'in the same words' as in the paper for Ball. He had also assumed that Stuart would not reveal his source, and that the universal convention of anonymity would be observed by Stuart not only for the 'Sybilline Leaves' but for the packet of political papers, including 'Observations on Egypt', irrespective of whether they were published in the *Courier* or as a pamphlet, Besides, he had urged Stuart not to disclose to anyone that he was writing official papers for Ball, and Stuart had honoured Coleridge's wish. For, on receiving the 'Sybilline Leaves' by Laing, he had simply announced in the *Courier* of 24 September 1804 that Coleridge's health had improved, and that Coleridge had written 'when upon a visit to Sir A. Ball, and mentions his intentions of proceeding from thence to Sicily'.

Coleridge, therefore, felt at complete liberty to work up for Stuart material used for Ball in the official paper on Egypt, as he had already done with the 'Sybilline Leaves', particularly as he was under the impression that his employment by Ball was temporary. Accordingly he incorporated large portions of the official paper closely, and integrated them, as part of the process of not reproducing them 'in the same words', into a framework marked by a *personal,* expansive form of writing in contradistinction to the objective, compact style of the official paper. At the same time he developed additional ideas out of the official paper, including the uninhibited advocacy of the annexation of Egypt and the extended discussion of Bonaparte's route to India via Egypt. He also entered into a characteristic little excursus on political slavery with reference to the Egyptian peasantry,[92] complete with a proposal for improving their plight, modelled on the information he had obtained in Germany for his 'history of the Bauers'.[93] The excursus was flavoured with poetic imagery and prolonged into well-argued, lengthy footnotes in the manner of the traditional political tracts and letters, thereby providing further proof not only of the form and intention of the July draft as a pamphlet for 'the public' but of the *two* styles that Coleridge adopted for the July and December versions. For the December version is without the footnotes as inappropriate or lengthy for a ministerial paper, which again Professor Erdman has failed to notice in his mistaken assumption that the July draft was 'an early, prolix, rough paper',[94] on which account even the poetic imagery in the slavery passage was allegedly 'erased' from the 'polished' December version.[95]

Finally, Coleridge inserted into the July draft a warning against 'the possession of the Morea by the Russians',[96] which again could not possibly have been written for Ball to be sent to the ministry, because that would have been another unwarranted interference on Ball's part in 'a subject that does not immediately relate to my official situation' in Malta. Moreover, it would have conflicted with the ministry's cardinal policy of bringing Russia into the Third Coalition, in proof of which a large fleet of transports was about to assemble in Malta harbour for an Anglo-Russian expedition to Naples against an expected French march on Rome and Southern Italy. Inevitably, therefore, Coleridge's warning in the July draft against Russian possession of the Morea is not to be found in the December version for the ministry, although the warning itself was perfectly proper for the projected pamphlet or for the *Courier,* which, in fact, did report the fleet of transports on 11 November in 'An Extract of a Letter from Malta', which

Professor Erdman has wrongly attributed to Coleridge[97] not only without grasping the significance of a reference to the transports in the very first sentence of the 'Extract' but in apparent unawareness that travellers and members of the garrison commonly sent home news of Malta and neighbouring countries in their private letters whence it passed to the newspapers.[98]

Moreover, although Professor Erdman has noted[99] the omission of Coleridge's warning against Russian possession of the Morea from the December version for the ministry, he has again made no attempt to account for it in a historical context. Instead, Professor Erdman has made the fundamental mistake of interpreting all these textual and technical differences between the July draft and the December version in terms of 'economy'[100] and of 'a movement' from the 'early, prolix, rough' July draft to the 'polished' December version. In consequence Coleridge has been represented as having removed 'excrescences' from the earlier paper,[101] including a pointed allusion that was obviously intended for 'the public' in England and that again could never have been written for Pitt's ministry, as it dealt with a famous 'Intercepted Correspondence'[102] that Coleridge, in his earlier anti-war journalism, had denounced in the *Morning Post* as an alleged forgery authorized precisely by Pitt's ministry.

The truth, therefore, about Coleridge's method of composition is the exact opposite of that postulated by Professor Erdman. Far from having been one of 'economy', it was a subtle technique of *expansion* by an old hand in the art of manipulating used or borrowed material and working it up, indeed, transforming it, with interpolated and altered passages bearing all the hallmarks of Coleridge's originality as *an acute and abstract thinker*. The opposite is also true of Professor Erdman's assertion that the December version is 'fuller of facts' and 'more sober in reasoning' than the July draft.[103] In fact, the 'passion' of Coleridge's reasoning—to use Professor Erdman's own word[104]—as reflected in Coleridge's style, is to be seen at its most unmistakable, if not intensest pitch, precisely in those passages that Professor Erdman has implied to be 'excrescences' in the July draft simply because they are not to be found in the December version for the ministry.

What could be more characteristically passionate, for instance, and at the same time 'sober in reasoning' than this argument[105] that evolved out of the sentence already cited from the July draft about a possible charge of 'dreamlike speculations' against Coleridge's 'reflections' on Egypt, and which was entirely omitted from the December version? How ardently Coleridge answers the charge, especially as it had evidently been thrown into sharper relief for him in Malta,[106] in a general context, as himself a man of 'theory' surrounded by military men of 'action' and 'experience':

> But if a readiness to act on mere presumptions of theory be the error that most easily besets thinking minds, a blind faith in false analogies of the past is often a still worse snare to the unthinking, who are too willing to consider what they choose to call experience as a cheap substitute for the necessity of thought altogether. Experience justifies us in anticipating the same or similar results from similar agents under similar circumstances; but will not authorize us to identify either the agents or the circumstances only because in both instances the country was Egypt, and the invading army belonged to France.

To interpret this passage and several others like it, together with the extended discussions and techniques already outlined, as 'excrescences', is to reveal a disturbing insensitivity to the working of Coleridge's mind and art. For these passages, taken together and collated with the December version, provide overwhelming *internal* evidence that it is inconceivable that Coleridge should have written them up and devoted such thought to them simply to discard them as 'excrescences'. That he did not do so can be proved from the *manuscript* of the July draft itself, which provides the decisive *external* evidence of Coleridge's method of textual *expansion*. For it shows him, especially in the latter part of the manuscript, literally working the additions and alterations into and out of the main body of the text. Even the footnotes on political slavery[107] can be seen growing into marginal enlargements preceding insertions of much greater length[108] as *direct extensions* of the text, complete with a rubric to 'read on at X in the margin'. To appreciate Coleridge's method, therefore, it is essential not only to collate the July draft with the December version for their textual and technical differences, but to examine the manuscript itself. For

Professor Erdman's transcription, however faithfully it records the additions, corrections and even the footnotes and rubric, cannot fully bring out *the actual process* of textual expansion. Moreover, Professor Erdman has misread the process as 'excrescences', even though he has noted that 'the second half of it [the manuscript] is being constructed before our eyes'[109] as part of what Coleridge himself called 'an induction of particulars' in an illuminating phrase at the end of the July draft,[110] which again is missing from the December version.

The 'induction of particulars', by which Coleridge meant detailed and 'sober reasoning' on contentious issues like Bonaparte's expedition to Egypt, was precisely his justification for the 'prolixity' which, at the end of the July draft, he feared that he had been led into. In consequence he was *at first* inclined to round off the draft with the kind of *apology* that was so common and conventional in the letters of the period from travellers in the Mediterranean and elsewhere.[111] But Coleridge then went on to explain that 'I must rest my excuse' for the 'prolixity' on 'the deep interest which the subject [of Egypt] excited in me, & deserves to excite in minds more capable of doing it justice'.[112] Accordingly Coleridge deleted the conventional apology in seeming confidence that his 'induction of particulars' had either rendered it superfluous or would serve to vindicate him. But Professor Erdman has not only missed the conventional apology as another feature of Coleridge's letter form of writing in the July draft but has misinterpreted Coleridge's deletion of the 'excuse' as proof that he was removing 'excrescences' from the July draft in a 'movement' towards the December version.[113]

It was Coleridge himself after all who described the July draft to Stuart as 'a valuable paper on the present state of Egypt much fuller of facts and more sober reasoning' than the lost official paper written for Ball to be sent to the ministry.[114]

His description, which complements the manuscript of the July draft as external evidence in refutation of Professor Erdman's assertions, occurs in a letter of August 1806 immediately after Coleridge returned to England from Malta and resumed his leader-writing for the *Courier,* precisely, as has already been suggested, to influence 'the public' with his newly gained knowledge of Mediterranean politics. In fact, after writing the letter to Stuart, he informed Mrs Coleridge[115] that he was dividing his time between a course of lectures and 'my Reflections moral and political grounded on Information obtained during two years resident in Italy and the Mediterranean'. There is no suggestion in Coleridge's letter to Stuart that he considered the July draft of 'Observations on Egypt' less valuable than the December version, or that its value derived from an Appendix that he had added to the December version, as Professor Erdman has asserted[116] in apparent forgetfulness that the Appendix in question was not with Coleridge at the time that he wrote to Stuart. For he informed Stuart that he had returned to England without all his political papers except the July draft of 'Observations on Egypt', which was 'valuable' and 'fuller of facts and more sober reasoning' *on its own merits*. In fact, it was *after* he made the comparison between the July draft and the lost official paper on Egypt, and pronounced the former to be more valuable than the latter, that he went on to state to Stuart that, 'for the rest of my papers, I must wait, till they come from Malta',[117] whither they had been sent back from Naples to avoid capture by the French in their march on Rome and Southern Italy.[118] The Appendix to the December version of 'Observations on Egypt' was 'with the rest of my papers' in Malta, so that Coleridge could neither have been thinking of it in crying up the value of the July draft to Stuart nor could he then 'draw' upon it for Stuart—again contrary to Professor Erdman's information.[119]

As for Coleridge's other statement to Stuart about the 'valuable paper on the present state of Egypt', Professor Erdman is equally incorrect in his interpretation of it. For Coleridge, in stressing that 'I collected every fact from respectable Eye-witnesses' for the paper, was surely thinking of *all* the eye-witnesses, *in print as well as in person*, on whom he had drawn for *all* the versions of the paper; whereas Professor Erdman[120] would restrict them to those whom Coleridge had consulted for the Appendix to the December version. But this interpretation is refuted by Coleridge himself in the very sentence of his statement to Stuart, for Coleridge claimed that he had collected 'not a few [facts] from Selim Effendi, the Mamaluke Minister at Malta',[121] who had been to hand for consultation, if necessary, for *all* the versions of the paper, as he

236

had arrived at Malta long before Coleridge.

NOTES AND REFERENCES

1 *EOT*, i. cxxiiin[9].
2 CRK/1/Gen./B/1-61.
3 GD51/1/84.
4 *CL*, ii. 1132.
5 *EOT*, i. cxxvii.
6 PRO, C.O.158/9/f.13.
7 *EOT*, iii. 179-87.
8 Cf. *CL*, ii. 1144.
9 Br. Lib., Add. MS. 37268 f.67.
10 PRO, C.O.159/3/17 May 1803; F.O.70/25/11 Nov. 1804.
11 *EOT*, iii. 214n[28], 198n[18].
12 Br. Lib., Add. MS. 37268, ff.51-6; PRO, C.O.158/7/451-59; F.O.70/25/ 11 Nov.1804.
13 *EOT*, iii. 205.
14 *ibid.*, iii. 198 & n[18].
15 *ibid.*, i. cxxvi. Prof. Erdman's reference (*EOT*, i. cxxvin[2]) to *S.T. Coleridge in Malta and Italy* for R. Southey's echoing Coleridge's 'imperialist idea' is inaccurate. It should read 'p.306' instead of 'p.308'. And Coleridge's 'new role of propagandist for imperialism' is defined in the same book on p.248, not 'p.258', as Prof. Erdman states (*ibid.*, i. cxxvin[2]).
16 *EOT*, i. cxxvi.
17 *ibid.*, iii. 198n[18].
18 *ibid.*, iii. 188 headnote, 2nd paragraph.
19 Br. Lib., Add. MS 37268, ff.51-6.
20 PRO, C.O.158/7/451-59.
21 *CL*, ii. 1146.
22 *ibid.*, ii. 1157n[1].
23 Cf. 'Verses addressed to J. Horne Tooke', *PW*, i. 151, ll.43-8.
24 Scottish Record Office, GD/51/1/814; GD51/1/815/1-2.
25 PRO, C.O./158/8/ff.1-4.
26 Cf. 'It was the fashion of the day to style Egypt the *key* of India, and Malta the key of Egypt' (Coleridge, *Fr.*, ii. 366).
27 Br. Lib., Add. MS. 34932, ff.181-83.
28 *Fr.*, ii. 293.
29 *EOT*, ii. 142n[2].
30 W. Hardman, *A History of Malta (1798-1815)*, 1909, 488-89.
31 PRO, C.O.158/9/f.13.
32 *EOT*, iii. 179-87.
33 *CL*, ii. 1145.
34 *EOT*, i. cxxvii.
35 *CL*, ii. 1164.

36 *ibid.*, ii. 1146.
37 *PW*, ed. J.D. Campbell (1893), APP.K, 550. STC's spelling of 'Sibylline' in 1817 differed from 'Sybilline' in 1804.
38 *CL*, ii. 1146.
39 *ibid.*
40 p.2, under 'naval intelligence'.
41 *EOT*, i. cxxiii.
42 p.2, col.4.
43 *EOT*, i. cxxiiin[6].
44 *ibid.*, iii. 179-87.
45 *Fr.*, ii. 369.
46 *ibid.*, ii. 368.
47 It is not even included in Appendix B, devoted to 'Related Manuscripts', in vol. iii of *EOT,* pp.179-214.
48 *EOT*, i. cxxivn.
49 *ibid.*, i. cxxivn[2]; cxxvn[4].
50 The reference should read 'pp.170-4', not 'pp.170-1', as given in *EOT,* i. cxxivn[2].
51 *EOT*, i. cxxivn[2].
52 *Fr.*, ii. 302.
53 *ibid.*
54 *ibid.*
55 *ibid.*, ii. 299.
56 Br. Lib., Add. MS. 37268, f.57.
57 *CL*, ii. 1146.
58 *Fr.*, ii. 306.
59 *CL*, ii. 1149.
60 Cf. *ibid.*, i. 645 & 464 headnote.
61 *Fr.*, ii. 187-96.
62 *CL*, ii. 1146-147.
63 *ibid.*, i. 464, 645.
64 *CN*, ii. 409, App.B, F.14.4. See D.Sultana, *S.T. Coleridge in Malta and Italy* (1969), 207-8.
65 *EOT*, iii. 188-89.
66 *CL*, ii. 1159, 1165.
67 *EOT*, i. cxxivn[5].
68 My italics.
69 *EOT*, iii.189n[1].
70 Cf. *Fr.*, ii. 306.
71 Cf. *EOT*, iii. App.B, 206.
72 *ibid.*, iii. 199.
73 *ibid.*, iii. 196.
74 *ibid.*, iii. 187 headnote, 189n[1].
75 *ibid.*, iii. 199n[21].
76 *ibid.*, iii. 189n[1].
77 *ibid.*, iii. 188 headnote.
78 *ibid.*, iii. 187 headnote.

79 *CN*, ii. 409, App.B, F.14.4.

80 *CL*, i. 464.

81 *Fr.*, ii. 187f, 236f, 256f.

82 Cf. *CL*, ii. 1147, 1149, 1160.

83 *EOT*, iii. 199.

84 *Fr.*, ii. 289.

85 *EOT*, iii. 190n[3].

86 Cf. *Fr.*, ii. 289.

87 Cf. *EOT*, iii. 201n[5].

88 *CL*, ii. 1178.

89 Cf. PRO, C.O.158/9/f.56; Ball Papers, Greenwich, CRK/1/Gen./B/7 July 1804.

90 *EOT*, i. cxxv; iii. 187 headnote & n[1].

91 *Contarini Fleming*, Bradenham ed. (1927), 166.

92 *EOT*, iii. 194-95.

93 Cf. *CL*, i. 469. Prof. Erdman (*EOT*, iii. 194n[14]) has completely missed this point.

94 *EOT*, i. cxxv.

95 *ibid.*, iii. 194n[14].

96 *ibid.*, iii. 197.

97 *ibid.*, ii. 31.

98 See, e.g., 'Extract of a Letter from the Mediterranean', *Courier*, 24 Sept., 1804. Even Coleridge's Malta friend, Captain Charles Pasley, was himself to send the *Courier* a set of anonymous political letters on Lampedosa (see D. Sultana, *S.T. Coleridge in Malta and Italy* [1969], 330-32). The *Courier* extract of 11 Nov. 1804 attributed to Coleridge by Prof. Erdman almost certainly originated from a traveller or officer *en route* from Upper Egypt and Syria, which were a closed book to Coleridge in terms of practical experience.

99 *EOT*, ii. 197n[16].

100 *ibid.*, iii. 188 headnote.

101 *ibid.*, iii. 188n[1].

102 *ibid.*, iii. 192.

103 *ibid.*, iii. 188 headnote.

104 *ibid.*

105 *ibid.*, iii. 197.

106 Cf. *CN*, ii. 2488, 2337, 2342, 2386.

107 f.103 & verso.

108 ff.123-24 & verso.

109 *EOT*, iii. 187n[1].

110 *ibid.*, iii. 199.

111 See, e.g., P. Brydone, *A Tour through Sicily and Malta* (1774), ii. 130, 165, 167.

112 *EOT*, iii. 199.

113 *ibid.*, iii. 187n[1], 188 headnote.

114 *CL*, ii. 1178.

115 *ibid.*, ii. 1181.

116 *EOT*, iii. 188 headnote.
117 *CL*, ii. 1178.
118 *ibid.*, & 1175.
119 *EOT*, i.cxxvii, ll. 1-2; *ibid.*, i.cxxixn[3]; *ibid.*, iii. 188 headnote.
120 *ibid.*, iii. 188n[2].
121 *CL*, ii. 1178.

Notes on Contributors

ERIC ANDERSON has recently been appointed Head Master of Eton College. He has edited *The Journal of Sir Walter Scott* (1972) and has written a number of short articles on aspects of Scott's work. At present he is editing for Yale University Press the Percy-Anderson volume of *The Percy Correspondence*.

JOHN BEER, who is Reader in English Literature at Cambridge University, is the author of *Coleridge the Visionary, The Achievement of E.M. Forster, Blake's Humanism, Blake's Visionary Universe, Coleridge's Poetic Intelligence, Wordsworth and the Human Heart* and *Wordsworth in Time*. He has also edited and contributed to *Coleridge's Variety* and has produced a new edition of Coleridge's *Poems*. For the *Collected Works of Coleridge* he has edited Coleridge's marginalia to Archbishop Leighton and is editing his *Aids to Reflection*.

GEOFFREY CARNALL is Reader in English Literature at the University of Edinburgh. His study of Southey's political attitudes, *Southey and his Age*, appeared in 1960. He has edited and completed John Butt's volume in the *Oxford History of English Literature: The Mid-Eighteenth Century* (1979).

JOHN GUTTERIDGE read English at Oxford and also studied at Queen's University, Kingston, Ontario. His doctoral thesis was on the Sources, Development and Influence of Coleridge's Conversation Poems. He is now editing Coleridge's Poems up to 1798 for a volume in the Longman series of Annotated English Poets.

ALETHEA HAYTER is a literary critic and biographer. She is a Fellow of the Royal Society of Literature and is on the Boards of Governors of the Old Vic and Sadler's Wells Theatres. Formerly she worked for the British Council in Greece, France and Belgium. Her publications include biographical studies of Coleridge and B.R. Haydon and a critical survey of Elizabeth Barrett Browning's Poetry. She is also the author of *Opium and the Romantic Imagination* and has edited Maturin's *Melmoth the Wanderer*, De Quincey's *Confessions of an English Opium Eater* and *Selected Letters of Edward FitzGerald*.

ALEXANDER KERN is Emeritus Professor of English at the University of Iowa. He was also Visiting and Fulbright Professor of American Literature at several universities in Europe, India and Egypt. He is the co-author of *American Literature* and *Sources of the American Republic* and the co-editor of *The Early Writings of Henry David Thoreau*. He has also contributed to *Myth and Symbol* and *Literature and Ideas in America*. At present he is writing *Coleridge and American Romanticism*.

241

MARION LOCHHEAD is a Fellow of the Royal Society of Literature. Her biography of John Gibson Lockheart appeared in 1954. Her other publications include *The Scottish Household in the Eighteenth Century* (1948), *Young Victorians* (1959), *The Victorian Household* (1964), *Episcopal Scotland in the Nineteenth Century* (1966), *Portrait of the Scott Country* (1968) and *The Other Country: Scottish Fairy Tales Retold* (1978).

ANN MATHESON, a graduate of St Andrews and Edinburgh Universities, is an Assistant Keeper in the National Library of Scotland, Edinburgh. She has recently completed a doctoral thesis on Theories of Rhetoric in the Eighteenth-Century Sermon.

H.W. PIPER is Professor of English at Macquerie University, Australia. His publications include *The Active Universe: Pantheism and the Concept of Imagination in the English Romantic Poets* and (ed.) *The Beginnings of Modern Poetry*. More recently, he has published a number of articles on symbolism in Coleridge's major poems and is preparing a book on the topic.

MARGO VON ROMBERG is a graduate in Classics and English Literature of the Universities of St Andrews and London respectively. At present she is completing a doctoral thesis on Verse Translations of Greek Drama in the Early Nineteenth Century.

DONALD SULTANA is Reader in English Literature at the University of Edinburgh. His publications include *Samuel Taylor Coleridge in Malta and Italy*, *Benjamin Disraeli in Spain, Malta and Albania* and *'The Siege of Malta' Rediscovered: An Account of Sir Walter Scott's Mediterranean Journey and his Last Novel*. At present he is editing the post-1800 poems of Coleridge in the Longman series of Annotated English Poets.

KATHLEEN WHEELER, who is a Research Fellow at Cambridge University, specialises in English and German Romantic literature. She has sub-edited volume two of Coleridge's *Marginalia* in the *Collected Works of Coleridge*, and is editing the 1798-99 poems of Coleridge in the Longman series of Annotated English Poets. Her impending publications include *The Creative Mind in Coleridge's Poetry* and *Sources, Processes and Methods in Coleridge's 'Biographia Literaria*.

Index

For reasons of space this is an index only of names and of the titles of Coleridge's works. No name is included which is referred to only in the notes.

243

Midnight', 137, 143-44, 192; 'The Improvisatore', 75; 'The Kiss', 152; 'Kubla Khan', 76, 107, 172-73, 175-76, 178, 180, 185-87, 192, 194, 197, 199; *Lay Sermons*, 41, 43, 72, 75, 105, 109, 181; *Lectures on Revealed Religion*, 183; Lectures on Shakespeare, 90, 99, 101, 105; 'Limbo', 193; 'Lines on an Autumnal Evening', 137; 'Love' ('Genevieve'), 52, 63; Marginalia, 56; 'Melancholy', 167; 'Ne Plus Ultra', 193; 'The Nightingale', 137; The Notebooks, 29, 52, 54-5, 83-4, 98-100, 141, 161-62, 164, 185, 200-1, 206; 'Observations on Egypt', 215, 224-36; 'Ode to the Departing Year', 183; *Osorio*, 195-96; *Poems on Various Subjects*, 152-53, 158; 'Reflections on having left a Place of Retirement', 139, 151, 158-60, 167; 'Religious Musings', 179, 183, 192, 194, 197; *Remorse*, 17-18, 22, 27, 34, 72, 105; 'The Rose', 152; 'Satyrane's Letters', 27-8, 34-5, 225, 228; *Sybilline Leaves*, 105, 108, 157, 219; 'This Lime-Tree Bower my Prison', 137, 141-42, 147, 151, 160-69, 181; 'To the Evening Star', 152; 'To William Wordsworth', 193, 208; *Wallenstein*, 51, 72, 81, 97-8; *The Watchman*, 145, 159; *Zapolya*, 18, 23-7, 29-30, 36, 57

Collier, John Payne, 53
Cooper, James Fenimore, 48-9
Corneille, Pierre, 102
Cottle, Joseph, 152-53
Cowper, William, 137-49, 161-63, 165
Crowe, William, 159
Cudworth, Ralph, 123, 154-57, 164

Dante, Alighieri, 75-6
Darwin, Erasmus, 185, 187
Davy, Sir Humphry, 50
Denham, Sir John, 87
De Quincey, Thomas, 130-31
De.cartes, René, 114
Dickens, Charles, 75
Disraeli, Benjamin, 231
Dryden, John, 44-5, 86, 88
Duff, William, 39

Edel, Léon, 127
Edwards, Jonathan, 113, 115, 117-18, 125
Eichlor, A., 84
Eliade, Mercia, 174, 179
Eliot, T. S., 130
Ellis, George, 81
Emerson, Ralph Waldo, 114, 118-27, 129-30, 133

Empson, William, 177
Erdman, David, 212-15, 217-19, 222, 224, 226-36

Fichte, Johann, 62, 107, 119
Fletcher, John, 89, 99, 140
Forstner, Lorne J., 174, 176
Fox, Charles James, 145, 223
Franklin, Benjamin, 115
Frere, Bartle, 91-2
Frere, George, 83, 90
Frere, John Hookham, 50, 53, 80-93, 96-8, 103, 109, 220
Freud, Sigmund, 172, 175, 177-78

Garnett, Richard, 74
Gerard, Albert S., 179, 182
Gillman, *Mrs*, 72-3, 91-2
Gillman, James, 72-3, 91-2
Gillray, James, 46
Godwin, William, 97
Goethe, Johann, 51, 101, 107, 130-31, 196
Gray, Thomas, 40
Graves, Robert, 172, 177
Green, James, 73, 101, 107
Grierson, Sir Herbert, 56
Griggs, Earl Leslie, 57, 82

Hamilton, Sir William, 81
Harding, D. W., 172, 177-78
Hartley, David, 100, 115, 118
Hayley, William, 149
Hazlitt, William, 29-30, 34, 38-47, 84, 138
Hawthorne, Nathaniel, 122, 129, 132-33
Hedge, Frederic H., 119
Hegel, Georg Wilhelm, 182-83
Herder, Johann, 116
Hobart, *Lord*, 215
Hobbes, Thomas, 129
Homer, 48-9, 87-8, 140
Hook, Theodore, 71-2, 74-6
Hooker, Richard, 125
Horace, 159
Humboldt, Wilhelm, 98
Hume, David, 100, 115, 118
Hutchinson, Sara, 200

Jefferson, Thomas, 115
Jerdan, William, 76
Job, 180
Johnson, Edgar, 56
Johnson, Samuel, 58, 77
Jonson, Ben, 89, 99, 130

245